T0393879

Cyrus the Great

Cyrus the Great was a celebrity of the ancient world, the founder of one of the first world empires in the ancient Near East, whose life and deeds were celebrated through the many stories told about him then and for millennia.

This book offers an analysis of these stories, locating them within the rich storytelling cultures of the ancient Mediterranean and the Near East. Although there are few fixed points in Cyrus' career, it is possible to see through these narratives the way his kingship developed so he became not just the instrument of the gods, but also their companion. Mitchell explores what these stories reveal about the different societies and cultures who engaged with the mythology surrounding Cyrus in order to examine their own conceptions of great men, leadership, kingship and power. Such was his celebrity in antiquity that the stories about his kingship have remained influential over the course of two and a half thousand years into the modern era.

Cyrus the Great: A Biography of Kingship is of interest to students and scholars studying the Achaemenids and ancient kingship, particularly as it is depicted in the literary and historical traditions of the ancient Near East, as well as those working on the Near Eastern world more generally. Scholars of Greek history in this period will also find much to interest them.

Lynette Mitchell is a Professor of Greek History and Politics at the University of Exeter, United Kingdom. She is the author of *The Heroic Rulers of Archaic and Classical Greece* and edited, with Charles Melville, *Every Inch a King: Comparative Studies on Kingship in the Ancient and Medieval Worlds*.

Routledge Ancient Biographies

To find out more about this series, visit: https://www.routledge.com/classicalstudies/series/ANCIENTBIOS

Cyrus the Great

A Biography of Kingship

Lynette Mitchell

Routledge
Taylor & Francis Group

LONDON AND NEW YORK

First published 2023
by Routledge
4 Park Square, Milton Park, Abingdon, Oxon OX14 4RN

and by Routledge
605 Third Avenue, New York, NY 10158

*Routledge is an imprint of the Taylor & Francis Group,
an informa business*

British Library Cataloguing-in-Publication Data
A catalogue record for this book is available from the British Library

Library of Congress Cataloging-in-Publication Data
Names: Mitchell, Lynette G. (Lynette Gail), 1966- author.
Title: Cyrus the Great : a biography of kingship / Lynette Mitchell.
Description: New York City : Routledge, 2023. | Series: Routledge
ancient biographies | Includes bibliographical references and index. |
Identifiers: LCCN 2022054298 (print) | LCCN 2022054299 (ebook) |
ISBN 9781138024106 (hardback) | ISBN 9781032470696 (paperback) |
ISBN 9781003384458 (ebook)
Subjects: LCSH: Cyrus, the Great, King of Persia, -530 B.C. or 529
B.C. | Iran--Kings and rulers--Biography. | Iran--History--To 640. |
Achaemenid dynasty, 559 B.C.-330 B.C. | Kings and rulers, Ancient.
Classification: LCC DS282 .M58 2023 (print) | LCC DS282 (ebook) |
DDC 935/.705--dc23/eng/20221109
LC record available at https://lccn.loc.gov/2022054298
LC ebook record available at https://lccn.loc.gov/2022054299

ISBN: 978-1-138-02410-6 (hbk)
ISBN: 978-1-032-47069-6 (pbk)
ISBN: 978-1-003-38445-8 (ebk)

DOI: 10.4324/9781003384458

Typeset in Times New Roman
by KnowledgeWorks Global Ltd.

Contents

Preface

This 'biography' on Cyrus has a rather strange life history of its own. As a Greek political historian, I first became drawn to Cyrus through the Greek texts, especially Herodotus and Xenophon, and especially how these Greek authors used Cyrus as a cipher for understanding Greek political ideas. In particular, I was interested in the ways in which he became a lens through which Greek political thinkers could understand kingship, especially in the age before Alexander the Great provided a new and dramatic model for rulership in the Greek world. When I was approached by Routledge to write a biography on Cyrus, I leaped at the opportunity, not knowing at all what I had taken on.

It quickly became apparent that this project was going to take me out of my comfort zone in the eastern Mediterranean and that my background in Greek political history was not going to be adequate for the task. I started by acquiring the new language skills needed and trying to tackle the immense bibliography of a different academic field. While this is a path well-trodden from the Greek world to the ancient Near East, for my part, I have found it a difficult one, and a long one, but one that has also been immensely rewarding.

I have approached this project as a Greek historian and in many ways, this has influenced my perspective on issues pertaining to the ancient Near East. There have been a number of recent books on Cyrus of Anshan. The question might well be asked whether there is a need for one more. However, in writing this book, I have tried to stay true to my main interest in ancient kingship. So, while this book on one level is about the stories and mythologies relating to Cyrus, on another, it is about what these stories can tell us about kingship in the ancient world, which is endlessly fascinating in its variety. It is on these terms that I hope this book makes a proper contribution.

There are a number of points over the last ten years when I have stumbled and nearly fallen (or just given up!). There are many people I need to thank for encouraging me to keep going and generously giving me help along the way. I hope the final outcome is worthy of their persistence! At the very beginning of this journey, Charles Melville and Diana Edelman were collaborators on various Cyrus and kingship projects. My colleague and friend Siam Bhayro gave me occasional tutorials on Akkadian over coffee. My colleagues in the Department of Classics, Ancient History, Religion and Theology at Exeter University have been unswervingly supportive and generous with good advice. Robin Osborne and Peter Rhodes just kept me going when I was despairing. Robert Parker, Dorothy Thompson, Paul Cartledge and Elspeth Dusinbuerre have all provided well-placed and kind words of encouragement when they were needed. Colin Matthews and Emma Kent kept me strong as well as providing moral support, but were thereby instrumental in getting this book done.

I also need to thank my travelling companions in Iran in 2014 on a tour put together by the company *Travel the Unknown*, which was an amazing journey of discovery of a wonderful country and generous people. Richard Stoneman, Richard Seaford, Mary Wilkins, Sue Thomas, Diana and Chloe Darke, I thank you for your companionship and all that I learned from your interests, curiosity and enthusiasm. There were also other kinds of companions on this journey of book writing who were irrepressibly supportive, especially the weekly 'lunch club': David Harvey, Chris Gill, Richard Seaford, Richard Stoneman, John Wilkins and Matthew Wright.

There are also many people who have read and commented on drafts of chapters, and of the whole text, not least Richard Seaford, Caroline Waerzeggers, Wouter Henkelman, Christopher Pelling, Ian Rutherford and Timothy Rood. Brian McDowell very carefully proofread the complete manuscript. These kind friends have saved me from many errors of fact, syntax, emphasis and judgement, and also contributed further ideas about how particular points could be developed. Any errors and failings remaining are of course my own responsibility.

Timothy Rood, Scarlett Kingsley, Fiona McHardy and Christopher Pelling were kind enough to allow me to read chapters ahead of publication. Sébastien Gondet provided me with a site plan of Pasargadae and permission to reproduce it. Andrew George gave me permission to reproduce a map of Babylon. Margaret Cool Root and Mark Garrison gave me the image of PFS 93* and permission to include it in this volume. Michael Athanson was responsible for all other maps. Irving Finkel very kindly allowed me to reprint here his translation of the *Cyrus Cylinder*. Thanks also to Harvey Phythian for helping with the index.

I must also thank Exeter University for allowing me Research Leave at various points over the last 10 years to work on this project and the Leverhulme Trust for the Research Fellowship which allowed it finally to be finished. The librarians at Exeter University and the Sackler Library in Oxford were always patient with my many requests. I am also grateful for the great perseverance of the editors at Routledge, who did not ever quite give up hope that this book would materialise. I am particularly grateful to Marcia Adams from the Press who kindly helped with all the questions and problems in the final stages.

I end with special thanks to Stephen and James without whose support and love, nothing at all would have been possible. Tragically, my lovely Stephen, whose interest in this project and encouragement never wavered, passed away after a short illness during the final stages of the production of this book. It is therefore dedicated, with the greatest love, to his memory.

LGM
May, 2023

Abbreviations, Editions, Languages and Translations

Abbreviations

In general, I have avoided abbreviations as much as possible in the interests of accessibility. However, the following abbreviations have been used:

ABC	Grayson, A.K. (1975a), *Assyrian and Babylonian Chronicles*, Locust Valley, New York.
BNJ	*Brill's New Jacoby* (available online at: https://scholarly editions.brill.com/bnjo/#:~:text=Brill's%20New%20 Jacoby%20is%20a,Jacoby%20or%20excluded%20by%20him.).
CAD	*The Assyrian Dictionary of the Oriental Institute of the University of Chicago.*
DK	H. Diels and W. Kranz, *Fragmente der Vorsokratiker*, 6th edition.
LSJ	H.G. Liddell & R. Scott (1996), *Greek English Lexicon*, 9th edition, with a revised Supplement, Oxford.
PF	Persepolis Fortification Tablets.
PFS	(*) seal documented by impression(s) on Persepolis Fortification Tablet(s); * indicates that the seal impression also includes an inscription.
SAA	State Archives of Assyria
Tod	M. Tod (1933) (ed.), *Greek Historical Inscriptions*, in 2 vols, Oxford.

Abbreviations of Persian Royal inscriptions are as in Kent, Old Persian (e.g. DB = Darius, Behistun)

Authors/texts in Greek and Latin:

Aeschin.	Aeschines
Aesch. *Pers.*	Aeschylus, *Persians*
Arist. *Nich. Eth.*	Aristotle, *Nichomachean Ethics*
Arrian, *Anab.*	Arrian, *Anabasis*

Diod.	Diodorus Siculus
Hdt.	Herodotus
Plut.	Plutarch
Plut. *Alex.*	Plutarch, *Alexander*
Plut. *Artox.*	Plutarch, *Artoxerxes*
Plut. *Aem.*	Plutarch, *Aemilius*
Q.C.	Quintus Curtius Rufus
Xen. *Anab.*	Xenophon, *Anabasis*
Xen. *Cyrop.*	Xenophon, *Cyropaedia*
Xen. *Oec.*	Xenophon, *Oeconomicus*
Val. Max	Valerius Maximus

Ctesias F 8d* The * indicates that the text may not be a genuine fragment of Ctesias.

Editions

For Babylonian cuneiform inscriptions, I have generally used the latest published editions from the Open Richly Annotated Cuneiform Corpus (ORACC: http://oracc.museum.upenn.edu/), either the hardback editions, or, where these are not yet available, the online editions.

Inscriptions from Iran:

Old Persian texts: R.G. Kent (1950), *Old Persian, Grammar, Texts, Lexicon*, New Haven.
Babylonian version of the Behistun inscription: E.N. von Voigtlander (1978), *The Bisitun inscription of Darius the Great: Babylonian version*, London.

For Greek and Latin texts, I have used the standard editions as appropriate (e.g., Oxford Classical Texts, Teubner editions, Les Belles Lettres, Loeb Classical Library).

For medieval texts:

Boccaccio, *De Casibus Virorum Illustrium*, P.G. Ricci & V. Zacarria (eds.) (1983), *Tutte le Opere de Giovanni Boccaccio*, vol. 9, Milan.
Boccaccio, *De Mulieribus Claris*, V. Brown (2001) (ed.), *Giovanni Boccaccio: Famous Women*, Cambridge, Mass.
Christine de Pizan, *Le livre la cite des dames*, É. Hicks & T. Moreau (2000) (eds.), *Le livre la cite des dames*, Paris.

Notes on Language

Akkadian: In order to aid accessibility, Akkadian spellings within the text have largely been anglicised (so that, e.g., š becomes 'sh', and Aššur becomes Ashur). Akkadian quotations, on the other hand, have been transliterated.

Greek: Greek names have usually been Latinised, except for the normal exceptions.

Translations

Unless otherwise indicated, translations (primarily of Greek and Latin texts) are my own.

List of Figures

Relative Chronologies

Relative Chronologies from the Late Eighth to the Early Fifth Century BCE of the Kings of the Neo-Assyrian and Neo-Babylonian Empires and Rulers based in the Zagros Mountains

	Assyrian Kings[1]	Babylonian Kings	Rulers in Central Zagros	Teispids	Achaemenids
730	Sargon II (721–705)				
720		[Marduk-apla-iddina II (720–710)]			
710	Sennacherib (704–681)	[Period of Assyrian domination of Babylonia including the destruction of Babylon by Sennacherib in 689.			
700					
690					
680	Esarhaddon (680–669)	Esarhaddon made his son Shamash-shum-ukin, brother of Ashurbanipal, ruler of Babylon in 672, although he later revolted against his brother.		[Teispes?]	
670	Ashurbanipal (668–631 or 627)				
660			Cyaxares (c. 653–585)		

(Continued)

650	Replaced by the obscure 'Kandalanu' (648–627)][2]	Cyrus (I) (son of Teispes?), 640s?[3]
640		
630	Ashur-etal-ilani (630–, or 626–623?) Nabopolassar (626–605)	
	Sin-shar-ishkun (622?–612)	
620	(Ashur-uballit II 611–609)[4]	
610		[Cambyses I?]
600	Nebuchadnezzar II (605–562)	
590		Astyages (*c.* 585–550)
580		
570	Amel-Marduk (562–560)	
560	Neriglissar (560–556) Labashi-Marduk (556) Nabonidus (556–539)	Cyrus II (*c.* 560–530)
550		
540		
530		Cambyses (530–522) (Bardiya/ Smerdis/ Taxyocares 522) Darius I (522–486)

Notes

1. After Kuhrt (1995), 479.
2. See Kuhrt (1995), 576–89; Beaulieu (2018), 193–218; Dalley (2021), 170–213.
3. See further Chapter 2.
4. Crown prince who could not become king because Ashur had fallen: Radner (2018).

Key Dates

Maps

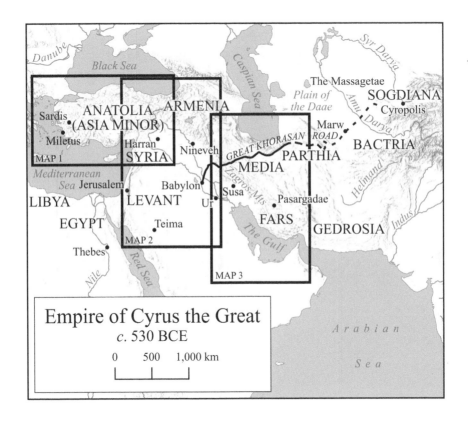

Empire of Cyrus the Great

c. 530 BCE

0   500   1,000 km

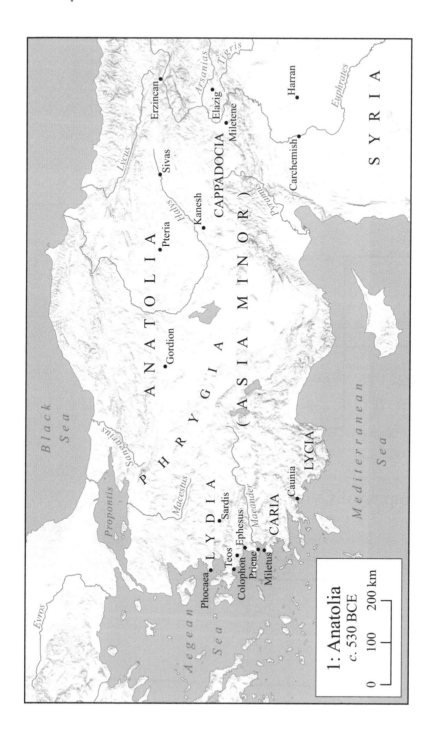

1: Anatolia
c. 530 BCE

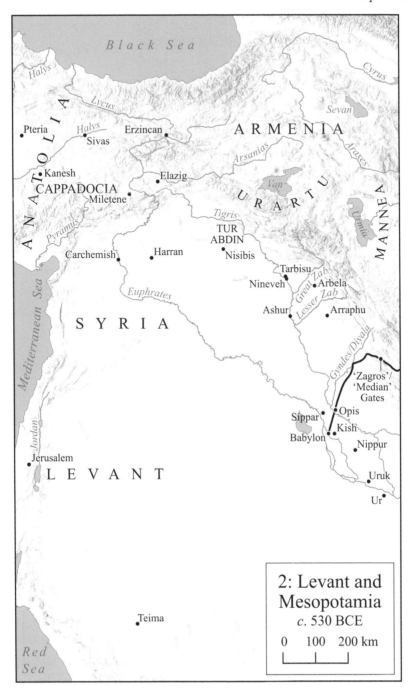

Black Sea

Halys

Lycus

ANATOLIA

Pteria

Halys

Sivas

Erzincan

ARMENIA

Sevan

Cyrus

Arsanias

Araxes

Kanesh

CAPPADOCIA

Miletene

Elazig

Van

URARTU

Pyramus

Tigris

TUR
ABDIN

Urmia

MANNEA

Mediterranean Sea

Carchemish

Harran

Nisibis

Tarbisu

Great Zab

Arbela

Euphrates

Nineveh

Lesser Zab

SYRIA

Ashur

Arraphu

Gyndes/Diyala

'Zagros'/
'Median'
Gates

Jordan

Sippar

Opis

Kish

Babylon

Nippur

Jerusalem

LEVANT

Uruk

Ur

Teima

Red
Sea

2: Levant and
Mesopotamia
c. 530 BCE

0   100   200 km

The Derbices

Caspian Sea

Aji Chay

MANNEA

HYRCANIA

Qezel Owzan

Mt Damavand

Rhaga

KHORASAN RD

PARTHIA

M E D I A

GREAT

ELLIPI   Ecbatana

Godin Tepe

Mt Alwand

Nush-i Jan Tepe

Mahidasht

Baba Jan Tepe

Karkheh

Z a g r o s

Tigris

Susa

Kabnak

Karun

KHUZESTAN

Euphrates

Shatt al Arab

Ur

M t s

Zohreh

Kur

Pasargadae

MAMA-
SANI

Dalaki

F A R S

The Gulf

Taoce

Mand

CARMANIA

Str of Hormuz

Pasargadae

Bolaghi Valley

Anshan/
Tal-i Malyan

Pulvar

Persepolis
(*c*.518)

Tol-i Ajori

Kur

0   20   40 km

3: Central and
Southwest Zagros
c. 530 BCE

0   100   200 km

1 Introduction

One of the most famous stories told in antiquity about Cyrus the Great was his decapitation by Tomyris, a queen of the Massagetae in central Asia, who put his head in a wineskin full of blood, and told him to drink his fill. This was a story which caught the imagination of the Greeks in the fifth century BCE, as well as the Romans five hundred years later. It became canonical in the middle ages in Europe, so much so that Tomyris became more famous than Cyrus himself. However, the storylines that transformed her into the victor over this great king were part of the complex storytelling that surrounded him from his own rise to power at the beginning of the sixth century until his death, and then were told again and again, even into modern times. While Tomyris, almost certainly a figure of mythology, takes on the dimensions of a historical queen, Cyrus was a historical figure who became mythologised, probably even in his own lifetime. Born somewhere at the beginning of the sixth century BCE, Cyrus the Great, King of Anshan, in the southwest Zagros Mountains (modern Fars, Iran), was a celebrity not just in his own time, but also over the millennia. The fame of his greatness was also not limited to the ancient Near East, but took on significance in other cultures, from ancient Greece and Israel to medieval Europe and beyond. However, that greatness was not always understood in the same way. As a result, we have not just one but many Cyruses.

Known initially for his military accomplishments, Cyrus went on to found what has been termed the first world empire, extending from Asia Minor in the west to perhaps the Indus in the east. We are justified in calling him an ancient 'celebrity' because of the ways in which his image as an 'owner' of historical agency was created and dispersed in his own time, and then in subsequent centuries. From the earliest stages of his career, when he came to the attention of those beyond the southwest Zagros where he was born, he was known as a divinely endorsed military 'fixer', although his image soon also had traction on a wider scale. While the stories of his birth and death had one kind of appeal in the Greek world of the fifth century, the conquest of Babylon had a completely different hold on the imagination of the Hebrew Bible, linked as it was to the destruction of Jerusalem. In the medieval period, however, it was not so much Cyrus but the Massagetan

DOI: 10.4324/9781003384458-1

queen, Tomyris, who arrested greater attention: he may have been great, but she, through this act of decapitation, showed herself to be greater.

The purpose of this book then is not really about uncovering what it is possible to know about this 'great' man and his life (which is actually disappointingly little), but what the stories about him reveal in regard to the different societies and cultures who found it interesting and important to engage with the mythology of his celebrity in order to explore their own needs and anxieties about great men, kingship, leadership and power – both powerful men and powerful women. It is not really a biography of a man, so much as a biography of the stories that surrounded his kingship.

Cyrus' celebrity continued, or at least was repurposed, into modern times, although not always easily or without controversy.[1] However, this monograph will concern itself with the stories of Cyrus largely from his own time in the sixth century BCE until the fifteenth century CE. It was at that point in the early fifteenth century, with the reintroduction of Greek texts in the Latin West, that the Cyrus tradition took on a new life and new trajectories that are beyond the scope of this monograph. Nevertheless, it is fair to say that Cyrus the Great is a celebrity who has occupied imaginations for two and a half thousand years. It is important to think about the nature of that celebrity, and what gave rise to it.

The Ancient Evidence

The first time we hear of Cyrus in any (more or less dateable) ancient text is in what is called the *Ehulhul Cylinder* (Figure 1.1), a cuneiform tablet produced at the court of Nabonidus, king of Babylon, probably sometime after 543 BCE (and before Cyrus' taking of Babylon in 539 BCE).

In this text, a foundation or building text, Cyrus is celebrated by Nabonidus for his victory over Astyages, 'king of the *Umman-manda*'.[2] According to Nabonidus, Cyrus was 'stirred up' by the gods Marduk and Sin to solve the problem of the *Umman-manda* at Harran in Syria, and, with his small body of troops, overcame the extensive *Umman-manda*. Significantly, as we shall see, Nabonidus gives all agency to Cyrus for putting an end to his problems at Harran. The *Ehulhul Cylinder* is an important document for this study, and we shall return to it on a number of occasions in the chapters that follow.

From the Greek world, we know that there were many stories and songs circulating about Cyrus' birth, life and death. As well as the narrative he provides in Book One, Herodotus in the fifth century says he knows three other stories about Cyrus' rise to power, but says that he will tell one told by those Persians who do not want to magnify the deeds of Cyrus (Hdt. 1.95.1). Likewise, he also knows 'many stories' about the death of Cyrus, although the one he chooses to tell (Tomyris and the Massagetae) he says is the 'most plausible' (*pithanōtatos*: Hdt. 1.214.5).

In Herodotus' *Histories*, Cyrus holds a programmatic place. As a baby and young man, he is protected by the gods: Harpagus, the Mede, who

Figure 1.1 The *Ehulhul Cylinder* of Nabonidus. © The Trustees of the British Museum.

rescues him from death and helps him vanquish Astyages, tells him so (Hdt. 1.124.1-2). However, while Cyrus is intelligent and compassionate, he is also ruthless, arrogant and finally unable to understand his relationship to the gods.[3] Just as Herodotus' Croesus becomes a model for Cyrus, in Cyrus' birth and death stories in Book One, Cyrus himself becomes the prototype for the tragic character of another Persian king: Xerxes.

In the late fifth/early fourth century, Ctesias, the Greek doctor at the Persian court, wrote a *Persica* in 23 books, which included material on Cyrus.[4] Ctesias' text itself is no longer extant, and understanding its original form and use of material on Cyrus is problematic. The first-century-CE Nicolaus of Damascus used Ctesias' text, probably together with other sources, to create his own universal history in 144 books. However, we also only have Nicolaus' text in summary form in a collection of historical texts commissioned by the tenth-century Constantine VII Porphyrogenitus of Byzantium (itself only partially preserved).[5] The distance then from Ctesias' *Persica*, at least insofar as we have it through Nicolaus, is substantial, and the possibilities that we are dealing with genuine Ctesian fragments on the face of it seem remote. However, there are good reasons for thinking (as we shall see in Chapter 3) that the 'Ctesian' material that has come down to us regarding Cyrus' rise to power seems to have been based on genuine Near Eastern stories about Cyrus, even if they have been redacted (and repurposed) more than once.[6]

Fortunately, however, Nicolaus is not our only source for Ctesias' Cyrus story. The ninth-century Byzantine official, diplomat, scholar and teacher Photius[7] also read Ctesias' *Persica* and, although he was not interested in the birth stories and only picks up on the Cyrus story with his defeat of Astyages, there are some reassuring points of contact with Nicolaus. Photius does also note more generally that Ctesias is at pains to distance his work from that of Herodotus (Photius 35b-36a = Ctesias T 8), a point which Diodorus seems to confirm (Diod. 2.15.2 = Ctesias F 1b). Differentiating his account of Cyrus (or Near Eastern history more generally) from that of Herodotus seems to be one of the driving motivations in Ctesias' selection of stories. Nevertheless, he does seem to be attracted (as is often remarked) to some of the more colourful stories surrounding Cyrus, or those about the cunning of Cyrus' servant and helper, Oebaras.[8] Although the reception of Ctesias' text is fraught with difficulties, it does seem that at least in those stories about Cyrus, there is a Near Eastern core (although that by no means makes them historical, as we shall see in later chapters). Yet, as Waters observes, these are Near Eastern stories for a Greek audience. He says: 'The *Persica* may be considered something more than a simplistic borrowing of or reception of Mesopotamian motifs. It is, rather, an appropriation of them'.[9]

Xenophon, in the fourth century, also knows that there were numerous stories and songs about Cyrus. He says at the beginning of the *Cyropaedia*: 'It is said and it is sung, even now, that in form he was most handsome, in soul most benevolent, most fond of learning, and most desirous of honour, so that he endured every labour and bore every danger for the sake of praise' (1.2.1). However, for Xenophon, Cyrus is an idealised leader. The extent to which Xenophon's account of the 'education' of Cyrus related to these stories and songs is probably very limited. Xenophon does use Near Eastern story motifs – the love story of Abradates and Panthea, for example – and other Cyrus narratives which may have Near Eastern origins, such as the capture of Babylon through the draining of the Euphrates (see further, Chapter 5). However, the storytelling of Cyrus' campaigns as we find it in Xenophon is almost completely ahistorical, and has its narrative trajectory (as we also find in Herodotus) towards the taking of Babylon after the final battle at the end of a year's campaigning against his enemy, the 'king of Assyria', at which point (and only then) he becomes a king in his own right.

However, while the picture of Persian kingship and society is broadly consistent with what we know from other sources, at least for the fourth century rather than necessarily the sixth, Xenophon's *Cyropaedia* is using Persia as the setting for an exploration of the science of good leadership, and Cyrus is the paradigm of a man who ruled a large and diverse empire.[10] In the *Cyropaedia*, he says that Cyrus had 'obtained obedience to himself in regard to a vast number of men and a vast number of cities' and so demonstrated that 'it was neither impossible nor difficult to rule men if one did it with intelligence' (1.1.2). The *Cyropaedia* is fictive history. In many ways, it is a 'boy's own' story of Cyrus' heroic deeds, particularly against the 'king of Assyria', whom he finally overcomes and kills with the taking of Babylon. However, within the context of his own relationship with his ineffective uncle Cyaxares, Cyrus shows the importance of obedience by submitting himself to Cyaxares' will (as he often points out to his followers), and tells others why it is important for him to do so, and for them to follow his example. In this way, he makes philosophical points about the need for a good leader both to secure and to show willing obedience.

Cyrus is also known from the Hebrew Bible, especially the books of *Isaiah* and *Ezra*, where he is portrayed as the destroyer of Babylon and the rebuilder of Jerusalem. Apart from the fact that the composition history of Biblical texts is complex (particularly *Isaiah*, which probably had three stages of composition as well as a process of later editing), Cyrus' representation as destroyer and rebuilder was, as we shall see in Chapter 5, theologically important within the Hebrew Bible, but probably does not help us toward understanding historical realities. Nevertheless, what these texts do show is how important Cyrus became in the Near Eastern imagination as a destroyer and a liberator – although there may be questions about the nature of this liberation.

The literary productions of Cyrus himself are very limited. Apart from the well-known *Cyrus Cylinder*, there are inscribed bricks in Akkadian from Ur and Uruk,[11] and also, perhaps, the alleged 'edict' (or edicts) of Cyrus regarding the rebuilding of the temple in Jerusalem recorded in the Hebrew Bible book of *Ezra* (*Ezra* 1.2-4, 6.2-5), although the authenticity of this edict has been doubted.[12] However, the *Cyrus Cylinder* itself is not a straightforward document, and its shaping needs to be understood within the ideologies of the Mesopotamian courts, and Cyrus' forming of his own distinctive, yet essentially Near Eastern, ideological position. We will discuss the *Cylinder* in detail later, especially as a product of the Mesopotamian scribal matrix. It is enough to say for now that the *Cylinder* also provides us with a story of Cyrus, one which he himself seems to have had a significant hand in producing, which articulates his vision of kingship, at least within a Mesopotamian context. For that reason alone, the *Cylinder* will be crucial to many parts of our investigation.

This apparent wealth of Cyrus narratives in the Greek, Biblical and Mesopotamian traditions, which (especially in the Greek tradition) have biographical characteristics, appear to present the possibility, by working our way through them on the basis of historical probability, of reconstructing a 'life' of Cyrus. This, however, is largely an illusion. Many of the stories we have in the Greek sources, for example, are just that: Near Eastern stories from a rich storytelling culture where the heroic figures of history (the kings) attracted many narratives to themselves, both positive and negative, about their deeds, and their relationship to the gods and their communities.[13] For example, the *Epic of Naramsin* tells the story of Naramsin's battle against the king of Apishal (Naramsin is 'like a raging lion' [*ki-ma ni-e-š-im-mi na-ḫi-ir-im*]: v.2), whereas in the *Curse of Agade* (which we will discuss in Chapter 5) Naramsin, in defiance of the god's will, attacks the temple of Enlil, who then sends the barbarous Guti to destroy Naramsin's city of Akkad.[14]

However, while many of these stories about ancient heroes are evidently ahistorical, at least in terms of 'what happened', they do give some indication of what we might call Near Eastern patterns of thinking about the past, and the didactic uses of the past for understanding the present and the future. In particular, they tell us a great deal about ancient kingship, and how kingship was positioned through storytelling, not only in the human plane, but even in the cosmos: kingship becomes the place of mediation (in different ways) between the gods and the mortal world.

These stories and the motifs from which they were formed were also constantly being re-told, re-copied and often re-shaped and re-purposed. Thus, the 'madness of Nabonidus' which is recounted in the *Verse Account of Nabonidus*[15] reappears in the Hebrew Bible's book of *Daniel*, although here it is the madness of Nebuchadnezzar.[16] Likewise, as we shall see in a number of chapters that follow, the stories about Cyrus that appear in our Greek authors are at the very least being chosen from the many possibilities available because of authorial need, but are also being re-shaped to suit narrative purposes. We should not take Herodotus' claims of 'greater plausibility' too seriously.

Cyrus, because of his actual human and historical presence, even though almost all the accounts of him are mythologised, becomes an important medium for exploring the relationship between humanity and the gods. As we shall see, because of the nature of what anthropologists call his 'metahuman' status (more on this later), and the different ways that his metahumanity was interpreted, he becomes an important figure not only for the Greeks to understand their own ideas about kingship and its relationship to the divine, but also in Babylon and Israel as well.

One of the major tasks of this monograph is to ask what kind of 'biography' it is possible to write of a historical figure like Cyrus, and if it is really possible to write one at all, particularly given the nature of the sources that we have about him. In that sense, a lot of this book will be about methodology. The materials that we have, because of their generally literary and theological nature (even building texts like the *Cyrus Cylinder*), need to be contextualised within their own literary and theological settings.[17] It is only by doing this work that we can really ask the bigger questions, also underpinning this book: what can a study of Cyrus and his kingship can tell us about Near Eastern kingship more generally, institutionally and in its relationship both to the gods and the community?

However, before we make a start on these larger tasks, we do need to consider first of all what we know about Cyrus, his deeds and his background in the Zagros mountains of southwest Iran.

Cyrus: The Background

There are very few fixed points in the life and career of Cyrus, the son of Cambyses, king of Anshan. Deinon, who wrote a *Persica* in the fourth century BCE, says Cyrus died when he was 70, having become king at the age of 40 and ruling for 30 years (*BNJ* 690 F 10). Although it is hard to confirm Deinon's claim (or on what information it was based), it is roughly consistent with most of the other sparse details we know about Cyrus' life, even though the round numbers on the face of it look suspicious.

Cyrus probably became king in about 560 or 559 BCE, a date calculated back from his death, which we know was in 530 BCE from the dating of Babylonian records (see Chapter 6).[18] Herodotus says he ruled for 29 years (1.214.3), and Ctesias, like Deinon, says he ruled for 30 years (F 9 §8), although Herodotus' date is generally preferred.[19] We also know from Babylonian Chronicles (at least as preserved from the Hellenistic period) that Cyrus defeated Astyages in 550 BCE (Year 6 of Nabonidus' reign), and that he became king in Babylon in 539 BCE (Nabonidus Year 17) (*ABC* 7 ii.1–4, iii.12–20). Almost everything else about Cyrus and his deeds is uncertain.

On the *Cyrus Cylinder*, Cyrus is called the king of Anshan. The city of Anshan had been an important Elamite city in the southwest Zagros, as one of the two major cities of the Elamite kingdom (the kings of Elam called themselves kings of Susa and Anshan from the second millennium down to the sixth century: see further Chapter 2). Nevertheless, Fars (where Anshan was located) in the first half of the first millennium was archaeologically 'empty'.[20] This fact suggests that, at least at the beginning of his reign, Cyrus' community in the southwest Zagros were pastoral nomads,[21] nomadism being an economic and social strategy, where, because of limited opportunities for agriculture, the basis of subsistence living was the herding of animals, primarily of sheep and goats, and the consequent need for periodic migration, even if it is combined with some sedentism and irrigated agriculture.[22] There is some debate concerning the beginnings of pastoral nomadism in the Zagros. While Potts has argued that the earliest pastoral nomads in Iran were horse-breeding Iranian speakers,[23] others have suggested that at some point in the first millennium, Iranian speakers came to live beside Elamites (who were probably already nomadic pastoralists) in the southwest Zagros, and that together they pursued pastoral nomadism, or a more blended form of pastoralism, as a way of life.[24]

In fact, nomadism is normally an economic strategy and resource-driven.[25] For this reason, there was not always a hard and fast distinction between nomadism and sedentary strategies: nomads could interact with settled communities and also move relatively swiftly from nomadism to settlement without necessarily passing through a transhumance phase. Herodotus says that in his time, some of the Persian tribes were involved in agriculture, and some were nomads (1.125.4). However, these differences may not be as clear-cut as Herodotus suggests,[26] and what we may see developing in the Zagros is a 'dimorphic' tribalism, which contains elements of the nomadic and the sedentary.[27] In fact, the nomadism of the Zagros was probably also a kind of 'enclosed nomadism', which is a phrase used to describe pastoral nomads who (unlike Bedouin nomads who exist completely outside other structures) are integrated at some level with more sedentary economic and social modes. In enclosed nomadism, as described by Rowton,[28] nomads and settlements have a symbiotic and interdependent driven relationship, in particular by the nomads' need for flour, and that of the settlers for the meat and other products of the herded animals, since villagers only had limited grazing land for pasturing their own animals. Nevertheless, Alizadeh, at least for the third millennium, argues for an 'enclosing' model of nomadism, where the nomadic tribes of the highlands of Elam dominated the settlements of the plains.[29] However, nomads could also be involved in agriculture, and research from other Near Eastern contexts has shown how quickly nomads could become sedentary and vice versa.[30]

Yet it seems that in the Zagros, the resources of nomadic pastoralism were also supplemented by warrior activities, probably of the elite. The seal of Cyrus son of Teispes (PFS 93*; Figure 1.2), probably the grandfather of our Cyrus (although that is not inevitable and will be discussed in more detail in a later chapter), is an elite object with a depiction of a warrior scene (with the warrior mounted on a horse),[31] suggesting that military success was a marker of status, and that military activity was used by at least some people to supplement the resources of the community.

As we will see in Chapter 3, Cyrus may have had some kind of dependent status in Astyages' army, an army which we also know seems to have been operating at least in the 550s around Harran (as recorded in the *Ehulhul Cylinder*). Harran was an important point on the trade routes north into

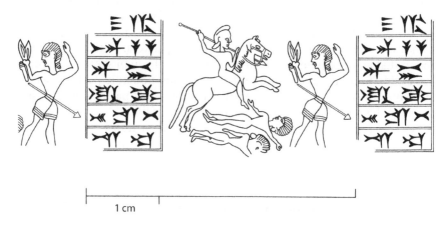

1 cm

Figure 1.2 Impression of the cylinder seal of Cyrus [I]. Courtesy of M.B. Garrison, M.C. Root, and the Persepolis Seal Project.

Anatolia and south into the Levant, so Astyages' army was possibly involved in some kind of extortion,[32] as well as creating problems for Nabonidus and his desire to restore the temple buildings there (temples that were destroyed by the Babylonians and the army under the command of Astyages' father, Cyaxares). That Cyrus himself was also a capable military commander is indicated by the fact that the Median elite of Astyages' army abandoned Astyages in 550 BCE, and went over to Cyrus, even though that was probably also due to the looseness of the Median confederacy, as we will explore further in Chapter 4. As we shall see in the next chapter, the move from pastoralism to at least a limited kind of sedentism happened quickly in Fars in the sixth century, probably as a result of Cyrus' access to the wealth of the Medes in Ecbatana, which seems to have been used for irrigating the Pulvar Plain where Cyrus was to build his 'garden palace' (which we will discuss in Chapter 2).

That the society in which Cyrus himself lived was in some sense nomadic and did not produce literary texts does not mean, however, that it was primitive, illiterate or unsophisticated. Despite little written evidence from the early part of the first millennium, we do have two cylinder seals from a period earlier than Cyrus: PFS 93* (already mentioned) and PFS 51. PFS 93* is inscribed, in Elamite: 'Cyrus son of Teispes, of Anshan'. The second cylinder seal is not inscribed (PFS 51), but Garrison has argued on stylistic grounds that it must be a companion seal for PFS 93*, and from the same workshop.[33] Garrison also identifies two other antique seals that he thinks come from roughly the same milieu (PFS 77* and PFS 1308*), and suggests that there must have been a specifically 'Anshanite' context (as opposed to Assyrian or Elamite/Susan contexts) in which these seals were produced.[34]

The very existence of these seals at all is suggestive of a society which had the resources to create or commission such high-quality glyptic art (Garrison comments on the quality of their carving), and, at least to some degree, needed to interact with other sophisticated (and probably sedentary, or largely sedentary) bureaucratic administrations and economies, probably the cities of the Elamite lowlands of Khuzestan.[35] Of themselves, the seals are prestige objects so suggest a society which had a level of stratification in which an elite needed and could use objects like these to mark out their status within the community. Through ownership of such high-quality seals, Cyrus (I), the original owner of the seal, was probably demonstrating within his own community his economic responsibilities and rights, a community which included not only the highlands, but also the sedentary and bureaucratised settlements of Khuzestan.[36] It is not necessarily surprising then that these seals were kept as heirlooms down to the reign of Darius I, where they then become symbols of continuity with an earlier dynastic heritage.

That there are no written documents from Cyrus II's Anshanite court, however, should not surprise us. Macdonald, in his discussion of the nomads of the pre-Islamic Arabian peninsula, has talked about why nomads do not generally use writing. He says:

> For a start, there are a number of severe practical difficulties. Writing materials are not readily available in the desert and have to be imported from the settled regions. In Middle Eastern deserts, the wind blows fiercely for at least half of most days and nights, with frequent dust or sand-storms, and the rains in winter and spring can be of tropical force. So, those who live in tents do not have much use for materials that can blow away, or be destroyed by dirt, wet and the attentions of hens, goats, dogs and rodents. It is no surprise, therefore, that nomadic societies living in these conditions have developed highly effective ways-of-life and social structures based on the use of powerful memories and oral communication, in which literacy can find no useful function.[37]

Conditions in Arabia were not the same as those for the pastoralists of the southwest Zagros Mountains of Iran, but it is obvious that the Zagros pastoralists did not have a need for writing, although the inscription on PFS 93* suggests that they were not illiterate. In fact, Macdonald also makes the point rather forcefully that writing is separate from reading: because one does not write does not mean that one cannot read, just as the written production of a text does not mean that its state is necessarily 'fixed', and cannot be influenced further. As Rosalind Thomas notes in her discussion of writing and oral poetry, in the context of a society which was overwhelming oral, ancient Greece:

> For the poet, the dictated performance might be only one performance among many and, since he was doing what he always had done, it is probably anachronistic to think that he would regard the written text as superseding all his own performances: after all, it recorded only one out of hundreds.[38]

It is even more to the point that even when what had become the Achaemenid court did begin to inscribe and even to develop an elaborate written administrative system, this written culture was not a literary culture, although it clearly operated in tandem with a lively and creative oral culture, as is evident from the narratives that found their way into Greek authors. Nevertheless, there are also indications that Cyrus and his own court, at least from the taking of Babylon in 539, were engaging deeply with Mesopotamian traditions.

The *Cyrus Cylinder*

This engagement with Mesopotamian literary traditions is particularly clear in relation to the so-called *Cyrus Cylinder* (Figure 1.3), a very important text that will be the workhorse for a number of the chapters that follow.

Figure 1.3 The *Cyrus Cylinder.* © The Trustees of the British Museum.

The *Cyrus Cylinder* is what is called a foundation text, which was (re)discovered in Babylon in 1879, although the precise location of its deposition and later excavation is unclear.[39] It is called a foundation text because the 'cylinder' (although it is not really a cylinder; Finkel has described it as 'barrel-shaped, slightly swollen in the middle')[40] of baked clay belonged within a Mesopotamian tradition of placing such inscribed clay objects as deposits within the structures of buildings or walls.[41]

The text of the *Cyrus Cylinder* was written in Standard Babylonian cuneiform, but the language, according to Stolper, 'is marked by exalted vocabulary, arch and stilted grammatical forms and archaizing usages. The sound of Cyrus' message was grand and old'.[42] Unlike Neo-Babylonian foundation cylinders (which were usually arranged in two columns, although the *Ehulhul Cylinder* of Nabonidus from Sippar has three columns), the text of the *Cyrus Cylinder* runs all the way along the long axis, in the manner of the cylinders of the Neo-Assyrian rulers of Babylon, and may have been influenced by the foundation inscriptions of Ashurbanipal to which the *Cyrus Cylinder* itself makes reference (43).[43] Nevertheless, Schaudig has argued that the language, signs and literary context of the *Cylinder* is very much Babylonian (rather than Assyrian) in character.[44] A full translation of the *Cylinder* by Irving Finkel (2013) can be found in Appendix A.

The *Cylinder* as it was received in the British Museum in 1879 was broken, although that was not necessarily the condition in which it was originally excavated.[45] In 1971, a fragment in the Yale Babylonian Collection in the United States was recognised as belonging to the *Cylinder*, and is now on long-term loan to the British Museum.[46] More recently, two further fragments were found in British Museum archives, although not of the *Cylinder* itself, but what was evidently a copy of the text of the *Cylinder* in one long flat tablet, a clear indication that the audience of the text of the *Cylinder* was not just 'the gods' or later kings involved in building works (such foundation texts often make reference to the building works of previous kings and the discovery of their foundation text, or to prospective kings who will find their texts), but was intended for wider publication and distribution, perhaps even throughout the territories of Cyrus' nascent empire.[47] Finkel suggests that at least the proclamation was 'likely to have been promulgated far and wide', even if the text was adapted for specific contexts as appropriate.[48]

We will return to the *Cyrus Cylinder* on a number of occasions throughout this book as the only literary output of Cyrus' reign of any length, which was created within what Carr has called the Mesopotamian scribal matrix, which centred on the scribal schools of Babylon.[49] However, if we are to understand the significance of its composition, and that of other traditions, especially oral traditions, arising out of the Mesopotamian literary milieu, we need to pause for a moment to consider how the Mesopotamian literary tradition was produced and perpetuated.

The Scribal Matrix: An Oral and Written Cultural Tradition

The Mesopotamian scribal education was for the elite, and based on the training of youths for ritual and administrative purposes.[50] Despite its apparent focus on written texts, Mesopotamian scribal culture existed within what has been termed a culture of 'ambient orality'. As Postgate notes in regard to Assyrian administration: 'most routine administration was not committed to writing, and what we do have is biased precisely because it records the exceptional'.[51] In the so-called scribal matrix, memorisation played a large part, as well as recitation. Scribal education involved not just copying, but also, through copying, the memorisation of a vast corpus of material, and scribal education relied on teachers instructing students verbally.[52] It is probably significant that despite the large number of copies of some of the foundation texts dating from the reign of Nabonidus – there are about fifty-three copies of the *Ehulhul Cylinder* for example – no two are identical,[53] which may suggest production from memory rather than verbatim copying.

Furthermore, although it now seems that at least functional literacy was higher than was once thought,[54] the performance of what we might call literary texts was an important part of their transmission. Cooper, for example, argues that Sumerian and Akkadian literary works were created by the scribes, who then instructed performers.[55] But it was not only literary works that were performed. Porter has also discussed the large numbers of copies of foundation/building texts that were produced in Assyria and stored in locations other than the building to which they refer.[56] An obvious Babylonian example, again, is the *Ehulhul Cylinder*, which mentions building works at Harran, as well as at Sippar, copies of which were stored at Sippar and Babylon.[57] Furthermore, Porter suggests that these documents (like the *Cyrus Cylinder*) were not only accessible as written documents, but also publicly declaimed.[58]

As a result, scribal education was not just about learning the grammar and writing systems of difficult languages, but also absorbing a cultural heritage. For this reason, one result of the memorisation of texts was the impact on the formation of new texts.[59] When scribes were called on to create new texts, they were able to draw on, from their memories, a variety of older texts, which they could reshape according to their current needs. For this reason, it should come as no surprise that texts from different periods, and even different genres, seem to 'echo' other. Beaulieu also points to the fact that even administrative and official texts could resemble, or contain allusions to, literary texts.[60]

The foundation text of Cyrus from Babylon, the *Cyrus Cylinder*, is written in this scribal tradition, so also often uses the phrasing of the building texts of Cyrus' Babylonian predecessors (including Nabonidus, who is reviled in the *Cyrus Cylinder*).[61] However, the *Cylinder* itself alludes to the Babylonian myth of creation, the *Enuma Elish*, in a way that compounds Cyrus' role as a divinely ordained 'fixer'.[62] In tablet VI of the *Enuma Elish*, Marduk has been made king of the gods and has ordered Babylon to be built. Then follows a list of his names, the first of which is Marduk 'who ... saved the gods, his fathers, from hardship (*it-ṭi-ru ina šap-šá-qí*)' (VI 123-6).[63] In the *Cyrus Cylinder*, we are told that, because of Nabonidus' impiety and improper rituals, and because he 'destroyed all his people with an unresting yoke' (6-8), Marduk sought out a righteous king, and grasped Cyrus by the hand (12). Marduk commanded Cyrus to march against his city Babylon, and 'like a friend and companion marched at his side' (15). Marduk then allowed Cyrus to enter Babylon without a battle, and so [Marduk] 'saved his city, Babylon, from hardship' (*it-ṭi-ru ina šap-šá-qí*). The *Enuma Elish* was recited to the statue of Marduk on the fourth day of the *akitu* festival, the New Year festival, which established annually the relationship between the priests and the king.[64] So, in the *Cyrus Cylinder*, not only is the Persian occupation of Babylon legitimated by Marduk's search for, and support of Cyrus, but also, as Haubold says, Cyrus' taking of Babylon too becomes 'the final act in the cosmic drama' being played out in the *Enuma Elish*.[65] We will explore further in Chapter 5 the implications of how Cyrus positions himself in this text as a cosmic warrior.

Within the scribal matrix there were also complex interactions between oral and folkloric motifs and literary texts, and motifs could move between the two kinds of traditions, changing shape and context as they did so.

An important example is the 'rags-to-riches' motif of royal texts, whereby rulers (or high-ranking officials) were attributed humble origins only later to rise to a position of great power. Although apparently folkloric in character, this motif was widespread in oral traditions surrounding the succession of kings (see further Chapter 3), and the motif of 'humble origins' was perpetuated and integrated into written productions within scribal settings.

A good example of the motif of 'humble origins' (which also shows the breadth of currency of this particular motif and its longevity) is the so-called 'autobiography' of Weni, a senior official in provincial Old Egypt. This text, inscribed on a stone slab carefully positioned within Weni's mortuary chapel at Abydos, describes Weni's rise from humble origins to becoming the 'friend' of the king. However, it was, as Janet Richards has argued, a carefully constructed piece of centralised royal propaganda to promote the special connection between Weni and the king in order to suppress competition by other members of the elite in provincial Abydos.[66] As Richards has shown, Weni's 'rags-to-riches' story is total fabrication and that by reading Weni's inscription alongside other elements in his burial chapel, it becomes clear that Weni was himself a member of a powerful elite family and the point of the propaganda exercise was to show that Weni was influential as the king's man, and so to reinforce the position of the king himself. Although this text looks like autobiography, it is, in fact, a scribal production to fit a political purpose, and is not actually historically biographical at all.

Nevertheless, Weni's autobiography does show how artful biographical and autobiographical material in public inscriptions could be, and how the temptation to read them at face value should always be resisted. Even when Nabopolassar, the first of the Neo-Babylonian kings, declares that he is the 'son of a nobody'[67] we should not necessarily assume that he was a complete unknown from a non-elite family, but that this kind of declaration was part of a well-known strategy of Mesopotamian kings to suggest that their origins were obscure, and allowed them to take on, or to exploit, the role of the 'stranger-king' (more on this later).[68] As we will see in Chapter 3, the pseudo-autobiography of Sargon (a well-known scribal school text) made such a claim about Sargon of Akkad.

What is important for us, however, is the pervasiveness of this motif. For example, it is used more than once in the Hebrew Bible, such as in the stories of Moses, the foundling who is adopted by the daughter of Pharaoh in *Exodus*, and David, the shepherd boy who becomes king in *1 & 2 Samuel*. Brian Lewis has compiled examples of variants on the basic story pattern from around the world.[69] As we shall discuss in Chapter 3, the versions of Cyrus' biography which emerge in parts of the Greek tradition also emphasised his humble origins, and have been linked to the written copies of the pseudo-autobiography of Sargon, providing a good example of interactions between oral and written traditions. The significance of this motif is both the indication of the charismatic qualities of the man who went from humble origins to high status and the implication of divine assistance. Herodotus'

Cyrus thinks that, because of the circumstances of his birth, the gods look after him, although it is also because of his misunderstanding of this relationship that he dies in battle against the Massagetan queen (see further Chapter 6).

However, there were other ways to talk about lineage. In the *Cyrus Cylinder* a different strategy is used, but still one that relies heavily on engagement with texts of the Mesopotamian scribal matrix. The second part of the text of the *Cylinder* is written in the first person, and begins with a strong, apparently personal, and autobiographical statement of Cyrus' identity (20-1):

> I am Cyrus, king of the universe, the great king, the powerful king, king of Babylon, king of Sumer and Akkad, king of the four quarters of the world, son of Cambyses, the great king, king of the city of Anshan, grandson of Cyrus, the great king, ki[ng of the ci]ty of Anshan, descendant of Teispes, the great king, king of the city of Anshan ...
>
> (Transl. Finkel)

The *Cyrus Cylinder* is a scribal text, and the level of input even Cyrus may have had in its production has been questioned. However, what is striking in this text is the use of royal genealogy to establish Cyrus' legitimacy. Although genealogies and royal titularies of this kind were more Assyrian in character than Babylonian (we will return to this issue in Chapter 2), Nabonidus did use such titulary in the *Ehulhul Cylinder*.[70] Nabonidus himself was a usurper,[71] and was very careful to situate his kingship as a seamless progression in relation to the previous Neo-Babylonian and even the Neo-Assyrian kings, especially Ashurbanipal, thereby showing his place in the sequence of 'Mesopotamian' kings.[72] As will be argued in Chapter 5, it is not accidental then that the *Cyrus Cylinder* also uses Assyrianising titulary, as the connection between the *Cyrus Cylinder* and the *Ehulhul Cylinder* are very close, and the *Cyrus Cylinder* is responding to Nabonidus' cylinder in a number of ways.

However, Cyrus' consistent choice of Assyrian-style titulary, and the fineness and delicacy of the intertextual reference to the *Enuma Elish*, and its potency, suggests that the Babylonian scribes in the production of the *Cyrus Cylinder* were prepared to concede quite as much as they were able to demand, and the text of the *Cylinder* must surely have been approved by Cyrus, just as Darius was later to approve the text of the Behistun text (DB §70). Cyrus is not just proclaimed as a legitimate ruler of Babylon chosen by Marduk; he is (like Marduk) Babylon's saviour, and even establishes himself as the special 'saviour' of Babylon.

Cyrus' relations with the Babylonians, and especially the priesthood, seem to have been relatively settled and secure. Negative propaganda about Nabonidus, in the form of the *Verse Account of Nabonidus*, also praising Cyrus' piety, was circulated. His son, Cambyses, ruled in Babylon as co-regent for a year after the conquest and probably fulfilled the requirements of the *akitu* festival in place of his father.[73] After that, while Cyrus himself may have visited Babylon three times (in 539, once between 538 and 534, and once in 531/30),[74] the rituals of the *akitu* festival were probably suspended, and the Babylonian priesthood seemed to have accepted the absence of their king.[75] Therefore, it is also necessary at this point to make some preliminary comments about ancient kingship, and the different ways that it presented itself in the ancient Near East.

The Many Faces of Kingship: Ancient Kingship in the Near East

One of the reasons kingship (whether ancient or modern) remains so interesting for modern analysis is because of not only its pervasiveness in world history, but also its fundamental relational quality between ruler and ruled and so its connection to leadership. Whenever one person is differentiated from others in a group, that relationship needs not just to be explained but also justified and given a framework within which difference can be limited. At the very least, it needs to be controlled, or the lack of limitation needs to be accepted, even in societies based on putative social and political equality. It is no accident that within the context of fifth- and fourth-century Athenian democracy, theories of positive kingship were developed in order to explain the need for, and parameters of, political differentiation among those who at least thought of themselves as politically equal.[76]

In fact, as Quigley has argued, the fundamental characteristic of kingship is that of 'separation' of 'the king' from 'the people', and that this relationship of separation is then negotiated and articulated through ritual.[77] In particular, he argues that it is the installation ritual that sets the person of the king apart from the rest of the community, and makes them extraordinary so that they stand outside conventional society.

The idea of separation which Quigley thinks is so important is also fundamental in the recent work of Graeber and Sahlins.[78] For them, however, kingship is about sovereignty, which (drawing on Schmitt's definition of sovereignty as the ability to determine the state of exception)[79] they define as the power of command supported by violence, or the ability to set the law aside. Importantly, they point to the violence implicit in kingship, which, even if never used, has potency, but which can be turned against the king himself. The king is able to hold this kind of sovereignty because he is set apart from the rest of the community, and simply through being the king (not through ritual) is a metahuman, and therefore has a natural association with divinity.

Strathern,[80] and Moin and Strathern,[81] approach the problem from a slightly different angle, through the lens of the Axial Age. They are also interested in sacred kingship, but understand it in the contrast between immanence and transcendence. On their terms, immanentist societies are those where the relationship (god-king-people) is accepted uncritically, and there is seen to be a 'natural' relationship where the king is accepted as sharing the powers of the gods, and is divinised. Transcendent societies, on the other hand, are those where the three-way relationship has been abstracted and critiqued so that the king does not function in society as a metahuman, but becomes the interpreter of divine will through critical reflection and external second-order media, such as holy books or law. In a transcendent society, the king is a figure of righteousness: he does not rule, but scripture or law does. However, they also argue that in immanentist societies, the divinisation of the king does not mean necessarily that he becomes 'a god'. Instead, the position of the king is more ambiguous. They say, 'kings are "in-between" things: already and evidently human, they are pushed part way into the sphere of the divine in order to intercede on our behalf'.[82]

In many societies of the eastern Mediterranean and Near East, kingship was the organising principle of the political community (although not always, and not everywhere). Broadly speaking, these societies were also immanentist in character, although there were movements towards modes of transcendent thinking, and there was no simple linear progress between immanence and transcendence. In archaic Greece, for example, Homeric kings ruled through divine law (*themistes*) which they received from Zeus (e.g., Homer, *Iliad* 9.96–9). Therefore, in the ancient world, for the most, we are dealing with kings as 'metahumans' at one level or another.

However, we do need to ask questions about their metahuman distance. To be a king, and therefore metahuman, is one thing. The other is to ask what kind of metahumans kings were, and in what relation to divinity kings were thought to stand. For some Greek rulers, for example, their divinised characteristics were thought to derive from their heredity: the Spartan and Macedonian kings, for instance, traced their descent from Heracles, and so from Zeus. Others retrospectively 'discovered' or 'recognised' their heroic/divine descent once they had achieved the status of the ruler on account of their deeds.[83] Alexander the Great, towards the end of his short life, was able to equate himself with Zeus (and even seems to have imagined himself wielding Zeus' thunderbolt).[84] Where along this spectrum can we place Cyrus or did he place himself?

In order to think about these questions, we need to begin by considering in more detail two dominant models of kingship in the ancient Near East (Assyrian and Babylonian) against which Cyrus needed to create and define his own particular royal ideology.

Kingship in Mesopotamia

In Mesopotamia, kingship was thought to come from heaven: the opening lines of the *Sumerian King List* state this quite clearly.[85] In fact, individual kings were chosen by gods, even before birth. Ashurbanipal, for example, goes so far as to say that, before his own parents were born, the god

Sin, 'who created me for kingship', had named him to rebuild Ehulhul (the temple of the god at Harran).[86] Likewise, Nabonidus says in the *Ehulhul Cylinder* that while he was in his mother's womb, the god Sin and the goddess Ningal decided his royal fate.[87]

However, despite the close, if complex, historical, cultural and religious connections between Babylon and Assyria,[88] there were also marked differences in their ideologies of kingship.[89] A fundamental difference between Babylonian and Assyrian kingship was their relationship to the temples, the priests, and so also the gods. The Babylonian king, in marked contrast to the Assyrian king who was initiated, did not have the authority to officiate as a cultic agent: he was not a priest and did not play an active part in a cultic ritual.[90] The varying relationship to the gods of the Neo-Babylonian and Neo-Assyrian kings exemplifies ideological difference suggested by Graeber and Sahlins, who have talked about these tensions in terms of the 'divinisation' or 'sacralisation' of the king:[91]

> Political struggle over the power of the king generally takes the form of a battle between two principles: divine kingship and sacred kingship. In practice, divine kingship is the essence of sovereignty: it is the ability to act as if one were a god; to step outside the confines of the human, and return to rain favor, or destruction, with arbitrariness and impunity. Such power may be accompanied by the theory that the king by doing so demonstrates he is an actual embodiment of some already-existing metahuman being. But it may not be; it could as easily be that by acting in this way, the king himself becomes a metahuman being. Japanese shoguns (a few anyway), Roman emperors, or Ganda kabaka could all become gods in their own right. To be 'sacred', in contrast, is to be set apart, hedged about by customs and taboos; the restrictions surrounding sacralized kings – 'not to touch the earth, not to see the sun' in Frazer's famous dictum – are ways not only of recognizing the presence of unaccountable divine power, but also, crucially, of confining, controlling, and limiting it.[92]

This variance between kings who had a divinised agency and kings whose agency was limited by their sacralisation, at least in its expression, is evident in the ways that Assyrian and Babylonian kings related to the gods. At least in their public writings, the Neo-Babylonian rulers emphasised their piety by maintaining the temples of the gods, and the rhetoric of kingship insisted that it was the gods who held agency in the defeat of enemies.[93] For example, despite his successful campaigning against the Assyrians at the end of the seventh century (known principally from a Babylonian Chronicle: *ABC* 3), Nabopolassar in his building inscriptions only rarely makes reference to his military success, and then is very careful to attribute it to the gods.[94] However, he also deliberately distances himself from seeking glory in such activities, instead emphasising his weakness and the gods' strength. For example, in a foundation cylinder outlining repairs to the city walls, he says:

> (As for) the Assyrians, who from distant days had ruled over all of the people and had made the people of the land suffer under its heavy yoke, I, the weak (and) powerless one constantly seeks out the lord of lords (Marduk), with the powerful strength of the gods Nabû and Marduk – my lords – I barred them from the land of Akkad and had (the Babylonians) cast off their yoke.
>
> (Transl. Weiershäuser and Novotny)[95]

Nevertheless, in the same cylinder, he even goes on to declare:

> Any king in the future, either a son or a grandson who comes after me, whom the god Marduk names for dominion over the land: Do not set your hearts on feats of might and power, (but rather) constantly seek out the shrines of the gods Nabû and Marduk so that they may kill your opponent(s).
>
> (Transl. Weiershäuser and Novotny)[96]

However, even though Babylonian kings also took part in annual kingship rituals as part of the *akitu* festival, which included the humiliation of the king at the hands of the priests as an indication of the delicate balance that needed to be maintained between the king and the priestly elite,[97] and charisma was channelled through the gods, in another building inscription Nabopolassar is sought out by god to become pre-eminent because of his piety:

> The god Shazu, the lord who knows the hearts of the gods of heaven and netherworld, the one who constantly observes the *ingenious behaviour* of the people, for me — the child who could not be found among the people — he observed my intention(s) and made me pre-eminent in the land where I was created. He called (my) name for dominion over the land and people, made a good *lamassu* walk beside me, (and) allowed (me) successfully to undertake everything that I did. He made the god Nergal, the almighty one of the gods, march at my side; he killed my enemy (and) cut down my opponent.
>
> (Transl. Weiershäuser & Novotny)[98]

He is great because the god makes him great. The Assyrian kings, on the other hand, confidently asserted (with the help of the gods) their personal greatness and strength. For example, the late tenth-/early ninth-century Adad-narari II says:[99]

> Great gods, who take firm decisions, who decree destinies; they properly created me, Adad-narari, attentive prince, [...], they altered my stature to lordly stature, they rightly made perfect my features and filled my

lordly body with wisdom. After the great gods had decreed (my destiny, after) they had entrusted to me the sceptre for the shepherding of the people, (after) they had raised me above crowned kings (and) placed on my head the royal splendour; they made my almighty name greater than (that of) all lords, the important name Adad-narari, king of Assyria, they called me. Strong king, king of Assyria, king of the four quarters, sun(god) of all people, I; son of Aššur-dan, appointee of the god Enlil, vice-regent of Aššur, who defeated all his enemies, son of Tiglath-pileser, king of [Assyria], holy offspring of Aššur-reša-iši, martial sovereign, trampler of criminals; at that time, by the edict of the great gods, my sovereignty (and) dominion were decreed (and) they named me to plunder the possessions of the lands. I am king, I am lord, I am powerful, I am important, I am praiseworthy, I am magnificent, I am strong, I am mighty, I am fierce, I am enormously radiant, I am a hero, I am a warrior, I am a virile lion, I am foremost, I am exalted, I am raging ...

(Transl. Grayson)

The son and grandson of kings, Adad-narari's kingship is given to him by the gods, who 'changed' (*ušutennu*) him so that he had a 'lordly appearance' (*nab-ni-ti* EN-*ti*) (6) as well as having the other virtues of a charismatic king.[100] This declaration is of charismatic kingship writ large. Simo Parpola has written of the Assyrian kings:

According to Assyrian royal inscriptions, kings were called and pre-destined to their office from the beginning of time. Their features were miraculously perfected in their mother's womb by the mother goddess, that is, the spirit of god, and their intellectual and physical abilities were perfected by the great gods, that is, the powers and attributes of god.[101]

The point about the Neo-Babylonian kings, on the other hand, was that they were charismatic rulers in their external-facing activities (e.g., Nabopolassar and the Assyrians, Nebuchadnezzar and the Levant, Nabonidus and Arabia). Nebuchadnezzar even seems to have built a palace in Babylon to house the war trophies of him and his father (the 'North Palace').[102] However, in terms of the home audience, extraordinarily, for the most part military success had to be repackaged for the local priestly elite in terms in which the Babylonian kings largely (if not entirely) effaced their agency in order to emphasise their piety in dealings with the gods.[103]

In fact, as a control on the absolute power of the charismatic king (whether Assyrian or Babylonian), Mesopotamian literature emphasised that kingship was the gift of the gods: whatever the charismatic qualities of individual kings, kingship came from heaven, and the gods could move kingship from one city to another without warning. It is significant that even the Middle Assyrian coronation ritual included the humiliation ritual of being slapped in the face by the priest. Pongratz-Leisten says: 'This humiliation was not so much a temporary degradation in status as in the Babylonian case, but was intended to stress the Assyrian king's inferior status vis-à-vis Aššur, i.e. his stewardship, with kingship being reserved for the supreme god'.[104] So the Assyrian kings, although having an 'in-betweenness' with divinity, could not claim a divinity such as that later to be claimed by Alexander the Great or his early successors where they became living gods,[105] or indeed perhaps Cyrus himself.

However, the lines between divinised and sacralised kingship were not absolute. Even the sacralised kings of Babylon could make play with divinising strategies in order to legitimise their positions, especially when their own right to rule was open to doubt. At this point, we need to introduce another anthropological phenomenon: the stranger-king, that is, a ruler who comes from outside the community, and whose violence (in usurpation) needs to be explained and controlled.[106] Marshall Sahlins, in his discussion of the phenomenon of the stranger-king, points to the fact that, by their nature, all kings are outsiders, or at least set apart from, their societies: 'royalty is the foreigner'.[107] Nevertheless, stranger-kings often come from outside the community and take power from their predecessors because of their own greater strength:

> The hero manifests a nature above, beyond, and greater than the people he is destined to rule – hence his power to do so. However inhibited or sublimated in the established kingdom, the monstrous and violent nature of the king remains an essential condition of his sovereignty. Indeed, as a sign of the metahuman sources of royal power, force, notably as demonstrated in victory, can function politically as a positive means of attraction as well as a physical means of domination.[108]

By marrying 'the princess' (the daughter of the king), the disorder and rupture caused by the usurpation are mediated and naturalised by integration into the natural and peaceful order of the community represented by its women and individualised in their princess.[109] One means of controlling the power of the stranger-king was through what Graeber and Sahlins have called 'adverse sacralization',[110] that is the king maintaining his metahuman status but being denied his human power by hemming him around with ritual.

The phenomenon of stranger-kingship was a feature of the Neo-Babylonian period. There were no less than three stranger-kings before Cyrus: Nabopolassar (who describes himself as 'the son of a nobody'), Neriglissar and Nabonidus. The Greek historian Berossus (*BNJ* 680 F 9a), writing in the third century BCE, told a story about the early sixth-century Neriglissar (who is known from other sources as an Aramaean tribal chief and a military commander in the army of Nebuchadnezzar at Jerusalem – so a real-life stranger-king)[111] that he married the unnamed sister of Nebuchadnezzar, and, on Nebuchadnezzar's death, overthrew the king's son, Amel-Marduk. Berossus' story sits on the cusp of storytelling and lived events. Did the actual stranger-king marry the princess, or was this just a later invention to naturalise his 'foreignness'?

It is interesting that in the *Babylon Stele*, Nabonidus (himself a stranger-king) makes no reference to the dynastic rupture caused by Neriglissar, but describes himself as the appropriate successor of Nebuchadnezzar and Neriglissar.[112] However, he does excuse his own insurrection against Neriglissar's son by saying Labashi-Marduk was untutored in the rites of the gods and that he had ascended the throne against the gods' will.[113] Nabonidus, who claimed, as we have seen, that he was chosen by the gods to be king when he was in his mother's womb, nevertheless used the 'divinising' strategies in his battle against the drive towards sacralisation.[114] Cyrus was later to use these very same weapons, although to even greater effect.

As we shall see, in the text of the *Cyrus Cylinder*, Cyrus denounces Nabonidus' own impiety and improper use of the rites (3–8). However, so far from trying to obscure his role as a stranger-king, Cyrus highlights it by declaring himself as a king of Anshan, descended from kings of Anshan. In this document, Cyrus cuts his own path. He is chosen by Marduk, who has searched the world for him (11–12), as the ultimate stranger-king. His position, however, is not naturalised by marrying the princess, but by becoming the active agent of the gods in their cosmic war, and (as we shall see) in this way, breaks the bonds of sacralisation (although he does also make concessions to them) to become a divinised king.

Cyrus' own background was very different from the kings of Mesopotamia, either the Assyrians or the Babylonians. In origin, he was apparently a nomadic pastoralist (rather than a city-dweller), even if a member of the warrior elite, and he came from a social, political and cultural world therefore at some level at odds with the cosmopolitan city-life of Mesopotamia. While Cyrus' community does seem to have been stratified, nomadic pastoralists practised not kingship as such, but a kind of 'pre-state' chieftainship.[115] However, with his military success, first with the largely Median army of the *Umman-manda* which brought to him the wealth of Ecbatana, and the swift move to at least a limited sedentism in Fars, Cyrus' position also changed. With the taking of Babylon, in particular, Cyrus was confronted with the nuanced kingship styles of Mesopotamia, which he had to navigate. It is certainly the case that Cyrus committed to at least part of the bargain struck in the text of his *Cylinder*: he undertook temple restoration work at Ur and Uruk, known from stamped bricks (see Chapter 2), which shows an attempt on his part to honour the routines of Babylonian kingship.[116] He also undertook irrigation works to the north of Babylon, and seems to have strengthened routes between Mesopotamia and Anshan/Fars through the development of a royal residence at Taoce on the Persian Gulf,[117] and kept an active interest in Babylonian religious matters in the years after the taking of the city.[118]

However, Cyrus is inventing a new style of particularly 'Near Eastern' kingship. Although the development is shadowy, and we can only glimpse its movement, part of the greatness of Cyrus was the swiftness with which he evolved from nomadic chieftain to 'King of Countries'. In the *Cyrus Cylinder*, Cyrus shows himself adept at negotiating the Mesopotamian scribal culture to his advantage, and is able to use this text to position himself not only as the pious ruler chosen by Marduk, but also as a cosmic warrior almost on a par with the god of gods.

Biographical Writings

So, how do we write a biography of Cyrus? But what is biography, or biographical writing, and how is it different from other kinds of writing? This is a question that needs asking not only in relation to ancient accounts of Cyrus and his deeds, but also of this book. What does it mean to write a biography of someone who even in his own life time had become so enshrouded by many different and conflicting stories about his deeds? Momigliano, in his seminal work on Greek biography, says that biography is 'some kind of history' and '[a]n account of the life of a man from birth to death'.[119] Hermione Lee, on the other hand, in her *Biography: A Very Short Introduction* says that 'If covering a "whole life" implies that biography should proceed chronologically from cradle to grave, then this rule has been so often broken as not to count',[120] and this point seems to be true for ancient biographical writing just as much as for modern biography.[121]

For Cyrus, as we will see, very little of his actual life can be reconstructed. In fact, part of the point of this book is to establish just how much we cannot say about Cyrus as a historical figure. His 'lives' as we have them in our sources are mostly legend rather than history. For that reason, it is not methodologically sound simply to choose one story in preference to another or to create composite accounts out of the various legends about him, any more than it is legitimate to try to find a historical account about Naramsin in the *Curse of Agade*. We certainly cannot genuinely reconstruct a cradle-to-grave narrative for Cyrus. For this reason, this book might be thought of as an anti-biography.

However, that does not mean that the stories of Cyrus' life, and about his deeds, cannot tell us interesting things about him, the ways in which the transition from pastoralist chieftain to the ruler of an empire was legitimised, and so about his kingship, just as the *Curse of Agade* also tells us about attitudes to kingship and the relationship between the king and the priestly elite in the Old Babylonian Period (second millennium BCE).

Although it is not possible to write a 'biography' of Cyrus in any straightforward sense, this book will use the conceit of a largely cradle-to-grave structure (apart from an initial chapter to clear the ground) in order to see what we can tease out of our sources about how Cyrus was representing himself and how he was being represented at various moments in his life and after-life. Because his life is written in stories, which make no attempt to rationalise themselves against each other, what we end up with is an array of different Cyruses. Although we may not learn as much about his actual life as a biography might suggest, there are many important and serious questions that can be asked about the nature of his kingship, and kingship more generally, in a Near Eastern cultural setting. As a consequence, rather surprisingly, a sense of the man, how he was understood, and the cultural context in which he became the ruler of a world empire, do emerge.

Notes

1. See, e.g., Ansari (2012), 21–2, 166–79; Steele (2022).
2. Weiershäuser and Novotny (eds.) (2020), Nabonidus no. 28.
3. See Pelling (2006).
4. Ctesias T 1–3.
5. See also Stronk (2010), 73–84.
6. On Nicolaus of Damascus (F 66) and Ctesias: Lenfant (2000), 304–9. On Ctesias and Near Eastern traditions, see Chapter 3.
7. On Photius, and the composition of his 'summaries', see Treadgold (1980), esp. 1–36; N.G. Wilson (1994), 1–22. Interestingly, Photius (145b-146b [189]) probably also read Nicolaus of Damascus' universal history, although he does not remember much about it; Treadgold (1980), 63–4.
8. E.g., the Persian women who display their genitals to their fleeing menfolk to remind them to be brave: Ctesias F 8d*§43; the puppet show at the siege of Sardis to frighten the Lydians: Ctesias F 9.4, 9a–c.
9. Waters (2017), 103.
10. Tuplin (2013); Atack (2020), 134–44.
11. Bricks from Ur: Schaudig (2001), 549; http://oracc.org/ribo/Q006654/ (accessed 25/10/2021); compare also Walker (1981), no. 115; bricks from Uruk: Schaudig (2001), 548; http://oracc.org/ribo/Q006655/ (accessed 25/10/2021). See also Kuhrt (2007a), 74–5.
12. Edelman (2005), 151–208.
13. See Grayson (1975b), 3–9.
14. See Westenholz (1997), no. 12 (*Epic of Naramsin*); Cooper (1983).
15. Schaudig (2001), 563–78; English translation: Kuhrt (2007a), 75–80.
16. See further Chapter 5 n. 60.
17. See especially Schaudig (2018); Schaudig (2019).
18. Note also Berossus, *BNJ* 680 F 10 which gives Cyrus a reign of 9 years from his conquest of Babylon.
19. E.g., Kuhrt (1995a), 2.656: 'Herodotus gives us very precise regnal years for Cyrus (29), which suggests he had access to a reliable (written?) source'; cf. Lenfant (2004), lxvi.
20. See, e.g., Ballati (2017), 36–7.
21. Most of the Kur River Basin is in the 200–400 mm isohyets range (Sumner (1972), 12), so that there is enough water for agriculture only if irrigation from rivers is also possible (van der Mieroop (2016), 7). On pastoral nomadism in the Kur River Basin, see also Sumner (1972), 250–2, 265.
22. Sumner (1972) has shown that in earlier periods irrigated agriculture did play a role in the economy of the Kur River Basin. On the issue of the archaeological 'invisibility' of nomads more generally, see Cribb (1991), 65–83; note also Finkelstein (1992).
23. Potts (2014), esp. ch.3.

24. See Miroschedji (1990); Henkelman (2008a), 41–57.
25. See Salzman (2002), 246.
26. See Briant (1990), 79–80.
27. Rowton (1976).
28. Enclosed nomadism: Rowton (1974).
29. A. Alizadeh (2010).
30. Saltzman (2002), 256–60; see also essays in Szuchman (ed.) (2009).
31. Briant (2002), 19–20; Xen. *Cyrop.* 1.3.3, who says that the Persians did not have horses, but this was almost certainly not the case.
32. Compare the Twareg of the Sahara: Sáenz (1991). See also Chapter 4.
33. M.B. Garrison (1991).
34. M.B. Garrison (2011).
35. See further Chapter 2.
36. See further Chapter 2.
37. Macdonald (2009), esp. 49–118, quotation from 51. cf. Lindner (1982).
38. Thomas (1992), esp. 15–51, quotation from 48.
39. Taylor (2013).
40. Finkel (2013), 11.
41. Taylor (2013), 64–6.
42. Stolper (2013), 42.
43. Taylor (2013), 67; cf. Stolper (2013), 41.
44. Schaudig (2018). He says (70) the language of the *Cylinder* is 'a beautiful and flowery Babylonian'.
45. Taylor (2013).
46. Finkel (2013), 13–5.
47. Finkel (2013), 15–24; cf. Stolper (2013), 48–9.
48. Finkel (2013), 18–23; see also Waerzeggers (2015), 190.
49. Carr (2005).
50. Carr (2005), esp. 17–46; van der Torn (2007); Jursa (2011), 184–204.
51. Postgate (2007), 338.
52. E.g., Carr (2005), 27–8.
53. Weiershäuser and Novotny (2020), 17–8.
54. For example, Simo Parpola makes the point that, even though scribal literacy was a specialist skill, in the eighth century at least functional literacy was probably widespread: Parpola (1997). Note also Charpin (2010); Veldhuis (2011). Cf. Jursa (2011), for widespread literacy among the priestly class at Babylon.
55. Cooper (1992), 114–5.
56. Porter (1993), 108–17.
57. Weiershäuser and Novotny (eds.) (2020), Nabonidus no. 28.
58. Note also Canepa (2015), 12.
59. Carr (2005), 34–46.
60. Beaulieu (2007), 141–2.
61. There is much discussion about the level of Cyrus' input into this text, given the context of its composition. Haubold (2007, 50–2) sees this as an essentially 'Persian' document. Kuhrt (2007b, 173–5), on the other hand, does not see in this document evidence of Persian policy (especially not of religious tolerance as the *Cylinder* has traditionally been understood), but instead draws out the way in which the Babylonians were able to exert pressure over Cyrus to fit into these Babylonian norms of royal behaviour in committing to the preservation of Babylonian rituals and temple buildings. Waerzeggers (2015, 191), in a similar vein, says that the *Cylinder* reads like 'a manifesto of conditional collaboration by the vanquished, rather than a charter of goodwill by the victor,' although it may be worth asking what kind of balance was struck between priests and king. Whether or not the Babylonian priests had rejected the rule of Nabonidus

because of his alleged preference for the moon god Sin over Marduk, as is suggested in more general terms by the *Cyrus Cylinder* and more specifically by the *Verse Account of Nabonidus* (Schaudig (2001, 553–78), it does seem that this document cuts a path between the new ruler's assertion of his position in his declaration of his heritage and his kingship (in unBabylonian terms), and his new subjects' requirements for a pious ruler, although Kuhrt (1990) argues that there is not strong evidence for priestly discontent with Nabonidus during his reign. The possibility has also been raised that it was based at least partially on a Persian document: Finkel (2013), 25. Schaudig (2018), however, places the document as a whole very much in a Babylonian context.

62. Haubold (2007), 50–2; cf. Schaudig (2001), 555 n. 906. See Schaudig (2018), esp. 72–6.
63. Talon (2005), 67.
64. Bidmead (2014); Waerzeggers (2015), 187–9.
65. Haubold (2007), 52; note also Bidmead (2014), 173.
66. Richards (2002).
67. http://oracc.org/ribo/Q005362/: no. 3.8, http://oracc.org/ribo/Q005366/: no. 7.4 (accessed 16/05/2022).
68. See Beaulieu (2018), 224–5.
69. B. Lewis (1980), 211–67.
70. Weierhäuser and Novotny (eds.) (2020), Nabonidus no. 28 i.1–6.
71. See Beaulieu (1989), 88–90.
72. E.g., Weierhäuser and Novotny (eds.) (2020), Nabonidus nos. 3 x.34–5, 28 i.39.
73. The discussion of the co-regency is extensive, but see, e.g., Oppenheim (1985), 558; Peat (1989); Zawadzki (1996). On Cambyses' role in the *akitu* festival: Tolini (2011), 125–45 (*pace* George (1996), 377–85).
74. Tolini (2011), 147–50.
75. Waerzeggers (2015), 199–202, although note also Bidmead (2014), 140–2.
76. L. Mitchell (2019).
77. Quigley (2005).
78. Graeber and Sahlins (2017).
79. C. Schmitt (2005), esp. 5: 'Sovereign is he who decides on the exception'.
80. Strathern (2019).
81. Moin and Strathern (2022).
82. Moin and Strathern (2022), 14.
83. L. Mitchell (2013a), 58.
84. See L. Mitchell (2013b); L. Mitchell (2022).
85. Glassner (2004), no. 1.
86. Novotny and Jeffers (eds.) (2018), Ashurbanipal no. 10 ii.29–32. Stol (2000), 83–9; Polonsky (2006), 308.
87. Weierhäuser and Novotny (eds.) (2020), Nabonidus no. 28 i.4–5.
88. See, e.g., Bottéro (2001); Crouch (2013); Pongratz-Leisten (2015); Finn (2017).
89. Ambos (2014).
90. Warezeggers (2011); Brisch (2022).
91. Moin and Strathern, on the other hand, make a slightly different distinction in the immanentist mode, where immanentist ('divinised') rulers are categorised as 'heroic' and 'cosmic' kingship: (2022), 14–5; note also Strathern (2019), 164–76.
92. Graeber and Sahlins (2017), 7–8.
93. See also Waerzeggers (2011), 729.
94. As we will see in Chapter 5, the destruction of cities was imputed not to the activities of the king, but to the gods' decision to abandon the city. Note also, however, especially the *Epic of Nabopolassar*, which adopts a different attitude to Nabopolassar's engagement with the Assyrians: see further Chapter 4.

95. http://oracc.org/ribo/Q005366/: no. 7.17–22 (accessed 24/03/2022).
96. http://oracc.org/ribo/Q005366/: no. 7.31–4, cf. http://oracc.org/ribo/Q005362/: 3.22–6 (accessed 24/03/2022). Note also Dalley (2021), 218–9.
97. Bidmead (2014), 77–83; note also Waerzeggers (2011).
98. http://oracc.org/ribo/Q005366/ Nabopolassar no. 7.8–16, note also 3.15–27 (accessed 16/05/2022).
99. Grayson (1991), 147: A.0.99.2 5–15.
100. Note also Pongratz-Leisten (2015), 440–1: '… high rank and status is intrinsically linked with perfection in outer appearance … Only the perfect royal body can be turned into a *body politic* and be entrusted with kingship by the gods'.
101. Parpola (1999).
102. Beaulieu (2017), 10.
103. Compare, however, an inscription from the reign of Neriglissar where the king gives the details of a campaign against an enemy (Weierhäuser & Novotny (eds.) (2020), Neriglissar no. 7; cf. no. 1 i.37–ii.4).
104. Pongratz-Leisten (2015), 438.
105. For Alexander the Great and Demetrius Poliorcetes as living gods, see L. Mitchell (2022).
106. On the 'stranger-king', see Sahlins (1981); Sahlins (2008); Graeber and Sahlins (2017), 5–7,
107. Sahlins (1981), 112.
108. Graeber and Sahlins (2017), 5.
109. Sahlins (1981), 122.
110. Graeber and Sahlins (2017), 8.
111. On Neriglissar as an Aramaean chieftan, see Beaulieu (2013), 32–7. For Neriglissar at Jerusalem: Jursa (2010a), 85. More generally, see also Da Riva (2013), 14; Waerzeggers (2015), 182–3.
112. Weierhäuser and Novotny (eds.) (2020), Nabonidus no. 3 v.14–24.
113. Weierhäuser and Novotny (eds.) (2020), Nabonidus no. 3 iv.34–42.
114. Even though Kuhrt (1990) has interpreted Nabonidus' 10 years in Arabia as a period of imperialist expansion, Nabonidus himself says very little about what he was doing in Arabia, or what his purpose was in going there: cf. Weierhäuser and Novotny (eds.) (2020), Nabonidus no. 47 i.22b–27a. On Nabonidus' activities in Teima, see Levavi (2020), 65.
115. Khazanov (1994), 164–9.
116. See Waerzeggers (2015), 195–7.
117. Irrigation works north of Babylon: Tolini (2011), 41–3. On Taoce: Henkelman (2008b); Tolini (2011), 73–7. For sea routes between Mesopotamia and the Persian Gulf, see Matthews and Nashli (2022), 19.
118. Jursa (2010b), 77–8.
119. Momigliano (1971), 6, 11.
120. H. Lee (2009), 8.
121. Pelling in his work on Plutarch, the great biographer of the mid first to mid second century AD, suggests that not even biography in its fullest sense has to cover the whole of a life but that political biography (as opposed to literary biography) did not always concern itself with births and deaths, because this was not the thing that was of interest in the 'life': Pelling (2011), esp. 301–2. On the genre of biography, see also Pelling (2022).

2 Cyrus

A Near Eastern King

Cyrus is often called a 'Persian' and the founder of the 'Achaemenid' empire. While he was certainly the second of these (because it was to become an empire dominated by an Achaemenid dynasty), that does not mean that Cyrus himself would have recognised this label. In fact, the realisation that the population of Fars, the geographical region in which Cyrus was born, was multi-ethnic in character, has raised significant questions in regard to how Cyrus would have perceived himself. These questions also have importance for how he imagined his style of kingship, especially as his empire grew to embrace not only the southwest and central Zagros region, but also Anatolia, Mesopotamia and central Asia as far as the Indus. So, in such a varied political and theological landscape, how might Cyrus have thought about who he was and who he wanted to become?

We will begin this chapter by looking at the question of his possible birth identity: did he self-define as Persian? Or Achaemenid? Or something else? What did it mean to be 'king of Anshan', particularly when the ancient Elamite city of Anshan no longer sustained a permanent population, sedentary structures, or political institutions? Was he actually Elamite? What was his connection to Parsua (one of a number of related toponyms for Fars)? Or Anshan? With the capture of Babylon, should we see Cyrus transforming himself into a Mesopotamian king? Or, in the formation of his ideology of kingship, was he trying to do something new? What we will see is that, far from subscribing to a 'Persian' ethnic identity, especially in an imperial context as 'King of Countries', Cyrus' identity seems to have centred on his self-identification as a 'Near Eastern' king.

Cyrus: A Persian?

Defining an individual's 'identity' is not an easy task, as it is so contextual. The identity that one is ascribed, or claims for oneself, in one context, could be different in another, and, in any case, most people have multiple identities. Likewise, both because of its shifting nature and subjectivity, 'ethnicity' is generally not an easy or satisfactory analytical category. While the fifth-century Greek historian Herodotus gave to one of his speakers

DOI: 10.4324/9781003384458-2

a definition of 'Hellenicity' on the basis of shared characteristics (shared blood, language, sacrifices, shrines and sacrifices to the gods and way of life: 8.144.2), these are not universal categories by which all ethnicities can be marked out, and it is not even at all clear that they were really certain in a Greek context either, except in a 'fictive' or imaginary sense.[1]

Modern analyses of ethnicity and ethnic identities are equally difficult.[2] Following the influential work of Jonathan Hall,[3] most ancient historians have understood ethnicity as a socially constructed group identification based on putative claims of shared descent. However, not all find this narrow means of defining ethnicity helpful and broader definitions based on social practice and cultural performance are now being explored, especially, although not exclusively, by archaeologists, who nevertheless recognise the difficulties in defining ethnic identity on these terms because of their mutability and 'complex situational dynamics'.[4]

Although there are references to 'Persians' (people from Parsa) in late seventh/early sixth century Neo-Elamite texts,[5] it is not clear when the idea of 'Persianness' crystallised as an ethnonym, ascribing certain characteristics to a group which also differentiated them from others, nor whether Cyrus would have called himself 'Persian', or even 'Achaemenid'.[6] Herodotus tells us the 'Persians' were organised in tribes (*genea*: 1.125.3), although even in antiquity, these tribes, some of which Herodotus also tells us were nomadic (1.125.4), did not necessarily represent descent groups, and Potts has suggested that instead, we should see them as political affiliations.[7] In fact, as we will see further in the next chapter, nomadic tribes may form on the basis of political or economic interest, but then retrospectively explain their formation through the idiom of kinship. Although Darius was later to declare himself on the inscription at Behistun as 'king in Parsa' and a descendant of Achaemenes,[8] and elsewhere as a 'Persian son of a Persian, an Aryan of Aryan stock' (DNa13–14, DSe 12–13), there is a discussion about what these labels mean. Widmer, for example, argues that *Pārsa* signifies here a multi-ethnic political group, while 'Aryan' refers to the descent group.[9] Inscriptions at Cyrus' palace at Pasargadae, in the Morghab valley on the Pulvar River plain, which describe Cyrus as 'Achaemenian' (CMa, CMc/DMa and DMc), are now generally thought to be additions made by Darius towards the end of the sixth century.[10] Waters concludes that Cyrus was not actually an Achaemenid and not related to Darius, although not all agree.[11]

Cyrus: King of Anshan

Whether or not Cyrus was an Achaemenid, it may be that we cannot really even call him 'Persian', even in its most basic sense of a 'man from Parsa'. At least at Babylon, Cyrus was styled as the king of Anshan and descended from kings of Anshan, which was the name for both a city and a region in the province of Fars in the southwest Zagros mountains. The city of Anshan was formerly a major centre in what Miroshedji has called the Elamite confederacy, which was ethnically, politically and culturally diverse, and which always had a loose unity.[12] In these Babylonian texts, Anshan is sometimes designated by the determinatives as a city (URU) and sometimes as a country (KUR), although the urban centre of Anshan was in fact deserted throughout the Neo-Elamite period, a point of great significance.[13]

Thus, on the *Cyrus Cylinder* (so in the period after the fall of Babylon), it is declared (20-22): 'I am Cyrus, king of the universe, great king, mighty king, king of Babylon, king of Sumer and Akkad, king of the four quarters, the son of Cambyses, great king, king of (the city of) Anshan, grandson of Cyrus, great king, king of (the city of) Anshan, a descendant of Teispes, great king, king of (the city of) Anshan, of an eternal line of kingship ...'. A building inscription from Ur likewise uses a similar style declaring that Cyrus is the son of Cambyses and king of (the country of) Anshan.[14] In a slightly earlier Babylonian text from Sippar, the *Ehulhul Cylinder* (after 543 BCE and before Cyrus took Babylon),[15] Nabonidus, the last king of Babylon, also gives Cyrus the title 'Cyrus, king of (the country of) Anshan'.[16]

This may mean that Cyrus as king of Anshan was a Babylonian view of Cyrus' heritage, although it is more probable that this is how Cyrus wished to style himself even before he took Babylon. This point seems to be suggested by the inscription on the cylinder seal from Persepolis, an heirloom (see Chapter 1), which says (in Elamite) that it is the seal of Cyrus of Anshan, son of Teispes (PFS 93*).[17] At face value, it would appear, and it is often assumed, that the Cyrus of the seal is the grandfather of our Cyrus named on the *Cyrus Cylinder*. Henkelman points out that this connection is not necessarily inevitable,[18] although the use of the seal at Darius' court does suggest that Darius was keen to show support for the 'Teispid' element in his family, or at least to enhance that link, which he makes in his genealogy on the Behistun inscription. If the Cyrus of the seal was an ancestor of our Cyrus, it looks like the identification with Anshan (although again it probably cannot refer to the city of Anshan in terms of a sedentary seat of power) is important.

Nevertheless, we need to account for this focus on the city in the *Cyrus Cylinder* (as opposed to the region or country of Anshan). From a Mesopotamian point of view, kings were identified with city culture and the king was closely associated with the gods. After 689 BCE, with the destruction of Babylon by Sennacherib and the complete neglect of the temples, later Babylonian Chronicles describe this period as 'kingless' 'because of the absence or destruction of the statue of Marduk, the tutelary deity'.[19] In that sense, the reference to Anshan as a city may reflect a Babylonian/Mesopotamian perspective of kingship, in the manner of the *Sumerian King Lists* (where kingship passes from one city to another), as Zournatzi argues.[20] Indeed, the apparent self-declaration of identity on the *Cyrus Cylinder* is written very much within a Near Eastern tradition of royal genealogy and royal titulary.[21]

Cyrus as an Assyrian King?

Cyrus' Assyrianising is often emphasised in scholarly literatures. The Assyrian influence on the cultures of the southern Zagros may date from the seventh century BCE: Garrison has discussed the iconography of the seventh-century seal (PFS 93*), used at the court of Darius, as having been influenced (at the least) by Assyrian models and Stronach discusses the variety of ways that the iconography at Cyrus' palace at Pasargadae has debts to Assyrian iconography.[22] It has also often been argued that it was based upon the Babylonian royal protocols of Ashurbanipal, rather than those of the Neo-Babylonian kings, although the Neo-Babylonian kings, and Nabonidus in particular, were also keen to reference Ashurbanipal in their inscriptions, as well other Assyrian kings.[23] Nabonidus himself repaired the statue of Sargon of Akkad in the Ebabbar at Sippar,[24] and made offerings, as also later did Cyrus.[25] The titles Cyrus uses on the *Cyrus Cylinder* are also Assyrian in character rather than Babylonian, although Nabonidus had also used some similar Assyrianising titles in the *Ehulhul Cylinder*, combined with more traditional Babylonian titulary.[26] In the lead-up to the complete conquest of Babylon (on which see Chapter 5), Cyrus also adopted the title 'King of Countries', switching quickly from the title 'King of Babylon', a move which Waerzeggers sees as Assyrianising.[27] Furthermore, Cyrus' Assyrianising at the 'palace' at Pasargadae (which almost certainly precedes the taking of Babylon in 539) already suggests that Assyria was a model for aspects of Cyrus' complex ideology of kingship, but Assyria is only one influence among many at Pasargadae.[28]

Cyrus and Elam

Some have argued that Cyrus was probably actually ethnically Elamite. Anshan itself had originally been an Elamite city and has been identified with Tal-i Malyan in the Kur River Basin.[29] Anshan had been, together with Susa, one of the principal cities of the Elamite confederacy, although by the beginning of the seventh century, Anshan was no longer under the direct political control of the Elamite kings: in 691 before the battle of Halule, the 'king of Elam' gathered together a confederacy of allies against the Assyrian Sennacherib which included (men from) Anshan.[30] From the middle of the second millennium, the king of Elam was styled as 'the king of Susa and Anshan', a title that was used down to the early sixth century, and revived by the Elamite rebel who opposed Darius I in the late sixth century, Atta-hamiti-Inshushinak, which is an indication of the ideological importance of the title.[31] While the Assyrians sacked Susa in 647 BCE, this did not mean that the Elamite state collapsed, and, although the reach of the Elamite kingdom may no longer have extended as far as Anshan in the years after the sack of Susa, the Elamite state seems to have retained indications of structure, stability and prosperity in the lowlands.[32] Further, although as we have noted, the city of Anshan itself seems to have been abandoned by the beginning of the first millennium BCE, highland Fars, in which the city Anshan was located, may still have been populated by nomadic pastoralists (or agropastoralists), who would leave little in the way of evidence in the archaeological record.[33]

It has also often been suggested that the name *Kur-aš* (in both Elamite and Akkadian texts, but which becomes Kuruš in Old Persian: e.g., CMa) is itself an Elamite name, that it was possibly a throne name and of a line of Elamite kings at Anshan,[34] although evidence from other contexts suggest that names are not always a good indication of subscription to ethnic affiliations in multi-ethnic settings.[35] Nevertheless, the links of the Persians and Cyrus to the Elamites, perhaps rather than the Medes, have recently been highlighted, and the ethnogenesis of the Persians as borne out of a mixed Iranian and Elamite heritage has been widely discussed.[36] The fact that the relief of the winged genius of Gate R at Cyrus' Palace at Pasargadae wears an Elamite royal robe is obviously significant,[37] as is the fact that, in the investment ceremony at Babylon after the taking of the city, either Cyrus or Cambyses wears Elamite robes (*ABC* 7 iii.26). It is also of interest that Herodotus (3.89.3) says Cyrus was called 'father' by the Persians because 'he was gentle and made everything good for them'. Whether or not Cyrus was truly gentle outside the idealised Greek imagination is another matter, but *abu*, 'father', was an Elamite royal title that was also used in Mesopotamia in the Old Babylonian period and has been linked to nomadic or tribal leadership.[38] Nevertheless, it is probably also important that, even after Cyrus is in control of Susa (which he was by the time of the creation of the *Cyrus Cylinder*: 30), he does not style himself – or is styled – as 'king of Susa and Anshan' (that is, ruler of the Elamite confederacy), but is being characterised in rather different terms.

But there are deeper questions at stake about what it may even have meant to be 'Persian' or 'Elamite' and how ethnic identities or group identities can shift and change over time and even carry different weight in new contexts. The focus on Anshan (whether city or country and whether strictly Elamite in this period or not) may occlude Cyrus' link with Parsa (Fars), which is also not straightforward. As suggested earlier, there is also the question of whether we should be talking about 'ethnicity' at all in this context, and what indicated 'Persianness' on a more general level: Darius may have called himself a man from Parsa, an Achaemenid, and an adherent of Ahura Mazda, but was this how the group defined itself? While the Greeks were happy to talk about 'Persians' from an etic (that is, external) point of view, the Greeks also found it difficult to distinguish between 'Persians' and 'Medes'. Even the administrative documents of the Persepolis Fortification Tablets do not seem to have made distinctions between Persians, Medes and Elamites (the three groups seem to have constituted 'us' in relation to 'them', that is other members of the empire).[39] Wouter Henkelman's work on the religious systems of Parsa as represented in the Persepolis Fortification

Tablets also shows the diversity of languages used and the variety of religious practices (including Elamite cult) in Parsa.[40] Even being 'Achaemenid' may have been an identity that adhered primarily to the royal family, which focalised its identity through the lens of Pars, rather than the inhabitants of Pars/Anshan more generally and it may have been the Achaemenids as a royal family that came to think of its principle religion as worship of Ahura Mazda (whether or not we can talk about Zoroastrianism),[41] and the principal language of kingship as Old Persian.[42]

Cyrus and Parsa/Parsua/Parsu/Parsumash

However, we even need to ask whether Cyrus considered himself a 'man of Parsa'. We have only two texts that link Cyrus himself with Parsa. In the *Nabonidus Chronicle* (*ABC* 7) Cyrus is styled both as Cyrus king of Anshan (${}^{m}Kur$-$aš$ $šar$ An-$šá$-an:7.2.1, without determinative, although at 7 ii.4 note ${}^{kur}An$-$šá$-an) and Cyrus king of (the country of) Parsu (${}^{m}Kur$-$aš$ $šar$ ${}^{kur}Par$-su: 7 ii.1, 15).[43] However, there are immediate problems in identifying Cyrus with Parsu rather than Anshan (or seeing them as strictly synonymous). In the first place, the copy of the *Nabonidus Chronicle* that we have dates from the Hellenistic period and Waerzeggers argues that it is a product of the Hellenistic Babylonians' interest in the transition from the rule of Nabonidus to that of Cyrus, as indeed she sees the *Nabonidus Chronicle* itself as a creation of the Hellenistic period without necessarily firm sixth-century roots.[44] In this reading, the association of Cyrus with Parsu could be anachronistic.[45]

The other link between Cyrus and Parsu seems to be in the Babylonian text of the Behistun inscription. Here Cyrus is given titles which do not appear in the Old Persian or Elamite versions.[46] Cyrus seems to be styled 'King in [the country] Parsu' (although Parsu is only tentatively restored in von Voigtlander's text),[47] and is given the title 'LUGAL KUR.KUR', 'King of Countries', which is the title that he uses at Babylon during the period of co-regency in dating formulae as distinct from Cambyses, who was given the usual Babylonian title 'King of Babylon'.[48] 'King of Countries' is also the title which *Darius* uses at Behistun and elsewhere (note the first paragraph of the Old Persian text of the Behistun inscription: DB §1.2). That Darius also calls himself king in Parsa may suggest that it was convenient for him also to apply the title to Cyrus to strengthen the link between them, even if it was not a title which Cyrus would have claimed for himself.

We should therefore be cautious in associating Cyrus with the toponym Parsa or with a Persian, rather than a proto-Persian, ethnic identity. There are significant doubts about the relationship between Parsa and Anshan. We have already noted the coalition formed against the Assyrians before the battle of Halule in 691. This coalition included men not only from Anshan, but also from Parsuash (together with men from Pashiru, Ellipi, the whole of Chaldea and all the Aramaeans).[49] This text clearly differentiates Anshan from Parsuash. The Acropole texts from Susa (late seventh/early sixth century) refer to groups of *parsip* (people from Parsa), but never Anshanites.[50] However, this raises another set of questions about where this Parsa/Parsuash should be located and how it might relate to other toponyms in Mesopotamian, Urartian and Elamite texts from the ninth century BCE (Parsu/Parsua/Parsamash/Parsumash/Parshua),[51] and in what sense these toponyms might be connected to ethnonyms.

A further complication is that there was also a region (and later an Assyrian province) to the east of Mesopotamia in the central Zagros region, called in Assyrian texts Parsua or Parsu(m)ash, which was annexed by Tiglath-Pileser III in the mid-eighth century, as well as a completely different region, probably named first in Assyrian texts of Shamshi-Adad V as Parsamash but certainly later by Sargon II (last quarter of the eighth century), as Parsumash, in the southwest Zagros. We also have other Assyrian references to Parsumash in the seventh century that associate Parsumash with a king called Kurash/Cyrus. In the mid-seventh century, Kurash, a king of Parsumash (sometime after the sack of Susa in 647 BCE), sent tribute and his eldest son as a hostage to the court of Ashurbanipal,[52] although there is no indication of the location of this Parsumash. Another text relating to Ashurbanipal, however, does say that Kurash was king of the country (KUR) of Parsumash, and that Parsumash together with the country (KUR) of Hudimeri lay 'on the far side of Elam', which from an Assyrian point of view must mean the southwest Zagros.[53]

These texts have been much discussed and there is very little consensus on how they should be understood.[54] It is very tempting to see these references to Kurash/Cyrus as Cyrus (I) of the *Cyrus Cylinder* and also the Cyrus son of Teispes of PFS 93*, although both the *Cyrus Cylinder* and the inscription on the seal say 'Cyrus' (who may not even be the same Cyrus) should be associated with the toponym Anshan (whether city or country), whereas the Assyrian texts associate Cyrus (who may, or may not, be our Cyrus' grandfather from the *Cyrus Cylinder*) with the toponym Parsumash. Furthermore, some have pointed to a possible chronological problem. If the Cyrus who sent tribute to Ashurbanipal was our Cyrus' grandfather, then the length of the reigns of Cyrus (I) and his son Cambyses must together have been about 86 years, although this is not impossible.

What comes out of a survey of these issues, however, is the instability of labels and the importance of geography, in forming, and then performing, culture. It is uncertain when Indo-European Aryan speakers came to the Zagros mountains, although they seem to have been there by the beginning of the first millennium. However, as has now long been recognised, it was not language that made them 'Persian', or at least this southwestern Zagros region was multi-lingual. Persianness grew out of the mixing of cultures, especially Elamite and Indo-European, in the southwestern Zagros mountains. It was the culture of the people in a geographical region in the southwestern Zagros that came to be called Parsa/Parsua/Parsumash, whatever the relationship between this region and the region of Parsua/Parsumash to the north in the central Zagros.

The relationship between Anshan and Parsua is more difficult to understand, but it is probable, as Henkelman and others have already suggested, that as toponyms, they represent different points of focalisation. This point, in particular, seems to be confirmed by the Babylonian text of the Behistun inscription, where it is *Darius* (or Darius' Babylonian scribe) who gives Cyrus the title of 'Persian king'.[55] Zournatzi is also probably right that the *Cyrus Cylinder* refers to the city of Anshan (where there was no longer a city) because 'the eternal line of kingship' was city based. It is also the case that all of these early identifications with Parsua/Parsumash are by outsiders; they are exonyms.[56] Darius is the first to call himself 'Persian', 'a man from Parsa'.

Cyrus and Anshan

Cyrus did associate himself with the region of Anshan. Although there can be no certainty, it is likely that Cyrus son of Teispes of the cylinder seal was Cyrus' grandfather (whether or not this Cyrus also sent his son to the Assyrian court). The seal is of high quality, as we have already noted. As well as for its economic and bureaucratic uses, it was also a marker of prestige, as the inscription itself would suggest. If the seal was not significant in some way, then we need to ask why it was kept in use in Darius' administration. This Cyrus (whether or not we want to call him Cyrus I) certainly self-identified with Anshan. As we have already noted, our Cyrus seems to have been associated with the country of Anshan as early as 550/549 when he defeated Astyages, as we know from the *Ehulhul Cylinder*.

However, it is also worth trying to unpack what this might have meant in the context of the apparent archaeological 'emptiness' of Anshan and Fars, nomadic pastoralism and the apparently sudden shift to some level of sedentism or at least irrigated agriculture. Excavations in the Mamasani region in Fars, on an important route from the highlands to Khuzestan, have shown evidence of a number of settlements, although, crucially, there is as yet no firm evidence of continuous occupation in the period between about 900 and 600 BCE (although, despite this break in the archaeological record, they were occupied at least in parts of the second millennium and during the Achaemenid period).[57]

On the other hand, sedentism in the Kur River Basin seems to have happened quite quickly in the mid-sixth century, as is represented both by Cyrus' 'palace' on the plain of the Pulvar River (a tributary of the Kur) and extensive irrigation works, the recently discovered monumental gate at Tol-i Ajori (a slightly larger copy of the Babylonian Ishtar Gate) and associated buildings, 3.5 km west of Persepolis and the residential palace at Toace on the Persian Gulf.[58] Cribb, in fact, talks about pastoral nomadism and sedentism as continuous and on a sliding scale.[59]

The building works at Tol-i Ajori and the development of the palace at Toace must surely be associated with the fall of Babylon to Cyrus in 539 BCE, but work at Pasargadae was almost certainly earlier. Although the building works at Pasargadae are not a palace in a conventional sense (more on this later), they and the associated irrigation works do represent a significant expenditure of resource and labour and a large population involved in agriculture. The traditional date for its building is after the defeat of Astyages in 550 BCE (*ABC* 7 ii.1–4); one story that is told places the location of the final battle at Pasargadae (in Ctesias/Nicolaus of Damascus on a mountain: F 8d*§35, 38–44) and Strabo gives the location of the battle as the reason for Cyrus building his palace-city there (Strabo 15.3.8), although it is on the plain (not on the mountain where Ctesias places the final battle). Building works could only have started after the fall of the Lydian empire and the defeat of the Greeks of Asia Minor since Lydian/Greek building techniques played such an important part in their construction.[60] Although the date of the fall of Sardis is uncertain,[61] it is generally assumed to be before the taking of Babylon in 539 BCE (although that is not inevitable), one of the few fixed dates in Cyrus' career.

Taken together, all of this suggests that what was meant by 'Anshan' must have been the region which encompassed the Kur River Basin, including the plain of the Pulvar River and the Persepolis plain. That Cyrus established his 'city' at Pasargadae in the north east of the Kur basin (rather than in the west and at the location of the city of Anshan, Tal-i Malyan) must surely have been strategic, taking advantage of the fertile alluvial plain of the Pulvar and serving as a means of controlling both human and natural resources. That the new palace city was on an important route is suggested by the excavation of what appears to be a significant Achaemenid way station in the Bolaghi Valley on the river route along the Pulvar from the Persepolis plain (and Tol-i Ajori) to Pasargadae,[62] and on the route north to Media (through Gabae/Isfahan).[63] The establishment of the new royal seat was soon accompanied by the growth of new towns and villages in the Kur River Basin.[64]

Cyrus' acquisition of Astyages' army seems to have been an important moment for the nomads of the southwest Zagros. The shift from pastoralism to irrigated agriculture (or at least partially so) needed a significant increase in resources, which seems to be part of the profile we are witnessing in the mid-sixth century, especially after Cyrus acquired the extensive resources of the Medes. It must surely also be significant that Cyrus' city is based around irrigated parklands, with no clear evidence for an urban space, although there is some evidence of a residential space to the east of the artificial lake.[65] It is probable that we should see Pasargadae as reflecting a swift movement from nomadism to sedentism, even if the permanent structures were those associated with the palace buildings and irrigated garden, about which we will have more to say later, while the 'populace' retained aspects of their nomadic heritage in a tent city, even if the relationship between city and palace was also carefully delineated and planned.[66]

Nevertheless, nomadism, as expressed through the moving court between royal centres, seems to have remained a feature of royal life into the fourth century, even though the details of the migrating court are vague and uncertain at best,[67] and during Cyrus' reign may have been limited. After the capture of Sardis, Herodotus says that Cyrus returned to Ecbatana (Hdt. 1.153.3), which suggests it was an important nodal point in his nascent empire, although the *Nabonidus Chronicle* also says that when he replaced Astyages as leader of the Median army in 547 BCE, he denuded the country (KUR) of Ecbatana of its wealth and took it to the country (KUR) of Anshan (*ABC* 7 ii.2–3). It seems he also visited Babylon three times after it came into his control, although Cambyses ruled there as co-regent for a year.[68] That Cyrus' reign seems to be marked by continuous military activity perhaps makes it premature to look too hard for a migratory pattern for his court. With the building of Cyrus' palace, however, we are possibly seeing that moment when a kind of agriculture-based sedentism, not separated from but possibly combined with pastoralism, had become symbolic of power. If we think of Cyrus' construction of his garden palace in terms of the 'enclosed' or 'enclosing' nomadism discussed in the previous chapter, we might ask: who was enclosing whom?

Cyrus' Garden Palace at Pasargadae: A New Kind of Kingship

The questions arising out of Cyrus' pastoralist background are important. In particular, it is striking how quickly his court moved at least to a kind of permanency and the expression of his kingship in the construction of the garden palace at Pasargadae, if indeed a 'palace' is an accurate way to designate what was evidently a specially and carefully designed spatial programme.[69]

But what kind of space was it? It was not a fortification, as, astonishingly, there is no perimeter wall. There is also no indication that the palatial buildings were used for administrative purposes (although it is sometimes assumed that it must have been an administrative centre for the empire), although there may have been within the gardens an area designated as a 'storage unit'.[70] It is also unclear whether the site as a whole, as distinct from Cyrus' tomb where later sacrifices were made (Arrian, *Anab.* 6.29.7), had religious significance beyond the generally numinous quality of secluded garden spaces (the purpose of the so-called *zendan* is unclear).[71] Nevertheless, taken as a whole, this palatial space itself is probably an indication that Cyrus was thinking of himself and his position in terms of kingship and the marking out of his metahumanity through the creation of separated space, at least, in some sense, from the rest of the community. He was no longer a nomadic chief, but a ruler of what was rapidly becoming a territorial empire with identifiable imperial structures. On this basis, the palatial space at Pasargadae provides an ideological statement of his kingship. As Irene Winter notes:

> The [Near Eastern] palace is ... set up as a mirror of the king. It is a physical manifestation of the ruler's power and ability to build; and at the same time, by having built so impressively, the ruler has further

demonstrated his power and ability to command resources, induce astonishment, and create a fitting seat of government – in short, to rule. The rhetorical function of the palace, as exemplified through its affect, is, I would argue, as essential as its residential, administrative, productive, and ceremonial functions.[72]

Nevertheless, Cyrus' palace was largely unlike its Near Eastern predecessors. Near Eastern palaces were immense multi-roomed buildings, which served multiple functions as the 'seat of kingship'. However, it did make a connection with Near Eastern royal ideology through its garden setting. Near Eastern palaces were often associated with gardens, and Karen Radner has shown how an important element of Near Eastern kingship was the king as 'gardener', and she argues that ensuring cultivation was one of the most important concerns of at least the Neo-Assyrian kings.[73] Gardens also feature in the reliefs at Assyrian palaces, especially of the later Assyrian kings. For example, a relief from Room H of Ashurbanipal's North Palace at Nineveh shows a mountain scene with trees and shrubs, a columned pavilion, canals, an aqueduct, paths and an altar (Figure 2.1).

Dalley has suggested that this garden is a representation of the garden (now mature) that Sennacherib built next to his new palace at Nineveh (and that they were the famous Hanging Gardens supposedly at Babylon),

Figure 2.1 Stone panel from the North Palace of Ashurbanipal (room H). © The Trustees of the British Museum.

although other possibilities have been suggested.[74] There were also gardens at Babylon,[75] even if not necessarily the Hanging Gardens which Josephus (*Jewish Antiquities* 10.11.1; *Against Apion* 1.19–20),[76] Diodorus (2.1.1–6)[77] and Strabo (16.1.5) describe. Nevertheless, it is clear that gardens, like palaces, were closely connected to kingship and their ideological positioning as spaces for gods and kings.[78]

At Pasargadae, the central conception turns around the garden, which is not just adjacent to the palace, or a kind of adjunct to the palace, but palatial buildings, whatever their functions, were incorporated within the garden space. Archaeological fieldwork at Pasargadae has revealed a number of monuments within a garden setting, covering an area of about 300 ha (Figure 2.2).[79]

Cyrus' tomb was known from antiquity to have been set within a cultivated grove of trees and an irrigated lawn (Arrian, *Anab.* 6.29.4; Strabo

Figure 2.2 Proposed archaeological plan of Pasargadae. Gondet et al. (2022). Courtesy of the authors.

15.3.7). Early excavation also revealed a formal rectangular garden (itself divided into two rectangles), about a kilometre to the east of the tomb, watered by stone irrigation channels (Figure 2.3).[80]

Stronach has suggested that these two rectangles would also have been divided into halves again so that together the four garden spaces would represent the 'four quarters of the world'.[81]

This garden could be entered by two small columned pavilions to the south of the rectangular garden, and what has been called Palace P to the north, which had a rectangular hall with five rows of six columns and two flanking porticos: the north portico had two small rooms at either end, and the south portico, which overlooked the formal garden, and in modern scholarship is sometimes called the 'throne portico' since there seems to have been a throne seat half-way along its length.[82] North east of the garden complex is a structure called the *zendan*, whose function remains elusive

Figure 2.3 Irrigation works, the formal garden, Pasargadae. Author's photos.
(Continued)

Figure 2.3 (Continued)

Figure 2.4 The Tall-i Takht. Author's photo.

and beyond that a large raised platform, the Tall-i Takht, with a lime-stone block façade, accessed by staircases.[83] To the south of the central garden was Palace S, a rectangular columned hall, surrounded by porticoes and with two corner rooms on the southwest side.[84] About 200 m south east of Palace S is Gate R, a free-standing rectangular building with a columned hall, two main entrances and two side doors.[85] Gate R is also the location of the 'four-winged guardian figure', a discussion of which we will return to shortly. What is important to note at the moment is that electromagnetic analysis, revealing ditches and canals, has shown that this central palatial area was set in a much larger garden complex that extended from the Tall-i Takht (Figure 2.4) in the north east and probably as far as Cyrus' tomb in the south east of the plain.[86]

This fact alone is extraordinary and unprecedented and demonstrates a unique conception in the Near East of royal space and 'city-scape'. The garden does not just become an extramural space where the king can express his royal and imperial position; it is the garden that frames that ideological positioning.[87] So, while Cyrus in the design of his garden palace can be seen to be drawing on Near Eastern exempla, he is also doing something very different: the garden itself becomes the palace (Figure 2.5).

Cyrus is the gardener-king: he is a king who situates his kingship 'in' the garden. But the 'garden palace' is not the only remarkable expression of Cyrus' royal ideology. It has long been noted that many of the architectural

Figure 2.5 View of the 'garden', from the Tall-i Takht to Cyrus' tomb. Author's photo.

elements at Pasargadae owe much to Anatolian, and particularly Ionian Greek antecedents, especially in some of the building techniques and aesthetic idiom of the stone-work.[88] Nevertheless, there are also other influences, for example, in what is perhaps the ziggurat-like shape of Cyrus' tomb and the columned halls of Palace P and Palace S.[89] That Cyrus drew on artistic and architectural influences from around his newly formed empire is hardly surprising, or that he made use of the labour and expertise of conquered peoples. Although Cyrus is often praised for his willingness to allow the Israelites to return from Babylon to Jerusalem (which may also have had political importance if he already had his sights set on Egypt), he was also prepared forcibly to detain Greeks from Asia Minor: Herodotus reports that Mazares, the Median general sent to subdue the Greeks of Asia Minor, 'enslaved' the people of Priene and Magnesia (Hdt. 1.161), which probably means they were deported.[90]

Figure 2.6 The winged figure at Gate. Reprinted from 'Illustrerad verldshistoria utgifven av E. Wallis', volume I (1875), 176.

However, the deliberately composite nature of his particular royal ideology, which does set him apart from his later Achaemenid successors, is the famous 'winged figure' at Gate R (Figure 2.6).

Gates were not only important liminal places in cities of the ancient Near East, but also sacral and public expressions of kingship.[91] This gate in particular (which is free-standing) was of monumental proportions (c. 28.5 m x 25.5 m), and Stronach calculates from the column bases that the height of the internal space was about 16 m.[92] It was one of the entry points for the formal garden and possibly marked off the public and residential areas from the royal space. That the gate was free-standing seems to highlight its symbolic nature.

The relief of the 'winged figure' was on the north east door jamb and faces inward towards the centre of the room. There were probably originally four such reliefs. The four-winged figure is generally Assyrianising in character – Sargon II had such winged guardians at his palace at Khorsabad – but it also wears an Elamite royal costume, and an Egyptianising headdress, which could be the result of Phoenician influence.[93] What the figure was intended to represent, however, is less clear. Nevertheless, as Waters suggests, 'the intersecting symbolism ... was another instance of a deliberately invoked ambiguity mediating the space – and at times there was no space – between royal and divine'.[94] As we will see in the chapters that follow, it was Cyrus' metahumanity, which he perhaps felt to varying degrees during his career, which was the mark of his new formulation of Near Eastern kingship; whether he would have called that 'Persian' kingship is a separate matter.

Notes

1. For example, from the mid-fifth century, the Macedonian kings claimed Greek identity based on their alleged descent from Heracles, a genealogy that was probably first 'invented' in the second half of the fifth century by the Macedonian king, Perdiccas, who was trying to fix Macedonian interests with the Greeks of the south, after his grandfather and father, Amyntas I and Alexander I, had fought on the Persian side during the Persian Wars. The claim of the Macedonian kings to be descended from Heracles was known to Herodotus (e.g., 5.17–22, 8.137–9). Borza thinks the Macedonian stories in Herodotus are suspicious, but that it was Alexander I who encouraged their pro-Greek slant in an attempt to redeem the Macedonians for their willingness to submit to the Persians and to assert his own Greekness among the Greeks of the south (Borza (1990), 105–15). However, Perdiccas was probably the first of the Macedonian kings unequivocally to put the head of Heracles on Macedonian coins: see Raymond (1953), 59–60, 163–5. Tellingly, in Herodotus, it is a 'Perdiccas' who founds the Macedonian royal dynasty.
2. See the collection of essays: McInerney (ed.) (2014).
3. Hall (1997); Hall (2002).
4. E.g., Mac Sweeney (2009), 101–26; T.S. Smith (2018); Düring (2020), 38–9.
5. On the Acropole texts from Susa, see Henkelman (2008a), esp. 5–6.
6. See Gates-Foster (2014).
7. Potts (2014), 88–9.
8. In the opening lines of the trilingual Behistun inscription, which records Darius' version of the events surrounding his succession, the Old Persian version says (§1–2):
   'I am Darius, great king, king of kings, king in Parsa, king of countries, son of Hystaspes, grandson of Arsames, an Achaemenian. Darius says: my father is Hystaspes; Hystaspes' father is Ariarmenes; Ariarmenes' father is Teispes; Teispes' father is Achaemenes'.
   While the Elamite version (probably the original version) is close to the Old Persian version (Parian (2017)), the Babylonian version is different (von Voigtlander (1978)):
   'I am Darius, king, son of Hystaspes, an Achaemenian, king of kings, a Persian man [LU], king of (the country (KUR) of) Parsa. Darius king, thus he says: my father is Hystaspes, the father of Hystaspes is Arsamenes, the father of Arsamenes is Ariarmenes, the father of Ariarmenes is Teispes, the father of Teispes is Achaemenes' (transl. von Voigtlander). The simpler titulary in the Babylonian version, however, replicates the Elamite titulary in DBa, which is

the inscription next to the figure of Darius in the relief: von Voigtlander (1978), 11 (notes on line 1). There is no Babylonian version of DBa, although the Old Persian version of DBa, which is directly above the Elamite, replicates the Old Persian of the main text: Kent (1950), 134–5. On the relationship in general between the Babylonian text on the one hand, and the Elamite and Old Persian versions on the other, see von Voigtlander (1978), 7.

9. See Widmer (2012); Windfuhr (2006). Elsewhere, however, 'Parsa' seems to be a descriptive toponym (e.g., DNa 43–7).

10. Stronach (2000), although see Vallat (2011).

11. Waters (1996); for the opposite view, see, e.g., Vallat (2011).

12. Miroschedji (2003), 18–9.

13. Sumner (1974); Sumner (1988), esp. 314; Potts (2016), 280, 310; Miroschedji (2003), 19. See also Carter (1994), 64–7 with Stronach (2018), 47–8.

14. Schaudig (2001), 549; http://oracc.org/ribo/Q006654/ (accessed 25/10/2021); Kuhrt (2007a), 75. Compare bricks from Uruk: Schaudig (2001), 548; note also Kuhrt (2007a), 74.

15. For the date: Weiershäuser and Novotny (2020), 140–1.

16. Weiershäuser and Novotny (eds.) (2020), Nabonidus no. 28 i.27: ᵐ*ku-ra-áš* LUGAL KUR.*an-za-an*.

17. For the translation 'Cyrus of Anshan', rather than 'Cyrus the Anshanite', see Henkelman (2011), 601–2, n. 70. There are many discussions of this seal and its inscription; for two important discussions, see M.B. Garrison (1991); M.B. Garrison (2011).

18. Henkelman points out the Cyrus of the seal may not even be a king in Anshan: Henkelman (2011), 602–3, n. 71 with 580–1.

19. Brinkman (1984), 67–9; cf. Kuhrt (1995a), 2.586.

20. Zournatzi (2011). Connection of gods to cities in Mesopotamia: Leick (2001), 107: 'Traditionally, as we have seen ... the gods dwelt within their cities; their temples were their houses and estates, where they lived with their spouses and children and servants... Mesopotamian religion never fully envisages the transcendental infinite presence of the gods; it needed to be tied to a place'. *Sumerian King Lists*: Glassner (2004), no. 1. Ideological function of *Sumerian King Lists*: e.g., Michalowski (2011), 14–6; van de Mieroop (2016), 46–8. Henkelman (2011, 610) is insistent that 'Anšan really was part of his (ie. Cyrus') titulature: it certainly was not an invention of the Babylonian scribes'.

21. On Assyrian and Babylonian royal genealogies, which name the father and grandfather, but then leap to the famous 'ancestor' as a way to fix the importance of the dynasty, see Rollinger (1999a), 184–5 and n. 162. See, e.g., Text 2 1.1–8 in Novotny (2014).

22. M.B. Garrison (1991); M.B. Garrison (2011).

23. On the royal protocols of the *Cyrus Cylinder* in comparison with those of Ashurbanipal and the Neo-Babylonian kings, see esp. Harmatta (1971). On the referencing of Ashurbanipal by Cyrus, see Finkel (2013), 25–6; Kuhrt (1983); Michalowski (2014). For references to earlier kings in the inscription of Nabonidus, see the summary of Weiershäuser and Novotny (2020), 7. See also Schaudig (2018).

24. Schaudig (2001), 590–5; Glassner (2004), no. 53.

25. Dedications by first Nabonidus and then Cyrus: Kennedy (1969), 79 (texts 1–4). See Kuhrt (2003), 356.

26. Weiershäuser and Novotny (eds.) (2020), Nabonidus no. 28 i.1–6.

27. Waerzeggers (2021).

28. See Stronach (2018).

29. Reiner (1973).

30. Luckenbill (1924), 88–9. On the connections between Susa and Mesopotamia on the one hand, and Susa and highland Fars on the other, see Amiet (1979).
31. Henkelman (2008a), 13–4 with 6–7; Henkelman (2011), 598–9; note also Potts (2016), 265.
32. See Henkelman (2003), 182–7; Henkelman (2008a), 1–63; *contra* (for example) Waters (1999), 102.
33. Carter (1994) argues that if we are to look for a location where strong contacts could have been made between Elamites and Iranians then Behbahan (possibly ancient Hidalu) on the borders of Khuzestan and Fars presents itself as a possibility, an idea developed further by Henkelman (2008a), 41–3. Note also Henkelman (2011), esp. 582–3.
34. Kurash as an Elamite name was first suggested by Andreas (1904) 93–4. More recently (with bibliography), see, e.g., Henkelman (2003), 194–6; Potts (2010), 21–2; Tavernier (2011), 211; Henkelman (2011), 585. Kurash as throne name: Henkelman (2003), 195–6; Henkelman (2008a), 56; Waters (2011), 290; Waters (2014), 171. Note also R. Schmitt (2000), 164–75 (although Schmitt thinks the practice of adopting throne names begins with Darius). Cyrus' Elamite lineage: Potts (2010).
35. In sixth-century Babylon, some 'Elamites' had Iranian names: Zadok (1976), 62–3. Likewise, not all Median 'lords' have Iranian names: Radner (2003), 63–4. On the other hand, the nephew of eighth-century King Daltā of the Ellipians did have an Iranian name: Henkelman (2003), 197–8. In a Greek context, the mother of the Greek historian Herodotus from Halicarnassus, which was a mixed Greek and Carian city, possibly had a Carian name, and his uncle was Panyassis (probably another Carian name), who wrote epic poems in Greek about the Greek foundation of Asia Minor. Whatever his name, Panyassis seems to have identified more closely with a Greek ethnic affiliation, than with any Carian admixture: Matthews (1974), 5–20; L. Mitchell (2007), 58.
36. E.g., Miroschedji (1985). Note also Henkelman (2011), 577–634, who wants to de-emphasis any supposed break between Cyrus' and Darius' alleged Elamite/Achaemenid heritage. An ongoing complication of the debate over the ethnogenesis of the Persians is the relationship between Parsua, Parsumash and Parsa, over which there remains no scholarly consensus: see, e.g., (as a representative sample of the debates), Levine (1974), esp. 106–12; Miroshedji (1985); Rollinger (1999b); Zadok (2001); Waters (2011); Radner (2013).
37. Álverez-Món (2010).
38. Hallo (1980), 194.
39. Henkelman and Stolper (2009).
40. Henkelman (2008a).
41. See especially de Jong (2010).
42. Canepa (2015), 14–5.
43. There may also be a reference to Parsu at *ABC* 7 iii.3 (see Grayson (1975a), 282 for suggestion, which is accepted by Glassner (2004), 236–7), although the text is fragmentary at this point and the toponym has to be almost completely restored. See further Chapter 5.
44. Waerzeggers (2015). Although the argument is constructed rather differently, Miroschedji (1985, 298) had already made a case for anachronism. Note also Zawadski (2010).
45. Waerzeggers (2017), 70 with bibliography in n. 19.
46. Von Voigtlander (1978), 13–4.
47. Von Voigtlander (1978), line 12.
48. For the titles given to Cyrus and Cambyses at Babylon, see the discussion by Tolini (2011), 140–5; note also Waerzeggers (2015), 184; Waerzeggers (2021); Beaulieu (2018), 248–9.

49. Luckenbill (1924), 88.
50. Henkelman (2008a), 56–7.
51. For an analysis of all the uses of the occurrences of these terms, see K. Alizadeh (2020). On the basis of the arguments regarding the *Nabonidus Chronicle* about Parsu by Waerzeggers and others (above), it is probably safe to remove this reference from the discussion: according to Alizadeh (2020, 31–2) that would leave only references to Parsumash and Parsumashians (the people of Parsumash) in the Assyrian sources, which Alizadeh identifies with the region and peoples of the borderlands beyond Elam.
52. Novotny and Jeffers (eds.) (2018), Ashurbanipal no. 12 vi.7–13.
53. Novotny and Jeffers (eds.) (2018), Ashurbanipal no. 23.114–7. See Diakonov (1985), 61–4 who thinks that *Parsūa* must be an Iranian word for 'borderland', cf. 67–8.
54. E.g., Miroschedji (1985), 268–78; Rollinger (1999b), esp. 118–22; Waters (2011); Henkelman (2011); Stronach (2013).
55. On the creation of the Babylonian text of the Behistun inscription, see von Voigtlander (1978), 7.
56. For a discussion of exonyms and autonyms in relation to nomads, see Tapper (2008).
57. Potts *et al.* (2009), esp. 178–83, 192.
58. Pasargadae: Stronach (1978); Benech, Boucharlat, Gondet (2012); Gondet *et al.* (2019); Gondet *et al.* (2022). Tol-i Ajori: Askari Chaverdi *et al.* (2014); Askari Chaverdi *et al.* (2017). Irrigation works on Pulvar River: Boucharlat (2014); Rigot *et al.* (2021); note also de Schacht *et al.* (2012). On the formation of the alluvial plain: Rigot (2010). It is interesting, and important, that the qanats in the Pulvar plain are almost certainly Islamic. Cyrus is often regarded as responsible for early qanats in Iran, but if this technology was available to him, he surely would have used it at Pasargadae. On the palatial residence at Taoce: Henkelman (2008b).
59. Cribb (1991), 14–8.
60. Nylander (1970); Stronach (1978).
61. See below.
62. Asadi and Kaim (2009); Colburn (2013). Works nearby were once thought to be part of the Achaemenid Royal Road (e.g., Briant (2002), 361), but are now considered to be connected to the irrigation works supplying the Pasargadae plain: Boucharlat (2014).
63. Henkelman (2008b); see also Matthews and Nashli (2022), 20 (Figure 2.12).
64. Potts (2016), 310.
65. A recent archaeological report on findings at Pasargadae postulates that this residential area must have been to the north east of Gate R and east of the lake (Gondet *et al.* (2019), 24; Gondet *et al.* (2022), 9–11, 16–7; but note also Benech *et al.*, 2012). Boucharlat previously argued (as did others before these more recent excavation works), that the residential and 'working city' must have been outside the garden and beyond the Tall-e Takht: Boucharlat (2020), 41. The date of the residential space north of the Tall-e Takht is still uncertain: Gondet *et al.* (2019), 16–7; Gondet *et al.* (2022), 12–3, 17–8. The residential space of the south slopes of the Tall-e Takht dates to the Late Sassanian/Early Islamic period: Gondet *et al.* (2019), 16–7; Gondet *et al.* (2022), 13–5, 18.
66. Boucharlat (2001); cf. Briant (2002), 256–8.
67. See Tuplin (1998).
68. See Chapter 1.
69. On the question of what (or what is not) a 'palace', see e.g., Tzonis (2018); Margueron (2019).
70. See Henkelman (2008a), 427–34.

71. See generally Henkelman (2008a), 430–41.
72. Winter (1993); note also Kertai (2015); Beaulieu (2017).
73. Radner (2000).
74. Dalley (1994). For Sennacherib's account of his building works at Nineveh, including the garden, see, e.g., Grayson and Novotny (eds.) (2012), no. 1. For other possibilities, see Amrhein (2015), 111 n. 51. Pollinger Foster (2004), 215 remains cautious about the location of the garden represented in the relief. Albenda suggests the representation of the aqueduct probably places the garden scene at Nineveh: Albenda (2018), 115.
75. Kuhrt (2001), 82–3; Beaulieu (2017), 10.
76. Josephus, *Against Apion* 1.19–20 = Berossus, *BNJ* 680 F 8a, although Berossus was only known to Josephus through the summary of Alexander Polyhistor.
77. This material is sometimes thought to derive from Ctesias, but is not included among the fragments edited by Lenfant (2004) or Stronk (2010); see Stronk (2010), 155 (*s.v.* 8).
78. Amrhein (2015), 111 n. 51; Pollinger Foster (2004).
79. Gondet *et al.* (2019), 2.
80. Stronach (1978), 107–12.
81. Stronach (1990a), 176.
82. Stronach (1978), 78–93, 110–2.
83. Stronach (1978), 11–23.
84. Stronach (1978), 56–77.
85. Stronach (1978), 44–55.
86. Benech *et al.* (2012); Gondet *et al.* (2019); Gondet *et al.* (2022).
87. See also Stronach (1990a).
88. Nylander (1970); Stronach (1978), *passim*; Boardman (2000), *passim*.
89. Nylander (1970), 99–101 thinks that it is the Etemenanki of Babylon which provides the inspiration for Cyrus' tomb, although others have suggested other possibilities: see, e.g., Stronach (1978), 39–43. Boardman (2(000), 53–60), rejects the model of the Mesopotamian ziggurat, and thinks antecedents must largely be found in Anatolia, although Kurht (2007b, 179), does think the Elamite ziggurat, Chogha Zanbil, is a possible proto-type. For the use of the 'columned hall' in Arabia, Anatolia, Media and Iran, see Gopnik (2010).
90. On the deportation of the people of Priene: van der Spek (2014), 258. It is important to note, however, that not all the people of Priene were deported or enslaved, since Bias of Priene spoke at a meeting at the Panionium soon after the conquest of Ionia was complete: Hdt. 1.170.
91. See May (2014).
92. Stronach (1978), 46; note also Codella (2007), 35–43; Waters (2022), 132–7.
93. Stronach (1978), 46–55.
94. Waters (2022), 137.

3   Cyrus' Birth Stories

In the centuries after his death, Cyrus remained a figure of fascination and interest, even in the Greek world far from the Zagros mountains. Many of the stories about Cyrus preserved in Greek texts came from the Near East. Herodotus says he was told his version of Cyrus' birth by Persians, as does Ctesias. As we will see, there is good reason to think that their stories are genuinely Near Eastern in origin, even if our Greek authors are retelling them for a Greek audience. Cyrus was remembered as a figure of importance, in the Greek world as well as in the Near East. This chapter will address the birth stories of Cyrus found in the Greek texts and contextualise them within the scribal matrix discussed in Chapter 1. One of the important points to emerge from this chapter is the complexity of the relationship between oral storytelling and written texts.

We will begin by looking at the birth stories as recounted in Herodotus and Ctesias and their Near Eastern antecedents, especially the stories about Sargon of Akkad. In the second half of the chapter, we will then consider what these stories tell us about ancient kingship and especially the kingship of Cyrus as he transitioned from a nomadic tribal chieftain to the ruler of a vast empire. As we shall see throughout the course of this book, Cyrus came to embody charismatic kingship. How he came to be a king of such proportions is what these birth stories are intended to explain, although not in the ways they purport. Nevertheless, their point is to show at the very least that not only Cyrus' career was blessed by the gods, but also that he had the charismatic credentials not just to control the army of the Medes, but an empire.

The Birth Stories

Among the Greek sources, the earliest of the birth stories for Cyrus come from Book One of Herodotus' *Historiai*. As we have seen, Herodotus says he knows a number of different accounts about Cyrus' birth (Hdt. 1.95.1). Many of these were obviously encomiastic in character (perhaps even exuberantly so) as he says he will recount the one told by Persians who do not want to exaggerate his deeds. Nevertheless, the one that Herodotus does

DOI: 10.4324/9781003384458-3

choose to tell is still heroic in character and opens the way for Herodotus to suggest that there had been divine intervention in Cyrus' birth and rise to power. That Cyrus felt himself cared for by the gods (and perhaps even to have some kind of divinity) becomes an important part of Herodotus' narrative concerning his death (Hdt. 1.124.1-2, 204.2, 209.3), as we shall discuss in later chapters.

The main account of Cyrus' birth and upbringing as given by Herodotus (1.107-130) is summarised as follows (although at least one other variant story seems to be embedded within it):[1]

Cyrus was the grandson of Astyages, the king of the Medes, who on account of a dream (that his daughter urinated so that not only the city was filled but the whole of Asia) gave his daughter in marriage to the Persian Cambyses, son of Cyrus (the Persians were at this time subject to the Medes), who he thought was noble but of an inferior social status ('less by far than a middle-ranking Mede': 1.107.2). However, when she became pregnant, he had another dream that a vine grew from her womb to cover all Asia. Because of the dreams, and what the dream interpreters told him they meant, Astyages arranged for the child to be exposed at birth. However, Harpagus, a member of the royal household, who had been given the job of disposing of the child, did not want the responsibility for the baby's death (because he was the baby's kin (*syngenēs*) and because Astyages was old and childless) so gave the newborn to a cowherd he knew to expose, a pastoralist (*nomas*) who lived in the mountains north of Ecbatana. As it chanced, the cowherd's wife had given birth on the same day to a still-born baby, so the cowherd and his wife switched the children. As a result, Cyrus was brought up by the cowherd of Astyages and his wife.

However, one day when Cyrus was playing 'kings' with the village children, he was elected 'king' by the others, since, Herodotus says, he seemed the 'most fitting' (*epitēdeiotatos*) for the position. However, one of the children, the son of a Persian noble, refused to take orders from Cyrus as he organised his 'royal court', and so Cyrus beat him. Cyrus was then brought before Astyages and forced to defend himself, which he did robustly. At this point Astyages recognised the character of the child's face and noticed that the child's answer was 'very free' (*eleutheriōtatē*). As a result, Astyages realised that Cyrus could not be the son of the cowherd, and must be his own grandson. All was revealed, Cyrus was restored to his natural parents, and Harpagus was punished by being served his own son for dinner.

Herodotus says that Cyrus grew up to be the bravest and the most loved of the Persians. Harpagus, who was looking for revenge, persuaded Cyrus to lead the Persians in revolt. Cyrus in turn convinced the

Persians by offering them two choices, a life of hard work and 'slavish' (*douloprepēs*) labour, or a life of luxury and ease. Cyrus said that he was divinely ordained to lead them, and if they followed him they would be free (*eleutheroi*). The Persians who welcomed the chance of freedom rose against Astyages and defeated him in battle. So, Herodotus has Astyages repine, the Medes were slaves who had been masters, and the Persians were masters who had formerly been slaves.

There is much about this story which is very Greek and is obviously aimed at a Greek audience. Christopher Pelling, while acknowledging the 'Oriental' origins of the story, explores the way that Herodotus has shaped the material for a Greek audience to suit his own narrative purposes against the background of Greek tragedy: 'the narrative has set [Astyages'] hopeless efforts against a background of cosmic inevitability. Herodotus has fitted this portrayal into a wider picture of a family at odds with itself, where affection and menace, boon and disaster, caution and overconfidence mingle with bewildering and devastating effect'.[2] Likewise, Chiasson argues that Herodotus sets Cyrus' birth story against a specifically Greek mythical background in order to 'make non-Greek events meaningful to a Greek audience; to enhance their importance and emotional impact through association with the primaeval age of Greek heroes; and finally to heighten the truth or persuasiveness (as the case may be) of a given account, as a means of confirming his own historiographic authority'.[3]

The 'hero exposed at birth' *topos* was well known in Greek mythology – Iamus, Oedipus and Ion, for example[4] – which might reflect the reality of child exposure on some level,[5] although Huys also explores other symbolic possibilities, including the suggestion that the exposed child is linked to Persian rituals at the installation of the king.[6] That these stories are about legitimation of rule is probably beyond doubt, but whether they reflect in a very abstract way the royal installation ceremonies of Persia or elsewhere is less certain, although part of the Babylonian royal legitimation ritual (which Cambyses took part in at least once: *ABC* 7 iii.24-8) probably included the ritual humiliation of the king before the gods as an expression of the king's piety.[7]

There is also another Greek birth story relating to Cyrus' exposure at birth in Isocrates (5.66), which takes a slightly different turn: Cyrus was exposed by his mother (of unknown origin) and picked up by a Persian woman and 'so changed his fortunes that he became master (*despotēs*) of all Asia'. In this case, Cyrus, a 'baby exposed at birth', does not appear to have noble birth at all, although he rises from humble origins to achieve greatness (which is the point of Isocrates' story). Herodotus also alludes to a story of Cyrus being suckled by a dog, which also suggests an 'exposed child' narrative,[8] although there is no indication whether or not it is also a 'humble birth' story. Both these stories, however, have behind them an indication that there is some other force at work, perhaps 'fortune' or 'the will of the gods', as a result of which the baby is discovered and reared.

However, there are also elements in Herodotus' story that appear to place it in a more Near Eastern context. In the first place, it is interesting that Herodotus' herdsman is clearly a pastoralist, who lives in the high mountains north of Ecbatana (Hdt. 1.110.1-2, 111.3), although, as we will see in the next chapter, the kind of nomadism practised in the central Zagros was probably transhumance and certainly an 'enclosed nomadism' where pastoralism was practised alongside settlement.

Herodotus also seems to know a genuinely Median version of the story (however else it might have been elaborated) because he knows the Median word for 'dog' (*spaka*: 1.110.1), which seems to be authentic,[9] whatever other errors he may have made in his understanding of Persian and Median language.[10] The apparently Median characteristics of Herodotus' story suggest, despite any Greek overlay, that it has Near Eastern origins; in any case, Herodotus' claim that this is essentially a story told to him by Persians seems to have some validity.

Connections have often been made between Herodotus' story of the birth of Cyrus and the Birth Story of Sargon of Akkad, preserved in a Neo-Assyrian script found at Nineveh possibly in Ashurbanipal's library,[11] but which was part of the curriculum in the earlier part of scribal education, along with only a limited number of other literary texts.[12] It runs:

Sargon, the mighty king, king of Akkade, am I.
My mother was an en-priestess(?), my father I never knew.
My father's brother inhabits the highlands.
My city is Azupirānu, which lies on the bank of the Euphrates.
She conceived me, my en-priestess mother, in concealment she gave me birth,
She set me in a wicker basket, with bitumen she made my opening water-tight.
She cast me down into the river from which I could not ascend.
The river bore me, to Aqqi the water-drawer it brought me.
Aqqi the water-drawer, when lowering his bucket, did lift me up,
Aqqi the water drawer did set me to his gardening.
While I was still a gardener, Ištar did grow fond of me,
And so for [...] years I did reign as king,
The black-headed people I did rule and govern.
With copper pick-axes, I did cut my way through the (most) difficult mountains.
I did ascend the high mountains,
I did traverse all the foothills,
The sealands, I did sail around three times.
Dilmun did submit to me (?) ...
The Great Wall of Heaven and Earth (?), I did ascend.
[(Its very) st]ones(?) I did remove [...]
Whatever king will arise after me,

[Let him exercise kingship for x years]!
Let him rule the black-headed people!
Let him cut his way through the (most) difficult mountains with
copper pickaxes!
Let him ascend all the high mountains!
Let him circumnavigate the sealands three times!
[Let Dimun submit to him (?)]!
Let him ascend to the Great Walls of Heaven and Earth (?)!
[Let him remove its stones ...]![13]

(Transl. Westenholz)

Here, of course, we see the exposure motif also used in both Herodotus' and Isocrates' accounts and also the 'rags-to-riches' motif, common, as we have seen in the first chapter, to many world cultures. The obvious parallel here is the Moses story from the Hebrew Bible book of *Exodus*, although the differences between the two stories have also been noted,[14] where, as here, the 'rags-to-riches' motif is combined with a story of the 'hero exposed at birth'. In both Herodotus' Cyrus story and the Sargon Birth Story (although not in Isocrates), the hero is of noble birth through his mother: both Lewis and Kuhrt point out that while Sargon's father is unknown – with the probable implication that the child was illegitimate – his mother was a high-status priestess.[15]

Nevertheless, just as there are similarities between the Sargon Birth Story and Herodotus' Cyrus story, there are also important differences. In the Sargon Birth Story, the baby is exposed by his mother (as in Isocrates' version), whereas in Cyrus' story, it is his grandfather who organises the exposure.[16] In Herodotus, the nature of the exposure of Cyrus is also different from the exposure of Sargon, although, as Redford has pointed out, this kind of shift could be because of the transference of the story from the river-dominated plains of Mesopotamia to the mountains of the Zagros.[17] In the Sargon Birth Story, as already noted, the father of the baby is unknown, although in Herodotus, when Mandane is of marriageable age, Astyages gives her not to a Mede worthy of his family, but to Cambyses, the son of Cyrus, who was of a good family, but 'beneath by far a middle-ranked Mede' (Hdt. 1.107.2, 111.5).[18] Nevertheless, Cyrus' nobility and true birth are later revealed by his 'fitness' to be king in his play with the other children (Hdt. 1.115.3) and by the fact that his answers under questioning were 'more free' (*eleutherōterē*) (Hdt. 1.116.1). In Isocrates, it is implied that he was just an abandoned baby (so not a 'hero exposed at birth'), who later by his own efforts rose to greatness; in fact, the point of the story in Isocrates is that if Cyrus could rise to greatness from humble origins, then so much more could Philip II of Macedon, with whom he is being compared.[19]

However, there is another, rather different kind of story about Cyrus' birth and rise to power in the late fifth-/early fourth-century Ctesias of Cnidus.

I paraphrase Ctesias' version here (as preserved in the Constantinian summary of Nicolaus of Damascus):[20]

> 'When the King of the Medes (Astibaras) died, his son Astyages, who is said to have been the most noble man after Arbaces, succeeded to the empire. But during his reign there was a great change, according to which the empire passed from the Medes to the Persians for this reason ...': F 8d*§1; cf. F 5.6
>
> Cyrus, a Mard by birth,[21] was the son of Atradates, a thief; Cyrus' mother, Argoste made a living by tending goats: F 8d*§3
>
> Cyrus was taken up by a man who 'beautified' the palace; this man moved him from the external 'beautifiers' (that is, the gardeners) to the internal 'beautifiers' and recommended him to their supervisor; this man often flogged Cyrus so he took himself to the lamp-bearer, who loved him and brought him close to the king as one of his lamp-bearers: F 8d*§4
>
> Cyrus distinguished himself and so began working for Artembares, who supervised the cup-bearers; the king, Astyages, asked Artembares who was pouring the wine so beautifully; Artembares said he was a Mard, a Persian, who gave himself to Atembares to be fed: F 8d*§5
>
> Artembares grew ill and suggested to the King that Cyrus should become his wine-pourer; Cyrus poured the king's wine night and day, and began to give a glimpse of his great moderation (*sophrosunē*) and bravery (*andreia*): F 8d*§6
>
> Artembares died after adopting Cyrus as his son; Astyages gave him all Artembares' possessions as if he had been his son, and Cyrus became great and his name known everywhere: F 8d*§7
>
> Astyages had a daughter whom he gave in marriage to Spitamas the Mede with the whole of Media as her dowry: F 8d*§8
>
> Cyrus sent for his father and mother; they came because he was a great man; Cyrus' mother told him about a dream: she seemed to be sleeping in a temple while pregnant with him; 'I appeared to urinate so much that the mass of urine became like the course of a large river which submerged the whole of Asia and reached as far as the sea'; a most learned Chaldean from Babylon said (when Cyrus told him about the dream) that Cyrus would enjoy highest honour in Asia, but that he should keep the dream a secret from Astyages: F 8d*§9[22]

Cyrus appoints his father as satrap of Persia and his mother as first in wealth and power among Persian women: F 8d*§10

Cyrus decided to make the Persians revolt and to try to depose Astyages: F 8d*§12

Cyrus meets Oebaras, who becomes his chief advisor: F 8d*§13-18

Cyrus asks Astyages' permission to go to Persia: F 8d*§20-23

Astyages' learns about the prophecy, and decides to kill Cyrus: F 8d*§24-6

Cyrus prepares a feast for the cavalry sent for him, and escape when they are asleep: F 8d*§27-8

*Sequence of battles with Astyages, Cyrus' father leading the Persian army; final battle at Pasargadae, Cyrus' ancestral home (*to patrōion oikēma: *F 8d*§41).*

[After the battles the excerptor provides a cross reference to a now lost text.]

'Many things having happened in between', Cyrus went to Astyages' tent, picked up his sceptre, and Oebaras placed Astyages' *kidaris* on his head: F 8d*§45[23]

Astyages was defeated and fled, 'because his power had been taken away by the gods'; Astyages was brought to Cyrus as a prisoner: F 8d*§46

The starting point of this story of Cyrus' birth is very different from that of Herodotus, especially in his relationship to Astyages. Photius makes the point explicitly that Ctesias says that Astyages was not related to Cyrus at all and that Cyrus married Astyages' daughter, Amytis, after executing her husband (36a = Ctesias F 9), both of which claims run directly counter to Herodotus' story. Further, although Cyrus rises from humble origins to overthrow the king, he is not a hero-exposed-at-birth, even though this was a motif that Ctesias used elsewhere in relation to Semiramis, the queen of the Assyrians. Semiramis, according to Ctesias, is the daughter of a goddess and a Syrian mortal; she was exposed at birth because of her mother's shame but was rescued by a flock of doves, brought up by cowherds and eventually married the king (Diod. 2.4.3-6 = Ctesias F 1b §4.3-6).

Despite the multiple layers of transition of Ctesias' text, there are good grounds for thinking that Cyrus' birth story attributed to Ctesias may be genuinely from Ctesias. Although Toher has argued that we cannot reconstruct

Ctesias' text from Nicolaus' because of the nature of Nicolaus' embellish-ments,[24] in this particular case, we are on firmer ground. In the first place, there is at least one point of contact between Nicolaus of Damascus (F 66.8), where Nicolaus (through Porphryogenitus) says that Astyages married his daughter to the Mede, Spitamas and Photius (who read Ctesias' *Persica* first hand) say that Astyages' daughter was married to the Mede (Photius 36a = Ctesias F 9.1).[25] Photius also says that Ctesias claims to have his information from the Persians (36a), which at least in relation to this story of birth and rise to power seems to be the case because of its link to Near Eastern traditions.

It has also long been recognised that the Cyrus story we have in Ctesias must also have Near Eastern roots because of its similarities to another of the stories of Sargon of Akkad from Mesopotamia, the so-called Sumerian Sargon Legend, found in fragments, dating from the Old Babylonian period:[26]

(*TRS* 73 obv.)

The sanctuary, [like] a cargo ship [   ].
Its great furnace [   ]
[So that] its canals would fore[ver flow with] waters of joy,
So that the hoe would be wielded in its agricultural tracts, the fields [   ],
So that the house of Kish, (which had been) like a ghost town, would be
    turned back into a settlement.
Its king, the shepherd Urzababa,
rose like the sun over the house of Kish.
(But) An and Enlil, by their holy command, authoritatively [*ordered*]
That his royal reign be alienated, that the palace's *prosperity* be removed.

At that time, Sargon – his city was the city [   ].
His father was La'ibum, his mother [   ] –
Sargon, happily [   ].
Because he was so born [   ]

(3N T296)

One day, after evening had arrived,
Sargon, when the offerings had been brought to the palace –
He (Urzababa) having lain down in the holy bed-chamber, his holy
    residence,
He understood, but would not articulate it, nor speak about it with
    anyone –
Sargon, having received the offerings for the palace –
He (Urzababa) had made the cupbearer responsible (for the offerings) – he
    (Sargon) took charge of the drinking chest.
Holy Inana was unceasingly working *behind the scenes*.

After five or ten days had passed, King Urzababa .... he was frightened
   in that residence,
Like a lion, he was dribbling urine, filled with blood and pus, down his legs,
He struggled like a floundering salt-water fish, he was terrified there.

At that time, the *cupbearer*, in the *temple* of Ezinu,
Sargon, lay down not to sleep, but lay down to dream.
Holy Inana, in the dream, was drowning him (Urzababa) in a river of blood.
Sargon, screaming, gnawed the ground.
When King Urzababa heard those screams,
He had them bring him (Sargon) into the king's presence.
Sargon came into the presence of Urzababa, (who said:)
'Oh *cupbearer*, was a dream revealed to you in the night?'
Sargon replied to his king:
'Oh my king, this is my dream which I will have told you about:
'There was a single young woman, she was high as the heavens, she was
   broad as the earth,
'She was firmly set as the [bas]e of a wall.
'For me, she drowned you in a great [river], a river of blood'.

[   ] U[rzab]aba chewed his lips, became seriously afraid,
He spoke to [...]. his chancellor:
'[   ] my royal sister, holy Inana,
'[   ] is going to put my finger into a ... of blood,
'[*The*]n she will drown Sargon, the *cupbearer*, in a great river.
'Belištikal, master smith, man of my choosing, who can write tablets,
'I will give you orders, let my orders be carried out!
'Let my instructions be heeded!
'Now then, when the *cupbearer* has delivered my *bronze cups* to you,
'In the Esikil/pure temple, the temple of destinies, *cast them in moulds* as
   if for figurines!'
Belištikal paid attention to his king's orders and
He readied moulds in the Esikil/pure temple, the temple of destinies.
The king spoke to Sargon:
'Go and deliver my *bronze cups* to the master smith!'

Sargon left the palace of Urzababa,
Holy Inana was unceasingly ⌐at his right side⌐.
When he had not come within five or ten *nindan* of the Esikil/ pure tem-
   ple, the temple of destinies,
Holy Inana turned around toward him and blocked his way, (saying:)
'Is not the Esikil/pure temple a holy temple? No one (polluted) with blood
   should enter it!'
At the gate of the temple of destinies, he (Sargon) met the master smith
   of the king.

After he delivered the king's bronze cups to the master smith –
Beliŝtikal, the master smith, ..., having *cast them in moulds* as if for
    figurines –
Sargon, after five or ten days had passed,
Came into the presence of Urzababa, his king,
Came right into the palace, firmly founded as a great mountain.
King Urzababa ..., he was frightened in that residence,
He understood, but would not articulate it, nor speak about it with anyone,
In the bedchamber, his holy residence, Urzababa was frightened,
He understood, but would not articulate it, nor speak about it with anyone.

In those days, writing on tablets certainly existed, but enveloping tablets
    did not exist;
King Urzababa, for Sargon, creature of the gods,
Wrote a tablet, which would cause his own death and
He dispatched it to Lagulzagesi in Uruk.

(*TRS* 73 rev.)

With the wife of Lugalzagesi ... [   ]
She ... [   ] her femininity as a shield [   ],
Lugalzagesi would not [*reply*] to the envoy, (and said:)
'Come now! Would he step within Eana's masonry?'
Lugalzegesi did not understand, so he did not talk to the envoy,
(But) as soon as he did talk to the envoy, the eyes of the prince's son were
    opened.
The lord said 'Alas!' and sat in the dirt,
Lugalzagezi replied to the envoy:
'Oh envoy, Sargon does not *yi*[*eld*].
'When he submits, Sargon [   ] *Lugalz*[*agesi*],
'Sargon [   ] Lugalz[agesi],
'Why does S[argon   ]?'

(Transl. Cooper)[27]

Drews, in particular, has made the connection between this Sargon Legend
and the story of Cyrus in Ctesias who is also a cup-bearer who overthrows
the king,[28] but this is not the only route of transmission for the Sargon-as-
cup-bearer story.

    This story thread itself has a long history since it is also known in other
Near Eastern texts, such as the *Weidner Chronicle* (which Glassner says cannot have been composed earlier than 1100 BCE), where Sargon is named as
Urzababa's cup-bearer who is given the kingship by Marduk,[29] and also in the
much older *Sumerian King List*.[30] There are also other important points where
the Sumerian Legend and the Sargon Birth Story touch on older narratives,

although picking up different themes. The Sargon Birth Story, for example, has a link back to the motif of king-as-gardener which is also found in the *Sumerian King List* (Sargon's father is a gardener),[31] an idea which also emerges in the Ctesian story of Cyrus, where the young Cyrus first arrives at the Median court as an 'outside beautifier'. That these stories 'cross-fertilised' in this way tells us something about the complexity of the interactions between oral traditions and written texts, a point we shall explore further in a moment.

Much, however, has been made of the alleged date and context of the composition of these two Sargon stories: the Birth Story and the Legend. Lewis argues (and it is commonly accepted) that the Sargon cycles (which he sees as versions of one basic story line) must have been composed and written down during the reign of Sargon II.[32] It is undoubtedly the case that by adopting this throne name, Sargon II was deliberately trying to identify himself with his Old Assyrian predecessor. However, Westenholz has shown that the original composition of the Sumerian Sargon Legend was almost certainly much older than the reign of Sargon II in the late eighth century, at least dating to the Old Babylonian period and drew on what she has called a 'cornucopia of sagas' about Sargon, that originally emerged from his reign onwards since even in his life time or soon after he acquired 'superhuman' status.[33] Furthermore, elsewhere she collects together a number of Sargon/Naramsin stories, which she thinks are scribal adaptations of what were essentially oral traditions, of which she writes:

> Considering this body of literature as a whole, the most striking feature is one of extreme fluidity and a most confusing lack of textual stability. Except for the manuscripts from Assurbanipal's Library … there are as many tales and tablets, with each tale witnessed by one manuscript only… The truth of the matter is probably that there were a number of stories about the Akkadian kings, each of them current in several variants.[34]

In fact, simply because we know them as written texts does not mean that these stories about Sargon did not have a previous life as oral traditions, or that they did not later circulate as oral stories once more, perhaps eventually to become the basis for stories about Cyrus and to be written down by Herodotus and Ctesias. The Cyrus story we have in Ctesias may also have been known to him in a written rather than oral form since Diodorus says that Ctesias consulted royal 'parchments' about ancient deeds (Diod. 2.32.4; cf. 22.5). Despite the fact that some have doubted Ctesias' access to written documents, there is little reason why this could not have been the case at the end of the fifth century. Darius at the end of the sixth century wrote his deeds on parchment to be distributed around the empire (DB §70), which continued to be circulated, as a copy of the Behistun inscription on papyrus dating to the end of the fifth century found at Elephantine indicates (a copy which also included the final paragraph of the inscription from Darius' tomb at Naqsh-i Rustam).[35] It is also the case, however, that Ctesias was aware of the inscription at Behistun, but attributes it to the growing tradition about the mythical Semiramis, rather than Darius (F 1b 13.2), so there were also disconnects at work between different forms of historiographical writings, even about records of the same events, which again seems to show how even stories that circulated in written form could be reappropriated and repurposed in both oral and written traditions.[36]

It has also been argued that the transformation of the Sargon stories into Cyrus stories should be related to Babylon, as the principal focus of the scribal tradition. Drews thinks that the Ctesian version of the Cyrus story has a decidedly Babylonian stamp on it (note the Chaldean dream interpreter who becomes for a time Cyrus' helper before he is supplanted – and killed – by Oebaras) and suggests Ctesias may have been at Babylon as the doctor of Parysatis (Ctesias T 7a, T 7aβ §3, cf. T 8b), the mother of Artaxerxes, who we know was Babylonian, and (according to Ctesias) spent time at Babylon after the murder of Stateira, Artaxerxes' wife (F 27.70, F 29b).[37] He also thinks that Ctesias' story must have been reshaped outside the scribal tradition: 'The milieu in which the Sargon story became the Cyrus story cannot, I think, have had access to a written tradition, for the written word ... would have held the story for Sargon against the claims of Cyrus, the new usurper'.[38] However, as we have seen, such a claim implies a rigidity about the scribal tradition which does not hold good.

Amelie Kuhrt also embraces the possible Babylonian context for the transfer of these stories from Sargon to Cyrus, but introduces a further step. She points out that Nabonidus, who is soon to be deposed by Cyrus, had already been drawing links between himself and Sargon to strengthen his own position in Babylon.[39] She argues: 'The prominence of Sargon in Nabonidus' reign shows that stories of the heroic world conqueror were particularly pronounced in the latest phase of the Neo-Babylonian empire, just at the time of Cyrus' conquest of Babylonia ... This ... appears to have led to the formulation of the story of Cyrus' rise into one analogous to that of Sargon'.[40]

She goes on to argue, since Cyrus' advent in Babylon was not disruptive, that, while the Cyrus story from Ctesias may have operated at the level of a popular moralising tale, Herodotus' version works at a 'royal, official level maintaining and confirming the socio-political fabric'.[41] Kuhrt further suggests that we should not make distinctions between written and oral traditions in the way that Drews does, although she too draws lines between oral and written traditions in a different way. While for Drews, the Sargon literature is written, but the Cyrus stories are oral folk tales, for Kuhrt Ctesias' Cyrus story is popular and moralising, so oral, while Herodotus' Cyrus story is official (and so had a written form?) just as had been its Sargonic predecessor, the Birth Story at least. She also suggests that Cyrus was responsible for the elision of himself with Sargon (just as Nabonidus had also connected himself with Sargon through cult).[42] The implication of Kuhrt's argument seems to be that Herodotus' Cyrus story also belongs in a Babylonian context for a Babylonian audience, but both she and Drews seem to suggest that there was a linear and even direct relationship between the Sargon stories and the Cyrus stories. That is unlikely, especially for the Sumerian Sargon Legend, which is only known from a small number of copies – and only a single copy at Nippur[43] – so probably was not widely circulated, at least in this form.

Furthermore, Babylon is not the only possible point of transition for the Sargon Birth Story to become an exemplar for the Cyrus story (if indeed there is a direct connection between the two stories). As we have already noted, the Sargon Birth Story was a standard element of the basic scribal education, which tradition was imported to other locations outside Babylon.[44] In particular, a scribal school in the Babylonian tradition of the middle Elamite period (1500–1100 BCE) has been identified at Kabnak (modern Haft Tepe), 16 km south east of Susa.[45] This scribal centre is another point at which the Sargon birth legend at least could have transitioned, or been repurposed, into the oral performance culture of the peoples of the Zagros. It is probably telling that both the Herodotean and Ctesian Cyrus stories omit Babylon from the 'sequence of empires': they both refer to the overthrow of Assyria by the Medes and then of the Medes by the Persians (e.g., Hdt. 1.95, 102-3, 106, 127-30; Ctesias F 1b §27.8; F 5 §34.6, F 6b*1),[46] which may make it unlikely that these stories took on their final form in Babylon, although different parts of them may have been influenced by Babylonian scribal traditions.[47] While at some point, both of the Sargon story cycles seem to have influenced to some extent oral stories about Cyrus, the transformation was probably neither direct nor simple and there may not have been a transformation as such at all, so much as a reforming of common story motifs. The story in Herodotus may be in the same general mould as the Sargon Birth Story, but they are not the same story. Similarly, the Ctesian story resembles the Sumerian Sargon Legend, or echoes it, but again they are important differences.

Nevertheless, the dynamic interplay between oral and written traditions in the creation of these stories is brought out most clearly through a consideration of the prophetic dream motif, which is an important element in three of our stories: the Sumerian Sargon Legend and both Herodotus' and Ctesias' Cyrus' stories. In the Sumerian Legend Sargon dreams that the goddess Inanna drowns the king in a river of blood, the dream terrifies Sargon, and it is clear to King Urzababa (who has had his own premonitions of disaster)[48] that it means Sargon will overthrow him. It is also important that Sargon's dream occurs in a temple. When Urzababa tries to arrange Sargon's death, the plot is foiled through the interventions of the goddess Inanna. It is the gods who take away Urzababa's kingship and give it instead to Sargon.

In Herodotus, as we have noted, Astyages, king of the Medes, had two dreams, one that his daughter, Mandane, urinated so much that the whole of Asia was flooded (Hdt. 1.107.1) and a second that a vine grew from her genitals to cover all Asia (Hdt. 1.108.1).[49] Both of these dreams were interpreted by the dream interpreters, although Herodotus only tells the outcome of the interpretation of the second dream, which was that Mandane's child would become king in place of Astyages (Hdt. 1.108.2). It is worth noting that in the Assyrian dream books, a dream of urination often related to children and could presage the birth of a child who would become king.[50] On this basis, Pelling has argued that the first dream is actually ambivalent in its meaning since, in the dream books, dreams of urination could be positive or negative.[51] Nevertheless, Astyages does take it negatively since it makes him afraid (Hdt. 1.107.2). Furthermore, Astyages was right to be afraid since the second dream threatens catastrophe for him, confirming his fears about the first dream, although, as Pelling points out, it is, in fact, Astyages' own actions that bring about the fulfilment of the dream prophesy.[52]

In the Ctesian account Cyrus' mother, this time Argoste, a Mardian goatherd (F 8d*§3), is the protagonist of the dream. Ctesias says that when Cyrus had already increased in power at Astyages' court, she reports a dream to Cyrus that she had when she was pregnant with him: she has a dream that she has a dream in a temple (a dream within a dream) in which (she says) she urinated so much that the mass of it was like to the course of a great river, which submerged all Asia, and Cyrus is warned not to tell anyone because of the danger this would present to himself (F 8d*§9).

Here we seem to see the interweaving of oral and written traditions. The Sargonic rivers of blood become Herodotean and Ctesian rivers of urine, probably under the influence of the Assyrian dream books. This may again point to a Babylonian phase for both Cyrus stories, but this is not inevitable since the dream books are also known outside Mesopotamia, notably also at Susa, which are in the same tradition as those from Assyria.[53] It could have been in an Elamite context that the rivers of blood became dreams of urination. The dreamer in the Sargonic version is the one who will overthrow the king. In Herodotus, it is the king who will be overthrown who dreams, but he dreams of Cyrus' mother. In Ctesias it is Cyrus' mother who dreams but she also dreams of the overthrow of the king and, moreover, she has her dream (at least she dreams that she does) in a temple, just as Sargon also has his dream in a temple.

What seems to be operating are sequences of dynamic oral traditions and a scribal tradition, which are interacting with each other at different points. There is no canonical version, or even direct lines of descent between different versions. Instead, the number of different stories reflect different stages of both their oral and written histories. Behind them all is the idea that kingship is given by the gods, just as it is also taken away by them and that human intervention can discover divine will through omens, but they cannot change it. This is also the theology of texts such as the *Curse of Agade* (an 'account' of the rise and fall of the city of Agade/Akkad) and the *Cuthean Legend* (the consequences of disregarding omens) and to a lesser extent in the *Sumerian King List* (although kingship comes from heaven, the gods take no explicit role in the way that it moves from one city to another).[54]

Grayson makes the point that Near Eastern stories centred on kings as heroes.[55] In the second half of the sixth century, Cyrus too had become another such heroic king, who attracted to himself stories about his kingship, which drew on and interacted with other Near Eastern kingship stories. What we now need to consider is what these stories might have meant in the Zagros Mountains that Cyrus himself was in the very act of repositioning on the Near Eastern stage.

Kingship Stories in the Zagros Mountains

The oral nature of Persian storytelling before the Sasanian period has long been acknowledged,[56] although whether or not they also kept written records, at least before the end of the sixth century, is less certain.[57] It has sometimes been argued that the stories that eventually appear in written texts had their roots in an Indo-Iranian or 'Kayanian' (pre-Achaemenid) tradition.[58] However, as we have seen, the oral traditions that reappear in the Greek sources have more complex roots, and share some elements with the written traditions of the Mesopotamian scribal matrix, even if some motifs are also Indo-Iranian (or even Elamite). In fact, the intermingling of the different strands of these traditions, both oral and written, are so complex and there are so many points at which different stories could influence each other, that there is probably little point in trying to trace 'descent' lines between story cycles.

Furthermore, just as there were a number of different, and not necessarily compatible, Sargon stories in the written tradition, in the oral traditions of the Zagros Mountains, there seem to be a variety of kingship stories, which were in general circulation and which also have points of contact with each other. For example, in Ctesias' narrative, Cyrus' Babylonian advisor, in a rather clumsy sewing together of motifs, is replaced by Oebaras (who later kills the Babylonian). When Cyrus first meets Oebaras, he is described as a man who has just been whipped (so of low birth) and carrying a basket of horse dung (F 8d*§13). Cyrus realises that meeting this man must be an omen,[59] and the Babylonian tells him that it is a good omen which indicates wealth and power.[60] Cyrus then keeps Oebaras with him as advisor, and Oebaras encourages Cyrus in the plan that the Babylonian had already suggested Cyrus adopt the overthrow of Astyages (F 8d*§12, 14-16). Oebaras then replaces the Babylonian as Cyrus' chief advisor and eventually becomes one of Cyrus' generals. There are at least two kinds of motif here: the omen foretelling Cyrus' success, and also Oebaras' own trickster 'rags-to-power' story.

The trickster figure and the omen motif had already appeared in Herodotus' story about Darius I's rise to power (although in Herodotus, the trickster-slave is Oebares).[61] As part of the crisis that results in the palace coup of the seven conspirators in Book Three, a decision has to be made about which of the conspirators will become king. Herodotus tells two versions of the story, both of which he says were told him by Persians (3.85-7). The plot of both stories is the same in general outline. Darius consults his slave-groom Oebares, and tells him that the conspirators have decided the kingship will go to the one whose horse was first to neigh at sunrise. Oebares then devises a plan using a mare to ensure that Darius' horse will neigh at the right moment (the two versions differ on how Oebares uses the mare to make the horse neigh). However, incidentally, just at the same time, the horse neighed, there was a stroke of lightning and clap of thunder, which the other conspirators recognised as confirmation of Darius' kingship (3.86.2).

It is striking that we have horse omens as well as other omens. Rollinger contextualises the story of the neighing horse within Babylonian omen literature: 'processional' omens, usually relating to the processions of the gods, which refer to neighing horses signifying regime change; cledomancy, the chance utterances of people or sounds of animals, which were taken to have ominous meanings; and the horse omens (Tablet 43) of the Mesopotamian *Šumma Alu*, or collections of private omens.[62] Rollinger comments on Herodotus' irony in constructing his story, especially in relation to Persian truthfulness, which the real Darius (rather than just the Herodotean one) makes so much of on the Behistun inscription (e.g., DB §4.57). Oebares 'trick', however achieved, also plays with the idea of Persian 'truth-telling'. Herodotus describes Persian education as riding a horse, drawing a bow, and telling the truth (1.36.2), but then, when the seven conspirators are deciding how to get past the bodyguard into the inner rooms of the palace, Herodotus gives Darius a philosophical disquisition on the 'necessary lie' (3.72.4-5).

However, the really ludic element of Herodotus' story, and a surprising one, is that, although Darius creates a false omen of the neighing horse, this is then confirmed by the real omen of the lightening and the thunder. Nevertheless, the point remains that Herodotus seems to be making use of actual Near Eastern material, not only the Near Eastern belief in omens (which he also seems to make fun of), but also stories about Darius' accession, which he says he has from Persian sources, and which connects with stories that were possibly already circulating about Cyrus. That we have Oebares/Oebaras in both story cycles surely cannot be coincidence, despite the differences in the stories.[63] These are narratives which are shifting and changing at each performance, whether oral or written, and motifs which are being reused and reshaped. What we need to consider next is what these stories might tell us about Cyrus' ideologies of kingship.

Stories of Accession and Succession: Charismatic Kings and Stranger-Kings

As we saw in the introductory chapter, ancient kingship was essentially charismatic, although charismatic qualities could be focalised through the divine (the gods have destroyed my enemies and therefore I am great) or through the person (I have destroyed my enemies because the gods have made me great). However, kingship based upon personal charismatic qualities created instability and problems for succession, especially if the kingship was to be maintained by the ruling family or clan. The problems were magnified when the ruling family was also polygamous. So, the number of possible successors were multiplied and the power of the ruled to assert limits on succession was weak.[64] As we have seen, Cyrus on the *Cyrus Cylinder* declares that his claim to kingship is based on the stability of patrilineal descent (20-1): Cyrus says that he is the son of Cambyses, a king of Anshan, who was himself the son of Cyrus (I), king of Anshan, who was the son of Teispes, king of Anshan. Although we have already noted that the title 'king of Anshan' is not straightforward, to all intents and purposes, Cyrus (II) is making clear that he is part of a ruling dynasty in the Zagros mountains. However one looks at it, Cyrus' claims at Babylon are at odds with the Cyrus stories in our Greek sources, and it is to these stories, and what they tell us about Cyrus' kingship that we now need to turn.

One feature of almost all the Greek Cyrus stories in their various versions (except for Xenophon's version in the *Cyropaedia*) is the motif of humble origins rising to great power (the 'rags-to-riches'/'rags-to-power' motif), although, as we have discussed, in Herodotus' Cyrus story, apparently humble origins (like Sargon's) are shown to obscure actual noble birth. This 'rags-to-riches' motif, as we have discussed, was itself a common feature of Near Eastern elite narratives.

Within kingship stories more generally, the 'rags-to-riches' motif helps solve one of the ideological problems of kingship: accession. The essential point about these stories is that heroic/charismatic qualities are revealed by the ability to overcome adversity: in order to legitimate his rule, the king must be better and stronger than anyone else. Thus, by his ability to rise from humble origins, the king has proven his right to rule. If he also comes from humble origins, then it also deals with questions of succession because the king has acceded to rule, not succeeded to it.

However, these 'rags-to-riches' stories could be used in combination with other motifs to create different storylines which legitimated accession. The implication of the dream prophecies is that (like Sargon, who is loved by Ishtar) the king is supported by the god. We have also seen how the 'exposed child' can be combined with the 'humble origins' motif, as in Isocrates' short vignette, although most versions of the 'exposed child' narratives are reserved for 'the hero exposed at birth' who later becomes king, like Herodotus' Cyrus, not only because of his own qualities (which was how his identity was uncovered), but also because of his inherently noble heritage, bolstering his legitimacy even further.[65]

However, legitimate succession was also important. What is interesting in Herodotus' story is that Cyrus' *royal* lineage is not Persian (Cambyses, his father, is Persian, but it is made very clear he is not royal), but Median. Cyrus is not a Persian prince, but a Median one. We have already noted the Median character of the story (the nomadic cowherd in the mountains above Ecbatana, the wife's name Spaco). That the baby Cyrus derives his noble status from his mother and grandfather is an important part of the storytelling, and legitimises his position in regard to the Medes, not the Persians, or at least not the Persians in the first instance. It is important to note, however, that Cyrus' claim to be a leader of Herodotus' Persians is because of his bravery (he was the 'bravest' [*andrēiotatos*] of his generation:

Hdt. 1.123.1). Here he is the charismatic leader pure and simple (although again he has no claim to Persian nobility). So, he has another 'rags-to-riches' moment, justifying the first one when his Median nobility was discovered.

However, for Herodotus, it is actually succession which is at stake, although he is interested in problematising it. The instigator of the coup against Astyages was Harpagus, a kinsman of Astyages, the 'most trustworthy of the Medes', and the steward of all Astyages' possessions (Hdt. 1.108.2). However (in another folk tale motif to explain Harpagus' treachery), Astyages had served up to Harpagus for dinner his dismembered son as punishment for the fact that Harpagus had not killed the baby Cyrus as he had been commanded (Hdt. 1.118-19). It was for this reason, Herodotus says, that Harpagus wanted revenge; and also because Astyages was oppressive in his treatment of the Medes, Harpagus had already met with members of the Median elite to persuade them to depose Astyages in favour of Cyrus (Hdt. 1.123). When all was in place, Harpagus encouraged Cyrus to march on Astyages; Astyages ('harmed by god' [*theoblabēs*]) appointed Harpagus as general of his army and marched out against Cyrus, only to have most of the army defect to Cyrus, or deliberately fight below their best (Hdt. 1.124-7). Herodotus then says Astyages himself led out all the remaining Medes, and in the battle that followed was taken captive (Hdt. 1.128). In this part of Herodotus' story, we seem to have a general sense of what did happen (the revolt of Astyages' army) combined with what Oswyn Murray has called 'the faithless vizier' motif.[66] Whether Herodotus put the birth story together with the faithless vizier story or whether they were already a single narrative when Herodotus encountered them, he is aware of their narrative incongruity and playfully has the captured Astyages mock Harpagus by saying that he could have made himself ruler, rather than handing the kingdom over to Cyrus, a Persian (1.129). It is through the mockery of Harpagus that Herodotus brings us back to the question of legitimate succession.

Although Astyages had previously recognised Cyrus as his grandson, he now rejects his right to succeed him because he is not a Mede. It looks like we have two layers of story here, one which is a Median story about succession, and another which transforms this story into a Persian one about accession. However, it is still the case, whatever Astyages' says, that Cyrus has a legitimate claim to be successor as ruler of the Medes by the fact that he is Astyages' grandson. Just as later, Herodotus was to poke fun at how the accession of Darius was to be achieved (more on this later), here he also undermines the succession story he has already set up for Cyrus so that he moves from being the legitimate successor to becoming the acceding stranger-king.[67]

Ctesias also creates a narrative of accession, although it works in a rather different direction since Cyrus is transformed from the stranger-king into the legitimate successor. In Ctesias' version, Astyages unwillingly allows Cyrus, his cup-bearer, to go to Persia, but after he has gone, he learns from the brother of the original Babylonian about the dream predicting that

Cyrus would overthrow him (F 8d*§16-26). Astyages then sent cavalry after Cyrus to bring him back. After initially tricking them, Cyrus (who had now acquired an army from his father, whom also Cyrus had made 'satrap' of Persia: F 8d*§10, 37; cf. 15 where Atradates is said to 'rule' Persia) defeated Astyages' cavalry force (F 8d*§27-9). Astyages himself then leads out another army against Cyrus, which suffers at the hands of Cyrus' army (F 8d*§33-4). After a final confrontation at Pasargadae (Cyrus home: F 8d*§41), Cyrus is declared king (of whom?) by Oebaras, Astyages' allies (who are not Medes) desert, Cyrus defeats Astyages, Astyages is taken prisoner, and Cyrus marries his daughter Amytis (F 8d*§45-6, F 9.1), from whom he would pre-sumably also gain control of Media. (Ctesias/Nicolaus of Damascus says that when Astyages married her to Spitamas the Mede, she brought with her, despite the fact she has a brother, all of Media as her dowry: Ctesias F 8d*§8, cf. 9.8.)

All of this is patched together, and struggles to maintain coherence, although whether it is Ctesias or his redactors who have done the patch-work in this written version is difficult to tell. There are also many folk-tale elements, which suggests that much of the story as we have it was generated at some level within the oral tradition. There are more omens: the song of Astyages' concubine (F 8d*§26), as well as lightning, thun-der and auspicious birds (F 8d*§41-2). In a prophetic act, even before Astyages has been defeated, Cyrus enters Astyages' tent, sits on the throne and Oebaras puts on Cyrus' head Astyages' *kidaris*, possibly a solid crenellated crown or a soft cap which only the king was allowed to wear 'upright' (F 8d*§45).[68] There are goatherds who become satraps and slaves that become generals (F 8d*§27, 32, 34-6, 40). Astyages only decides to kill Cyrus, recently his favourite, when he realises that Cyrus intends to unseat him (F 8d*§21-2, 25-6). Astyages also forgives Cyrus' dying father, the former thief, because he had been a good satrap (F 8d*§36-8). Cyrus tricks the cavalry sent to bring him back by giving them a feast, and escapes while they sleep off their hangovers (F 8d*§27-8), a popular motif we find elsewhere.[69] The Persian women force the retreating Persian army to return to battle by lifting their skirts to reveal their genitals (F 8d*43-4). Despite the inconsistency and lack of narrative flow, the central thread of the story is to explain the historical fact of how Cyrus was able to replace the Median king.

In the first place, he does so because of his worth. Oebaras says that Cyrus is more worthy to wear the *kidaris* because god had given it to him on account of his excellence (*aretē*), just as the Persians are more worthy to rule (*basileuein*) than the Medes (F8d*49). This is another story of charismatic accession: because the god willed it, the Mardian goatherd can become king because of his excellence, just as in the Hebrew Bible, the shepherd boy David, the former favourite and armour-bearer, of king Saul, was anointed by God, grew in military strength, eventually replace the weakened king (*1 Samuel* 16–*2 Samuel* 5).

Nevertheless, whatever the detail, the Ctesian Cyrus story tells us some of the same things about kingship as Herodotus' story and the Sumerian Sargon Legend: kingship must be earned, and it is the best man who rules (because that is what is divinely ordained). Further, there is a moralising and didactic core to this kind of story: just as the gods can move kingship from city to city, so also they can move it from the Medes to the Persians. However, it is important that in Photius' account of Ctesias' story, Cyrus honours Astyages as a father, and marries Astyages' daughter Amytis (F 9.1). By marrying the princess, accession becomes succession.

Whether or not Cyrus was actually the grandson of the real Astyages is probably impossible to determine.[70] Photius says that Ctesias makes the point that he was not, but also the logic of Ctesias' narrative (a simple 'rags-to-riches' story which is unlikely to have any more basis in reality than Herodotus' narrative) means that he cannot be, so the Ctesian claim is simply justifying his own story. On the other hand, the idea that he could be Astyages' grandson as the result of a marriage between two leading families in the Zagros is not implausible. Cyaxares, Astyages' father, is said to have brokered a marriage between Astyages and the daughter of Alyattes as part of a peace deal and alliance (Hdt 1.74.3-6), and other exogamous elite marriages are known.[71]

But this misses the point of these stories, or misses the point of the ideological problem they are trying to solve, which is to do with accession/succession, and the fact that Cyrus, within this storytelling, was on a number of levels a 'stranger-king'. Herodotus says as much when he has Astyages deny Cyrus' right to succession in Media, just as Ctesias has Oebaras crown Cyrus with Astyages' *kidaris*. One solution to the problem posed by the stranger-king was by justifying his role through kinship in one way or another.

However, Cyrus was not just a stranger-king in storytelling, but also in historical reality at least in terms of Astyages' army, a position that needed to be legitimised. It is often said that nomads see themselves bound together by ties of fictive kinship. Khazanov, in particular, has described how nomadic societies used pseudo-kinship and lines of descent as a means of expressing social relations.[72] He says:

> The mobility of nomads and the permanent instability of the pastoral economy give rise to a fluid social organization, which is capable of change and which has the requisite segmentary means with which to accomplish this. In the majority of nomadic societies the most appropriate principle for this turns out to be descent, in which the structuring role of the relations of kinship is conceptualized. Thanks to the application of the principle of descent, the complex and multi-level character of the social organisation of nomads is often expressed in the aggregate of separate segments, discrete descent groups of different genealogical depth which, if the need arises, are capable of fission or fusion.[73]

The establishment of kinship and dynasty, whether fictive or not, as a means of justifying rulership was important. In Photius' summary of Ctesias, he says that when the Bactrians learned that Astyages had become Cyrus' father and Amytis his mother and then wife they submitted themselves willingly to him (Ctesias F 9.2). We can also see its importance in the *Cyrus Cylinder* in Cyrus' declaration of his place in the Teispid dynasty (whether or not that is exaggerated as some have claimed). We also see it in the way Darius later is careful to marry into Cyrus' family, two of his daughters (Atossa and Artystone) and one of his granddaughters (Parmys) (Hdt. 3.88), and appoints Xerxes (Atossa's son) as crown prince, despite the fact that he had other sons by his first wife (Hdt. 7.2).

It is in these kingship stories about Cyrus that we see those bonds of fictive kinship being formed (or reformed), explored, problematised and resolved, even if in very different ways. That Herodotus' story, in particular, seems to have been at heart a Median one also would fit very well with other Median elements of the story that we have already noticed, and the Median character of the story is generally accepted.[74] As we will see in the next chapter, the Median army seems to have played a very important role in Cyrus' career, as well as in the coup of Darius, whatever its actual form, that took place in 522. It is with the army of the Medes in lived reality, who also existed in the Near Eastern imaginary as the semi-mythical *Umman-manda*, that Cyrus at least towards the beginning of his career needs to justify his position as stranger-king. The Cyrus stories, with *this* historical reality at their heart, are both problematising as well as trying to resolve the issues of Cyrus' kingship, especially as part of his transition from a nomadic chieftain to the ruler of an empire. While at Babylon, Nabonidus needs his inscriptions to emphasise his piety, in the Zagros Mountains, there are complicated stories of personal charisma and kinship that need to be told.

In this chapter, we began by looking at the number of narratives of various kinds about Cyrus' birth and rise to power that were circulating in the Greek world in the fifth century. Nabonidus in the 540s had already understood Cyrus' significance, although he may not have realised that Cyrus' Median army was soon to be turned against him, or perhaps he was trying to avert the dangers posed by Cyrus through his very public declaration of a positive relationship between himself and Cyrus, and their shared (if rather different) connection with the gods: as we have seen there were fifty-three copies of the *Ehulhul Cylinder*. It is striking that, as we shall see in later chapters, Nabonidus is keen to present himself as the pious (and passive) Babylonian king, whereas Cyrus (like the *Umman-manda*) is himself marked by violence. There is a coded message by Nabonidus for the Babylonian elite in the *Ehulhul Cylinder* about what Babylonian kingship should look like, and it is not the kind of kingship represented by Cyrus in the *Cyrus Cylinder*. We will unpick this code, and how Cyrus trumps Nabonidus, in Chapter 5.

We have looked at the role of the Mesopotamian scribal matrix and oral tradition in creating the different stories of Cyrus' birth and upbringing, and finished by considering what these stories tell us about different aspects of legitimate kingship among the people of the Zagros: both its charismatic character, and how charisma had to be balanced against kinship, even fictive kinship. Against the background of Near Eastern story motifs, like those found in the Sargon stories, Cyrus is being placed in a wider Near Eastern context of kingship, in which he is also in control of the *Ummanmanda*, who in the seventh- and sixth-century Mesopotamian context were understood as the Medes. It is to Media and the Medes that we turn in the next chapter.

Notes

1. This is a story about Cyrus being suckled by a bitch: Hdt. 1.110.1, 122.3; cf. Justin 1.4.10–14, so Asheri, in Asheri *et al.* (2007), 162.
2. Pelling (1996), quotation from 76.
3. Chiasson (2012), quotation from 232.
4. For a collection of 'exposure' stories in Greek literature: B. Lewis (1980), 157–71.
5. Patterson (1985).
6. Huys (1995), 13–24.
7. Bidmead (2014), 77–86.
8. See n. 1 above.
9. R. Schmitt (2015), 253.
10. Harrison (1998), esp. 3–9; Munson (2005), 56–63. On Herodotus' access to Persian sources, see D.M. Lewis (1997).
11. See especially B. Lewis (1980), 2; Westenholz (1997), 36–49. Lewis argues that the original date of composition of this text may be as early as Old Babylonian period (c. 2000–1600 BCE), but cannot be earlier because of language use, especially *šarru dannu*: B. Lewis (1980), 98–101, but note Hallo (1980), 193.
12. Gesche (2001), 147–9; Beaulieu (2007), 140.
13. Although Lewis originally suggested that the Birth Story continues after the 'blessing', because on tablet B, the inscription continues into another column (although this column is very fragmentary), Longman argues that this second column is an unrelated text: Longman (1991), 58–9, but see Westenholz (1997), 36 (who thinks Longman's suggestion 'most unlikely').
14. B. Lewis (1980), 263–6.
15. B. Lewis (1980), 38–42; Kuhrt (2003). In the *Sumerian King List* (Glassner (2004), no. 1), Sargon's father is not only known, but said to be a gardener, itself an import royal motif, as we have seen.
16. Huys notes that, while they are distinct variants of the 'exposed child' motif, they do overlap because they both lead to the motifs of death and rescue: Huys (1995), 44–5 with 40–1.
17. Redford (1967), 227.
18. It is probably worth noting in passing at this stage that on the Babylonian *Cyrus Cylinder*, Cyrus is said to be the son of Cambyses, the son of Cyrus, but it also said that Cambyses, like his father and grandfather before him, were kings of Anshan. Xenophon in the *Cyropaedia* also names Cyrus' father as Cambyses, although here king of the Persians.
19. See Haussker (2017).
20. Photius, who also summarises Ctesias, is not interested in this part of his text.

21. The Mardians were a Persian tribe: Hdt. 1.125.4.
22. Note also F 8d*§17–19, where Oebaras kills the Babylonian in order to replace him as Cyrus' advisor.
23. On the *kidaris*, see further below.
24. Toher (1989); note also Stronk (2010), 3: '... we have, up to now, probably only a few proper fragments of Ctesias' *Persica* ... Everything else ... is, in fact, only an interpretation and/or adaptation – or at best an unbiased and reliable quotation or *epitome* – by a third party...'.
25. Lenfant (2004), 305.
26. Edited by Cooper and Heimpel (1983). For a brief analysis of the story line, see Westenholz (1983), 328.
27. Cooper and Heimpel (1983).
28. Drews (1974).
29. Glassner (2004), no. 38.
30. Glassner (2004), no. 1.
31. Glassner (2004), no. 1.
32. B. Lewis (1980), 104–7.
33. Westenholz (1984).
34. Westenholz (1983), 331.
35. We know that these copies were written in a variety of languages; for the Aramaic version (and its date) found at Elephantine, see Porten and Yardeni (1986), 59–70; on the inclusion of the final paragraph from Naqsh-i Rustam, see Sims-Williams (1981). On DB Aram. see also Tavernier (2001). We also know that copies of administrative texts from Persepolis were recorded in Aramaic on leather: e.g., Henkelman (2008a), 93; Azzoni and Stolper (2015).
36. Tuplin (2005, 236–7) suggests that Ctesias must have even seen the Behistun inscription and its relief, although Ctesias' description of it (Semiramis accompanied by 100 *doryphoroi*, spear-bearers) seems to suggest that his knowledge of the monument was mixed, and that, whatever he knew about the realities of it and its image, he was engaging with a number of oral traditions since he also includes an account of Darius' accession which is a mixture of the account of DB, the Herodotean version, and another separate version.
37. Drews (1974), 391–2. Parysatis owned estates in Babylonia: Xen. *Anab.* 1.4.9; see also Stolper (2006).
38. Drews (1974), 392.
39. Kuhrt (2003), 354–6.
40. Kuhrt (2003), 355–6.
41. Kuhrt (2003), 356. Waters (2017, 64) broadly approves.
42. Kuhrt (2003), 354.
43. Cooper and Heimpel (1983), 67.
44. Carr (2005), 47–61.
45. Pedersén (1998), 120–3.
46. Herodotus thinks of Babylon as Assyrian (e.g. Hdt. 1.106.2, 1781) but that only makes the case stronger for other stages in the story formation outside Mesopotamia.
47. Nevertheless, there are other explanations for the omission of Babylon from the sequence of empires. Johannes Haubold (2013, 78–98) makes the interesting argument that the 'sequence of empires' is implicit in a Babylonian worldview as found in the *Babylonian Stele* (Weierhäuser and Novotny (eds.) (2020), Nabonidus no. 3) of Nabonidus and his *Ehulhul Cylinder*. He argues that the piety of the Babylonian kings means that, standing aside from the depredations of temples and shrines enacted by the *Umman-manda*, Babylon becomes a passive bystander in the business of empire building. However, there are

other accounts of the 'sequences of kingdoms/empire', which do show connections with Babylon (e.g., the Hebrew Bible book of *Daniel* includes Babylon (*Daniel* 2, cf. *Daniel* 7)).

48. Compare Urzababa's premonition of disaster with that of Naramsin's in the *Curse of Agade*: Cooper (1983), 243 *s.v.* line 87.

49. This story, or part of it, was also apparently known to Charon of Lampsacus (*BNJ* 262 F 14), although Asheri (in Asheri *et al.* (2007), 157) thinks that Charon only knew the second dream; Ceccarelli (2014) concedes that the fragment of Charon may be a doublet.

50. Oppenheim (1956), 265; Bottéro (1982), 12.

51. There was a specific urination dream in the Assyrian dream book which prophesied that a child would become king: Oppenheim (1956), 265; Bottéro (1982), 12 n. 8.

52. Pelling (1996). Note also Aesch. *Cho.* 526–33, 928–9; Soph. *El.* 417–23, where negative outcomes are prophesied through dreams.

53. Oppenheim (1956), 256–61.

54. Cooper and Heimpel (1983), 69–74. On the *Curse of Agade*: Cooper (1983), esp. 7–10. On *The Cuthean Legend* (or 'Naram-Sin and the Enemy Hordes'): Westenholz (1997), 263–368. On the passivity of the gods in the movement of kingship in the *Sumerian King List*: Cooper (1983), 29, but note also 8: '… the impetus for the *Curse of Agade* and the reasons for its propagation may be sought in a political and religious ideology that held that there needs to be only one legitimate divinely sanctioned king of Babylonia at any given moment. This ideology, which can be traced back to the great Lugalzagesi inscription, permeates the *Sumerian King List*, the Ur laments, the so-called royal hymns, and much else'.

55. Grayson (1975b).

56. For example, Boyce (1968), 31–2.

57. For a summary of the arguments, see Llewellyn-Jones (2010), 58–65.

58. Nöldeke (1930), 3–9; Boyce (1954); Yarshater (1988), 8–12.

59. On omens of 'meeting' (of the type, 'if a man encounters …'), see Köcher *et al.* (1957–1958), 68–9.

60. For these omens as genuinely Near Eastern, see also Panaino (2009).

61. Rollinger (2018).

62. Rollinger (2018), 140–2. On Babylonian 'procession omens' more generally: Schaudig (2008). On cledomacy: Oppenheim (1954–56). For the *Šumma Alu* more generally: Freedman (1998). For the 'horse omens' of Tablet 43 (which do not necessarily combine neighing and horse excrement as Rollinger suggests, although still confirm the importance of horse omens): Freedman (2017), 16–31.

63. See also Waters (2017), 69.

64. Comparison of ancient Macedonian and Spartan kingship is helpful here: see, generally, L. Mitchell (2013a), 30–2, 104, 137–41.

65. See Huys (1995), esp. 34–5

66. Murray (2001), 42.

67. It is probably only later, perhaps in the reigns of Darius or Xerxes, when 'Persianness' became firmly established as an identity, at least for the ruling family, that the Median story of Cyrus was reshaped again (perhaps by Herodotus himself, or perhaps by the storytellers in the Achaemenid court) to make it a 'Persian' story, even though that then created the oddity of succession, at which Herodotus makes fun.

68. On the complexities of royal headwear, see Shahbazi (2011); Calmeyer (2011).

69. Especially in Herodotus' account of Cyaxares' defeat of their Scythian overlords (1.106), Cyrus' initial victory over the Massagetae (1.207.6–7, 211), and Xenophon's account of the taking of Babylon (*Cyrop.* 7.520–1). Herodotus also

uses a similar trick in the story of the thieves of Rhampsinitus' wealth (2.121), and Charon of Lampsacus in the settlement of a border dispute between the Lampsacenes and the Parians (*BNJ* 262 F 17): Gera (1993), 261 and n. 227. Compare also the fourth-century Greek strategist, Aeneas Tacticus, who suggests attacking the enemy when they are eating and drinking wine, which will make them recalcitrant: 16.5–6.

70. There are reasons for being suspicious of Herodotus' account. Mandane's name (which appears in Herodotus, possibly Charon of Lampsacus, and Xenophon) may be what is called a 'speaking' name: *manda* = the Median woman (Asheri in Asheri *et al.* (2007), 157), although Armayor (1978, 152) connects the name with Mannanda of the Persepolis Fortification Tablets. Amytis, on the other hand, in Ctesias (F 9.11–14) is said to be the mother of Cambyses and Tanyoxarces (Smerdis in Herodotus: e.g., 3.30, and Bardiya on the Behistun inscription: §10 26–35), although in Herodotus, their mother is Casandane (2.1, 3.2–3). As Lenfant notes (2004, lxi), the logic of Cyrus' relationships in these traditions (with Mandane and Amytis) is similar in setting up a relationship between Cyrus and the Medes, and this must surely be the important point at least in terms of storytelling about Cyrus. Cyrus does not style himself as 'King of the Medes' or 'King of Media' in Babylonian texts, although it may be that that is how he could be styled by others in different contexts. Nabonidus refers to a king/kings of the land of Media who sends to him in peace in 543 BCE (Weiershäuser and Novotny (eds.) (2020), Nabonidus no. 47 i.42–45a), and this surely must be a reference to Cyrus, even though Nabonidus does not name him. Our sources are also completely inconsistent on whether Astyages had a son: Herodotus says he was without sons (1.109.3); Ctesias (through Photius) says that Astyages' daughter Amytis, who married Cyrus, had a brother, which naturally implies he was Astyages' son (Ctesias F 9.3); Xenophon gives him a son, Cyaxares, who inherits the kingdom when Astyages dies a natural death (*Cyrop.* 1.5.2).

71. Henkelman (2008a), 36.

72. For example, Khazanov (1994), 138–44.

73. Khazanov (1994), 139.

74. Murray (2001), 38.

4 Cyrus and the Medes

Cyrus is often said to have been the first 'world empire builder'. However, we know very little about how or when he acquired most of his empire, although he became ruler of territories that extended from Asia Minor in the west probably at least to Cyropolis in Sogdiana to the east (cf. Arrian, *Anab.* 4.3.1; Strabo 11.11.4),[1] if not Gandhara in the Hindu Kush, which appears in Darius' list of countries of the empire on the Behistun inscription.[2] It is also likely that Cyrus planned a campaign to Egypt, although that was finally accomplished by his son, Cambyses, after Cyrus' own death.

Nevertheless, we do know that Cyrus saw his project of conquest in imperial terms, at least by the taking of Babylon in 539 BCE. Although known in most Babylon texts as King of Anshan (even the *Cyrus Cylinder*), even before the complete taking of Babylon on 16th Tashritu (in fact the day before), he appears to have abandoned the normal title 'King of Babylon', which he acquired after the fall of the Babylonian Sippar (on 14th Tashritu), to style himself (or be styled) 'King of Countries'.[3] This seems to be the moment at which he sees and understands his imperial ambition.

As we have already noted, most of the key dates for Cyrus' transformation from a nomadic chieftain in the southwest Zagros to the ruler of an extensive empire are uncertain, although there are two fixed points: the defeat of Astyages, king of the Medes, in 550/49 BCE, and the acquisition of Babylon in 539 BCE. In this chapter, we will consider in detail Cyrus' relationship with the Medes, especially with the army which revolted from Astyages. It was this army, under the leadership of Astyages' father, Cyaxares, which together with the Babylonian Nabopolassar brought down the mighty (if by then uncertain) Assyrian empire.

In this connection, an important theme of this chapter is the need to understand the geography of the eastern Mediterranean and Near East, and the routes of communication between each of the subregions, in order to have any chance of unpicking what the principal actors were doing and why. To that end, we will begin by considering the location of Media in the Zagros and the development of Median influence in Syria and Cappadocia, and so consider what a Median 'empire' might, or might not, have been. We will then turn to Cyrus' relationship with the army which Astyages

DOI: 10.4324/9781003384458-4

inherited from Cyaxares, which Cyrus himself was able to use effectively as the basis of his growing power.

Media and the Medes

Cyrus' first steps towards control of central Asia began with the Medes, with the defeat of Astyages, the king of the Medes in 550/49, when the army under his control defected from the leadership of Astyages to Cyrus. This army had been instrumental in bringing down the Assyrian empire, and was to become central to Cyrus' own success. Before we consider further Cyrus' relationship to this army, we need to look first at its probable nature and its relations to the geographical space of Media.

The extent of the region of Media is elusive and seems to have changed during the period of Assyrian domination in the ninth and eighth centuries BCE, or at least Assyrian perceptions of its boundaries changed.[4] However, the core of Median territory seems to have extended along the Great Khorasan Road (Maps 2 and 3; note also the Index Map on xv, where continuation of the road beyond Media is indicated by a broken line), and was bounded by Mannea to the north, to the south by Ellipi and Elam, and to the east by Mt. Bikni, whose identification is uncertain, although Mt. Alwand near Hamadan/Ecbatana has been suggested as has Mt. Damavand between ancient Rhaga (near Tehran) and the Caspian Sea; Darius on the Behistun inscription says that Rhaga was in Media (DB §32 2.71-2),[5] and it was also on the Great Khorasan Road according to the much later Isidore of Charax (*BNJ* 781 F 2.7).[6]

Because the mountain ridges of the central Zagros run parallel to each other in a north west to south east direction, they are difficult to cross from west to east and access to the Iranian plateau is mainly along the tributaries of the Tigris.[7] The Great Khorasan Road, for example, ran through Mesopotamia along the river valley of the Diyala (Herodotus' Gyndes) and entered the Zagros mountains at the 'Zagros' or 'Median' gates (cf. Strabo 11.13.8), and then followed a system of valleys to the Alwand mountain range and Ecbatana just to its east (cf. Diod. 19.19.2).[8] It is significant that Behistun itself, where Darius was later to place his imperial relief and inscription, was on this road. The city of Harhar, which was on the western edges of Media, and sometimes included in Media by the Assyrians, was probably in the Mahidasht, also on the Great Khorasan Road.[9]

The first mention of the Medes is on the Black Obelisk, an inscription which details the campaigns of Shalmaneser III in 835 BCE.[10] However, it is unclear whether the ethnonym 'Median' was an exonym given to the peoples of the central Zagros by the Assyrians, or whether it was an autonym which the people of this stretch of the central Zagros took for themselves.[11] It is also difficult to see what made them 'Median', especially in Assyrian terms, although Radner suggests that what distinguishes them from their neighbours was that they rode horses (rather than used horses for chariots).[12]

The Assyrians also encountered them living in cities with dynastic 'city-lords' (*bēl āli*), whose names were not exclusively – or even predominantly – Indo-European, from whom the Assyrians were able to extract tribute.[13] The first man named as a 'Mede' in the Assyrian royal inscriptions was Hanaṣiruka, probably the 'ruler' of the royal city of Sagbita which was destroyed by Shamshi-Adad V (823–811 BCE), along with (allegedly) 1,200 dependent settlements.[14]

The important Median city of Ecbatana was known in antiquity for horse breeding, agriculture and animal herding (Polybius 5.44.1; cf. Hdt. 7.40.3 for the horses of the Nisaean plain). Tribute and plunder extracted from them by the Assyrian kings included large numbers of horses and (in the eighth century) Bactrian camels, cattle, sheep and (in the seventh century) lapis lazuli.[15] Nevertheless, it is becoming widely accepted that the Medes themselves were not nomadic in its strongest sense, but probably practised transhumance in complex migrations from what Greco has called steppes to river valleys, steppes to mountains, and mountains to plains,[16] but all of which existed beside a predominantly settled lifestyle in cities and villages.[17]

Ecbatana (modern Hamadan) was the principal Median city, but forts have been found at Baba Jan Tepe in Luristan and Nush-i Jan Tepe south of Hamadan, and a fortified palace at Godin Tepe,[18] although all seem to have been peacefully abandoned, possibly at the end of the seventh century.[19] Radner suggests that the *bēl āli* of the Assyrian royal inscriptions were 'robber barons' (the 'city lords') who settled along the trade routes that passed through Zagros mountains, especially the Great Khorasan Road.[20] For her, the eighth-century Assyrian description of the 'strong Medes' as those 'who roam the mountain(s) and the desert like thieves' should be understood as traders who travelled across the desert with camels, rather than seeing this as a reference necessarily to a nomadic way of life.[21]

Major questions, however, hang over the political organisation of these settlements. Herodotus says these were organised as *genea*, sometimes translated as 'tribes', although 'descent groups' are generally thought to be more appropriate in this context (Hdt. 1.101.1), particularly as the *bēl āli* were dynastic.[22] At the end of the eighth century, Sargon II tried to bring the region into his imperial system,[23] but, although these structures were not maintained, at the end of his reign, Esarhaddon (681–669 BCE) was able to demand loyalty from at least some Median cities when he required them to swear loyalty to the crown prince, Ashurbanipal.[24] As Liverani points out, the existence of these separate inscriptions for different city lords demanding loyalty seems to indicate that Media was still divided into separate chiefdoms in the first quarter of the seventh century.[25]

However, by the end of the seventh century, there are two phenomena which need to be reconciled. As we have seen, on the one hand, at least some of these Median 'cities' were peacefully abandoned. On the other, at the end of the seventh century, the Medes suddenly appear as significant actors in Mesopotamia on a wider stage, and not as subjects of the Assyrians, but as aggressors with the sudden appearance of Cyaxares, as king of an army which is called in Babylonian sources the *Umman-manda*, the 'army horde', which plays an active role in the military downfall of the Assyrian empire. The transition of the Medes from town/city dwellers under the control of independent chiefs to a unified and effective military force under the control of a single leader is both swift and opaque, although whether this military organisation is also translated into centralised political control is less certain.[26]

Nevertheless, it seems that Cyaxares was able to create an effective army, even if its main objective was opportunities for plunder and booty rather than territorial gain and control in a straightforward sense. The sources for the period from the rise of Cyaxares and his *Umman-manda* to the final defeat of the Assyrians in 609 are quite varied, but not particularly consistent, especially in the weight they place on the activities (or lack of activity) of the Babylonians. In 614 BCE, a Babylonian Chronicle, *The Fall of Nineveh Chronicle* (*ABC* 3) tells us that an army from Media was operating in Assyria, in the same year as Nabopolassar had also, apparently independently, conducted successful campaigns against Assyrian cities (Nabopolassar had driven the Assyrians out of Babylon, and become king in 626 BCE: *ABC* 2.1-15), although the Babylonians had returned home before the Medes arrived (*ABC* 3.1-23). Firstly, the Median army moved against Arraphu (south of Arbela) before heading towards Nineveh, taking the city of Tarbisu (*ABC* 3.23-5). According to the *Chronicle*, the Medes then sacked Ashur before the Babylonians had time to get there, after which Nabopolassar and Cyaxares met and made a peace agreement with each other (*ABC* 3.24-29). It is also possible that Nabopolassar and Cyaxares may also have cemented their relationship with a marriage between the daughter of Cyaxares and Nebuchadnezzar, Nabopolassar's son (Berossus, *BNJ* 680 F 8a 141).

Nineveh was taken and destroyed in 612 BCE, and its destruction was so effective that when the Athenian general Xenophon passed the site of the city in 401/0 (Xen. *Anab.* 3.4.10), he did not recognise it for what it was. Nevertheless, we have different versions of who was responsible for its destruction and the fallout. In the building tablets of Nabopolassar himself, although the general tone is very understated, his actions are at the command of the gods Marduk and Nabu and no mention is made of the Medes.[27] On the other hand, whatever we make of the date of composition and provenance of the *Fall of Nineveh Chronicle*,[28] it is written so as to emphasise the role of Nabopolassar in the destruction of Nineveh, although Cyaxares (here called king of the *Umman-manda*) and his army are said to have helped, but are not given a role in the plunder or destruction (*ABC* 3.38-43, 47).

If we turn to the Greek texts, Herodotus attributes the fall of Nineveh completely to the Medes (1.106.2), although he also suggests that the campaign took place a considerable time later than 612.[29] Herodotus' comments are also very brief, and come from a rather odd perspective, where Babylon is an *Assyrian* city, which Cyaxares (according to Herodotus), although he subdues all Asia, was not able to take (1.106.2). Ctesias also thinks the Medes had the principal responsibility for the destruction of Nineveh and the fall of the Assyrian empire (F 1b§21.8, F 5§32.5), although he seems to grudgingly concede the Babylonians helped. However, his chronology is so protracted and distorted and his cast of characters is so different from our other evidence to make it historically worthless (the last king of the Assyria is the effeminate and luxury-loving Sardanapallus/Sarandapallus, the Median general who defeats him is Arbaces (who ruled about 150 years before Cyaxares), and whose Babylonian supporter was Belesys).[30]

In the next (and final) phase of conflict, the new Assyrian ruler (although as a crown prince rather than king),[31] Ashur-uballit II, together with his Egyptian allies, withdrew to Harran in north Syria – Sin-shar-ishkun, successor to Ashur-etal-ilani, who was himself the successor of Ashurbanipal, seems to have died at Nineveh. Ashur-uballit was forced out of Harran by a combined army of the Babylonians and the *Umman-manda* (the Medes) in 610 BCE; according to the *Fall of Nineveh Chronicle*, the Babylonians plundered and garrisoned the city (*ABC* 3.58-65),[32] although Nabonidus was later to say in the *Babylon Stele* that the full responsibility for the plundering of the city and the destruction of the temple lay with 'the fearless king of the *Umman-manda*'.[33]

In 609 BCE, the *Fall of Nineveh Chronicle* tells us Ashur-uballit returned with his Egyptian allies. It seems that after some initial success, they were not able to take (or at least hold) Harran (*ABC* 3.66-69), and Ashur-uballit is not heard of again. As an end note that will have significance in later chapters, we are also told in a later chronicle, which does seem to belong to the same series as the *Fall of Nineveh* Chronicle,[34] that in 608 and 606 BCE, the Babylonians were campaigning on the one hand in Urartu, and on the other, around Carchemish, west of Harran, where in 605 BCE, Nebuchadnezzar, as Babylonian crown prince, inflicted a decisive defeat on the Egyptians at Carchemish on the Euphrates, opening up the possibilities for domination in the Levant (*ABC* 5.1-5; for preliminaries, note also 4.16-26).[35]

Most commentators have generally accepted the Babylonian chronicle as most accurately representing reality, and that seems reasonable, at least insofar as it seems to present a balance between the perspectives of our different kinds of sources. Haubold makes the important point that there is no single view of what happened in these years,[36] and there was not just one image of this important king. Stories of Nabopolassar's passivity (according to Nabonidus) are belied by other stories of the first of the Neo-Babylonian kings, especially the *Epic of Nabopolassar*, which, although only known from one small and late fragment, seems to delight in Nabopolassar's violence against the Assyrians.[37] It probably is not really surprising that Nabopolassar (or his supporters) would want to emphasise the Babylonian perspective (or indeed that Nabonidus would want to play it down for other reasons, as we have seen). However, what *is* actually more surprising is that both Herodotus and Ctesias (both Greeks from Greek cities which had known Persian domination in Asia Minor), with multiple Babylonian versions to draw on, wanted to make more of the involvement of the *Medes*, with the Babylonians only playing at best a supporting role.

The Median 'Empire' (?)

We have already noted that Herodotus also knows about Cyaxares and his army and their action against the Assyrians (1.106.2), but tells what seems to be a rather different story from what we know from other evidence of political development in Media. In his account 'the Medes', originally living in villages, were united as a *Mēdikon ethnos* by Deioces, who they decided to make their king (*basileus*), and established Ecbatana as a fortified city from where, keeping himself hidden away, Deioces exercised his rule (1.96.1-98.3, cf. 1.101.1). According to Herodotus, Deoices, on his death, was succeeded by his son Phraortes, who subjugated the Persians and campaigned against other *ethnea* of Asia, including the Assyrians before being killed in battle (Hdt. 1.102.1-2). Phraortes (who Herodotus says ruled for 22 years: 1.103.2) was then succeeded by his son Cyaxares, who reformed the army and united 'all Asia up to the River Halys (in Anatolia)' (Hdt. 1.103.2-3). After an interlude in which the Medes were subjected to the Scythians as they themselves were laying siege to Nineveh (Hdt. 1.103.3-106.1, 4.1.2-3), Cyaxares and the Medes in turn defeated the Scythians by means of the trick of inviting them to a feast, making them drunk and then killing them (on the popularity of this motif, see Chapter 3), and then themselves turned against the Assyrians and subjected all Assyria except for Babylon (Hdt. 1.106.2). It is worth noting that Ctesias also has a story about a war between the Scythians (although in Ctesias, they are Sacae) and the Medes in the reign of Astibaras (who as the father of Aspandas/Astyages must be Cyaxares: Ctesias F5 (Diod. 2.34.6)), although the story is used as a vehicle to introduce the romance of the warrior queen, Zarina/Zarineia.[38]

Doubts have been expressed about a number of Herodotus' details. Although the Medes did attack Nineveh in 614 (*ABC* 3.24, and here the text specifies KUR.*Ma-ad-a-a*),[39] the Medes also did not become the inheritors of the Assyrian empire as Herodotus suggests, although the attitude of the Babylonians to the Assyrian centres is also debated,[40] just as his insistence that the Scythians brought down the Median empire creates even more chronological problems.[41] Most importantly, however, there have also been significant doubts expressed over whether there was ever even a Median 'empire' of the kind described by Herodotus (cf. Hdt. 1.102.1-103.2). In particular, Sancisi-Weerdenburg, in her important and influential article of 1988, says: 'To put it bluntly, if it were not for Herodotus and his successors, the very existence of a Median state would be unknown to us'.[42]

Nevertheless, despite the importance of these reservations, the question of why (as already suggested earlier) the Greek sources would understand

Near Eastern history in this way still needs to be explained. It is probably significant that Ctesias (who hopelessly muddles the detail) still has roughly the same general pattern. This shared story patterning has to have come from somewhere. While it is unclear what kind of 'domination' (as Tuplin suggests we should call it)[43] the Medes might have exercised after the fall of the Assyrian empire, we should not just dismiss Herodotus' account of them, even if that account also should not be taken at face value.

It is also important to note that much of the search for a Median 'empire' has been linked to the search for a shared Median material culture, but that assumes an 'empire' would necessarily express itself in material terms in what has been termed a 'culture of empire'.[44] The Assyrian Empire, for example, is often considered to have achieved cultural and political homogeneity by enlisting the allegiance of the elite, whether Assyrian or from conquered territories, even if there is a disagreement about the imperial strategies through which this homogeneity was achieved.[45] The search for any kind of Median culture, however, has been elusive, and there is little evidence of shared experience apart from living in the region along the Great Khorasan Road, and participation in the army of the *Umman-manda*. For that reason, there is always the possibility that we should be thinking about shared activity rather than shared culture when thinking about the Medes.

It certainly seems that the influence of the Medes (or at least the *Umman-manda*) may have been felt beyond Media proper and they do seem to have had extended their reach to places outside Media. Herodotus says that the Cappadocians (north of Harran) were 'obedient (*katēkooi*)' to the Medes, which brought Cyaxares into conflict with the Lydians against whom he subsequently fought a series of battles (Hdt. 1.72.1-2, 74.1-3). Although the date of the final battle is uncertain, it should probably be assumed that negotiations brought the conflict as a whole to an end (whether or not we believe in Herodotus' eclipse).[46]

There is also some evidence that the Medes may have had influence in at least some parts of Armenia, and perhaps even as far as Hyrcania and Parthia (note DB §35 2.92-8). The Urartian state in Armenia, which first emerged as a unified state in the late ninth century and withstood a number of incursions by the Assyrians,[47] probably failed by the mid-seventh century,[48] although whether its collapse was caused by Scythians, Medes, or internal problems is disputed.[49] There is some slight archaeological evidence that the Medes had influence in Armenia after the collapse of Urartu.[50] Possibly more substantial is the fact that in the Behistun inscription, in respect of the revolts against Darius of 522 BCE, the response to the revolt of Phraortes (who notably claimed a familial link with Cyaxares) of Media is played out in Armenia as well as in Media, just as later a Sagartian also claims dynastic links to Cyaxares (DB §24 2.13-§33 2.91). Tuplin also thinks it significant that Media, Armenia and Cappadocia are listed together in the earliest of provinces of the Persian Empire (DB §6 1.15-16), that in the iconography of Persepolis the 'gift bearers' from these three provinces are dressed similarly, and

> [t]he fact that the Behistun narrative (DB 26-30, 34) deals with Armenian events as part of "what [Darius] did in Media" (i.e. suppress the Median rebels, Fravarti and Cicantakhma)... Armenia is clearly so strongly associated with Media that the narrator does not feel the need to note explicitly that Armenians sided with Fravarti – and so strongly that their suppression required major effort.[51]

In addition, in the early years of Nabonidus' reign, the army under the command now of Astyages (Herodotus says he was the son of Cyaxares) were certainly making a nuisance of themselves as far away from Media as Harran in Syria. As we have already noted, there are different accounts of the involvement of Cyaxares' army in the destruction of the city and the temple in 610 BCE: while the *Fall of Nineveh Chronicle* (*ABC* 3) says that the city was looted by the Babylonians (although the implication is that the *Umman-manda* were also involved since they had also been at Harran with the Babylonians: *ABC* 3.63-5), Nabonidus for his part (since he wants to emphasise Babylonian piety and deflect blame for impiety) claims that it was the *Umman-manda* who plundered Harran, and that Nabopolassar, the king of the Babylonians, was grieved by what they had done.[52] We will return to Nabonidus' account of the taking of Harran in the next chapter, but, for now, however we understand these different texts, it is clear that from Nabonidus' accession in the middle of the sixth century, control of the city was at least contested so that Nabonidus was not able to undertake the planned rebuilding work of the temple that was needed after its earlier destruction.

From a Mesopotamian point of view, Harran was an important city both strategically and symbolically (Map 2). The god of Harran, Sin, the ancient Sumerian moon god, was closely connected with Mesopotamian kingship.[53] Ashurbanipal had rebuilt the temple of Sin, the Ehulhul (which had previously been renovated, as Ashurbanipal tells us, by Shalmaneser III),[54] and, as we have seen, it became the last outpost of the Assyrian empire. Nabonidus was also later to rebuild the temple after its destruction in 610, and made careful reference to the building works of Ashurbanipal,[55] so connecting himself to the Assyrian heritage of the city, and also to Assyrian kingship. In fact, the Neo-Assyrian kings were also personally involved with the cult of Sin, to a degree which within the Neo-Assyrian empire only bears comparison with their interest in the cults of Babylonia.[56] Nabonidus formed his intentions for the veneration of Sin at Harran in the early years of the reign,[57] and Holloway guesses that Nabonidus' interest in the cult of Sin at Harran was linked to its 'demonstrated empire-building qualities' in the Assyrian West.[58] It was also the natal home of his mother Adad-guppi (who was born during the reign of Ashurbanipal), who possibly served as a priestess in the temple, and saw the temple's destruction in 610.[59]

The city was also an important nodal point for routes across northern Mesopotamia, and also routes from the Levant, and through Cappadocia into Anatolia.[60] In the Hebrew Bible, for example, Abra(ha)m settles for a time at Harran on his way from Mesopotamia to the Levant and Egypt (*Genesis* 11.31-12.10), and major routes from northern Mesopotamia connected Harran and Melitene/Melid (in Cappadocia, near modern Malatya), which gave access north to Anatolia and especially Asia Minor in the west.[61] After the fall of the Assyrian empire, while the Babylonians may have taken general control, by the 550's Medes were in control of Harran, at least insofar as they were able to prevent Nabonidus' building works (Nabonidus says that the *Umman-manda* surrounded it)[62], and so presumably controlled routes north to Miletene, another important intersection between the Taurus Mountains and Euphrates for roads into Anatolia, the Halys River and the city of Kanesh (a city in central Anatolia which had important Assyrian trade connections).[63] They may well also have had access to the roads running west to east in northern Mesopotamia, as well as the routes from northern Mesopotamia into Armenia, particularly those which had been used by the Assyrian kings.[64]

Nabonidus' work at Harran was delayed until after his 10-year sojourn in Arabia because the *Umman-manda*, now under the leadership of Astyages, were causing problems for the Babylonians,[65] and Beaulieu thinks they must have had control of the city.[66] The distance of Harran from Ecbatana was substantial, and there is the question of how the *Umman-manda* gained (and maintained) access to the city, especially if they were based in Media. One possibility was that Astyages and his army (coming from Media) approached the city by following what was to become the Persian Royal Road from where it met the Great Khorasan Road at the river valley of the Diyala, to a point near Nisibis (modern Nusaybin) and then followed roads on an east-west axis to north western Mesopotamia.[67] Another possibility is that he approached Harran through Armenia and Cappadocia: Tuplin argues that when Cyrus later came into conflict with Croesus, he came to Cappadocia through Armenia, along either the Erzincan-Sivas road or further south on the Van-Elazig highway.[68] Deciding which route probably depends on how much control the Babylonians were actually able to exert over the roads of northern Mesopotamia. At least in 547, we know that Cyrus was able to access routes on the western side of the Zagros, since, whatever his destination, the *Nabonidus Chronicle* says he crossed the Tigris below Arbela (*ABC* 7 ii.15-16). Rollinger, on the other hand, argues that Cyrus (and so his army) did not have control of Urartu/Armenia until 547,[69] but as already discussed a mid-seventh-century date is usually agreed for the collapse of Urartu.

Nevertheless, Harran had to be accessed by Astyages and the *Umman-manda* by one route or another, which opens up an approach to the problem of the alleged Median empire by asking what is meant by 'empire'. The Assyrian empire, for example, is often viewed in terms of 'a spread of land' which has impervious borders (as seen on most maps of the Near East), what

Liverani has called the 'ink stain' model of empire; this territorial model is appropriate at points at the height of the Assyrian empires. However, the spatiality of some phases of the Assyrian empire have also been discussed in terms of a 'network empire', that is a 'network of communications over which material goods are carried', along which nodal points are not necessarily contiguous.[70] This model of a network empire may also work very well for understanding how the Medes may have controlled the central Zagros, especially as we have already seen that the Median cities were located along the corridor of the Great Khorasan Road, and their influence may have extended east, perhaps as far as Rhaga, and even as far as Hyrcania and Parthia.[71]

So, although Herodotus seems to be thinking of Cyaxares' 'empire' in territorial terms, it may make more sense to see him both controlling routes of communication between the Halys in Anatolia, Armenia (which Zimansky has described as a network of highways and fortresses),[72] and across the central Zagros. Even if Cyaxares' control of Armenia is uncertain, it may be that the *Umman-manda* did reach Cappadocia by roads through Mesopotamia, especially if his ally Nabopolassar allowed him access.

We should possibly not even be thinking of Cyaxares' 'empire' in terms of political control over territorial states at all. Rather, it is likely that what Cyaxares was able to exact from Median city-lords was not so much political control as loyalty to a military leadership of a confederated army, perhaps in return for booty. It certainly seems to be booty which was the reward for the Assyrian incursions. It is also striking (and important) that in our Babylonian sources Cyaxares' army is generally called the *Umman-manda*. While it is often overtranslated as 'Medes', what it actually means is 'foreign army hordes' or 'enemy hordes',[73] and by the end of the seventh century, may have included other ethnic groups as well as Medes.[74] We will return to the importance of this descriptive label for the army in Mesopotamian literature in the next chapter. In any case, in Nabonidus' *Ehulhul Cylinder*, Astyages is called 'king of the *Umman-manda*/LÚ.ERÍM.-*man-da*' (28-9), an army which itself comprised 'kings' (LUGAL.MEŠ),[75] and who together were preventing the rebuilding of the temple of Sin.[76] If Herodotus is right that Astyages was the son of Cyaxares (there seems to be little real reason to doubt it), and he succeeded to his father's position over the army, he probably at least also had access to the roads that connected Harran to Mesopotamia, Anatolia, and perhaps even Armenia.

Cyrus and the *Umman-manda*

All of this becomes important for considering Cyrus' relationship to this army of the *Umman-manda*. The *Ehulhul Cylinder* claims that Cyrus 'scattered with his own few troops (*i-na um-ma-ni-šu i-ṣu-tu ... ú-sap-pi-iḫ*)' the vast army of the *Umman-manda* (28). Likewise, the *Cyrus Cylinder* says that Cyrus made the country of Gutium and the *Umman-manda* submit at his feet (13) (Gutium in Mesopotamian literature is often a general and imprecise designation of the mountainous Zagros region to the east; in the *Curse of Agade*, the Guti are 'a people who know no inhibitions, with human instincts, but canine intelligence and monkeys' features – Enlil brought them out of the mountains'; we will have more to say about Gutium and the *Umman-manda* on the *Cyrus Cylinder* in the next chapter).[77]

However, it is not at all clear that we should take the claim that Cyrus defeated the Medes in battle at face value. At first glance, this picture of conquest over the enemy horde (of the Medes) seems to fit with some of Herodotus' and Ctesias' more general comments about the Persians having once been subject to the Medes, and then overcoming the Median army in battle. However, even the full story as presented by these two Greek authors is not that simple, as we shall see.[78]

The apparent picture of outright conquest, however, also needs further exploration. The *Nabonidus Chronicle* suggests that Astyages marched against Cyrus in 550/49 BC for conquest (*ABC* 7 ii.1: *ana ka-ša-di il-lik-ma*), which would also make Astyages the aggressor (apparently contradicting the accounts of both Herodotus and Ctesias). However, as we have already discussed in the previous chapter, the *Chronicle* also says that Cyrus was successful against Astyages not because of military success over Astyages' army as such, but because the army rebelled, and Astyages was handed over to Cyrus as a prisoner (*ABC* 7 ii.2). As we have also seen, although the details vary considerably, both Herodotus (1.108-128) and Ctesias (F 8d*§46) both present a similar kind of story: that Astyages' campaign against Cyrus (who had himself rebelled) collapsed because leading members of the army were no longer willing to support Astyages' rule and transferred their allegiance to Cyrus, all of which suggests that the revolt of the army might have some historical reality.

It is also possible, as mentioned in the previous chapter, that Cyrus held some kind of vassalage in Astyages' army, and that he did himself revolt before the rest of the army also revolted. This scenario is not necessarily inconsistent with the Babylonian texts, in which Cyrus is always a king in his own right. In fact, the *Ehulhul Cylinder* confirms Cyrus' position as king of Anshan (27). Although at this point, the Akkadian is difficult to interpret,[79] it may also suggest that, although he was king of Anshan, he held some kind of subservient position in Astyages' army (27), which itself appears as we noted earlier to be a confederated army of a number of 'kings' (LUGAL.MEŠ: 25; cf. Ctesias F 8d*§45-6; *Jeremiah* 25.25). In any case, the *Ehulhul Cylinder* suggests that Cyrus first acted against Astyages as early as the third year of Nabonidus' reign, that is in 553 BCE, so three years before he defeated Astyages and the army defected,[80] which also seems to be suggested by the more extended sequence of battles of other Greek accounts, as Briant has pointed out.[81]

However we understand Cyrus' political or familial relationship with Astyages,[82] the picture that seems to emerge is of internal problems within

Astyages' army. The confrontation between Cyrus and Astyages led to a revolt in 550/49 within the army, displacing Astyages as 'king of the *Umman-manda*' in favour of Cyrus, a reconstruction which is also consistent in general terms with what we find in Herodotus and Ctesias. The willingness of the army to go over to Cyrus speaks to the precariousness of any leadership based on charisma: a charismatic leader is only as good as his charismatic qualities relative to other charismatic leaders. Furthermore, Flannery has discussed how rivalry between chiefdoms in nomadic and pastoralist societies operated at the level of the tribal chiefs, rather than between the tribes themselves.[83] It seems that, whether or not he was a vassal (or indeed the grandson of Astyages), Cyrus' leadership had become preferable to the army to that of Astyages, who in the Greek accounts is an old man when he has to deal with Cyrus (e.g., Hdt. 1.109.2-3).[84] That the leadership of the army could be changed in this way is probably also consistent with the fact that it had only been formed only 50 or 60 years before by Cyaxares, who was obviously another charismatic leader. It may well have been that in the earlier years of his reign, Astyages had managed to hold this army together – that he was able to cause trouble for Nabonidus at some distance from Media at Harran suggests that – but possibly the appearance of an experienced, energetic and ruthless military commander (Cyrus would probably have been about 50 years old when he replaced Astyages in 550/49, so not a young man as our Greek sources suggest, and had probably become king of Anshan – whatever that meant – 10 years before) made it easy for the army to defect.

Cyrus' control over the army solved Nabonidus' problems with the Medes at Harran, although that was probably not where the final confrontation with Astyages took place. Herodotus has two battles but is not very clear where they occurred (somewhere between Ecbatana and Fars: 1.127-8). Ctesias (through Nicolaus of Damascus) places a sequence of battles in Fars, which culminate in the mountains around Pasargadae (F 8d*§30-45), which Ctesias also says was Cyrus' ancestral home (F 8d*§41: *to patrōion oikēma*). Likewise, the *Nabonidus Chronicle* has Astyages marching out against Cyrus (*ABC* 7 ii.1). Strabo also places Cyrus' last confrontation with Astyages at Pasargadae (15.3.8), where he built his palace (although he could be inferring the battle from the location of the palace). Nevertheless, that the shift in the control of the army was felt as far away from the Zagros as Harran in Syria does suggest that Astyages' reach had also been extensive.

Astyages, at least initially, seems to have survived the confrontation with Cyrus. The *Nabonidus Chronicle* says that the army took him prisoner and they handed him over to Cyrus (7 ii.2). The *Ehulhul Cylinder* also suggests that Astyages was kept at Cyrus' court as a captive.[85] Likewise, Herodotus says Astyages was captured (1.128.3), but that Cyrus kept him unharmed at his court until he died (1.130.2). Nicolaus of Damascus, who seems not to be following Ctesias at this point, notes that Astyages was taken as a prisoner of war (F 66.46).[86]

Photius' account is the most detailed. In his summary of Ctesias, he says that Astyages' daughter and husband hid the Median king in the palace at Ecbatana (Ctesias F 9.1), but that Astyages gave himself up when his family was threatened with torture. Although Oebaras bound Astyages in chains, Cyrus released him and 'honoured him as a father'. Amytis, the daughter of Astyages, Cyrus initially honoured as a mother, but then, having killed her husband, married her. We later learn that Astyages had been sent to Barcania (F 9.6; F 9a), which seems to be a city in Media, or at least adjacent to it (cf. Q.C. 3.2.5).[87] Meanwhile, Photius/Ctesias says that Cyrus attacked the Bactrians, but that when the Bactrians heard that Astyages had become the father of Cyrus, and Amytis his mother and wife, then they gave themselves up willingly to Amytis and Cyrus (F 9.2). Next Cyrus made war on the Sacae, and captured the king, Amorges. Amorges' wife, Sparethe, then assembled an army against Cyrus and defeated him, capturing Amytis' brother and sons, who were later released in exchange for Amorges (F 9.3). Amorges then campaigned with Cyrus against Croesus (F 9.4). Cyrus, now in Persis (Fars), sent for Astyages, but he was killed on the journey by one of Cyrus' eunuchs (on the advice of Oebaras!) (F 9.6; F 9a).

It is difficult to see what we can draw from this account about actual historical events, but there are some tropes which are probably quite revealing about patterns of behaviour. We know from Herodotus that Cyrus was called 'father' and that being 'gentle', he contrived all things well (3.89.3). The 'gentle' ruler (especially the 'gentle shepherd') was itself a trope of both Greek and Near Eastern kingship (the Greek examples probably deriving from the Near East). As we have already seen in an earlier chapter, 'father' was also a title of Elamite kings, and linked to nomadic culture.[88] While we have already discussed the fact that Median culture was probably based on transhumance rather than pastoral nomadism, we have also already considered how in nomadic societies, kinship terms could be used as a way of explaining (and adjusting) relationships within the community, especially in order to confirm and legitimise leadership.[89] So, we find that Astyages becomes Cyrus' 'father' (that is, father-in-law) whether that was in reality true or not, although it is probably the case that Cyrus did marry a daughter of Astyages. Darius I married daughters, and even a granddaughter, of Cyrus to legitimate his kingship (and the succession), in circumstances which were also (at best) irregular.[90] Alexander the Great was later to do the same in relation to the family of Darius IIII,[91] just as Ada, the Hecatomnid queen of Caria, also adopted Alexander as her son as a means of securing her rule as his vassal (Arrian, *Anab*.1.23.8).[92]

However, what is more interesting is how fictional kinship and other kinds of reciprocal relationships could become a strategy for easing political relationships. Cyrus, it seems, makes Astyages his 'father/grandfather/father-in-law' either through a real or (perhaps) fictional relationship – through myth-making or complex marriage relationships. This relationship (whether fictive or not) then becomes the basis for another set of political relationships with political consequences, which are also then wrapped up in the terms of fictive kinship and reciprocity. If we return briefly to the birth stories discussed in the previous chapter, that is exactly what these stories were intended to do as well: to explain and make right in kinship terms a succession achieved by other means.

Cyrus at Sardis and the Medes in Asia Minor

After the capture of Astyages in 550/49 BCE, Babylonian control over Harran and the heartland of Assyria seems to have become more secure,[93] at least temporarily, so that Nabonidus was able to rebuild the temple of Sin, although he apparently did not do so until he returned to Babylon from Teima in 543, so at least six years after Cyrus' final confrontation with Astyages. Cyrus' victory over Astyages seems to have at least neutralised the Median problem at Harran, even if mainly by a leadership change in the army.

Until the taking of Babylon in 539 (or perhaps the year before), Cyrus' relationship with Nabonidus seems to have been positive, and mutually beneficial. From the *Nabonidus Chronicle*, we know that Cyrus was campaigning again in 547/6. It was long thought that this was the year of his campaign in Lydia, but the cuneiform is damaged and an alternative reading of Urartu has gained recent support, although there is still no consensus.[94] Cyrus' crossing of the Tigris below Arbela could have taken him in either direction, west towards Harran (and so into Cappadocia),[95] or north to the upper Tigris and Urartu (as Rollinger suggests) from routes across the Tur Abdin,[96] although, as we have seen earlier, Urartu by this period was a kingdom that had seriously declined, so that there was no longer much of a united kingdom to conquer, or indeed a king (cf. *ABC* 7 ii.17).

Wherever Cyrus was headed, that he crossed the Tigris below Arbela suggests he had access to the northern Mesopotamian road system from the junction where the Great Khorasan Road met the Royal Road (noted earlier), just as Cyaxares seems to have done. Beaulieu thinks Cyrus was probably even an ally of Nabonidus as early as 553, although not all agree.[97] In the so-called *Harran Stele*, Nabonidus talks about his return to Babylon in 543 (after a period of ten years at Teima in Arabia) and the rebuilding of the temple of Sin at Harran. He says that the kings of Egypt, Media and Arabia, as well as 'all the hostile kings' (*nap-ḫar* LUGAL.MEŠ *na-ki-ru-tú*) send to him for goodwill and peace.[98] The contrast between the kings of Egypt, Media and Arabia and the 'hostile kings' itself suggests that the first group of kings were (at least) not hostile.[99]

Otherwise, we know little more of Cyrus' career with certainty until the taking of Babylon.[100] Photius/Ctesias says that after his victory over Astyages, Cyrus campaigned in central Asia against the Bactrians and Scythians before taking Sardis with the help of the Scythian Amorges (F 9.2-4),[101] although Ctesias' account is usually assumed to be hopelessly garbled, and it is interesting that the taking of Babylon is not included at all.

Herodotus appears to delay these campaigns until after the capture of Sardis (1.153.4, 177), although his phrasing is also so vague that he may be talking about new uprisings or just even possible plans: for example, Herodotus says Cyrus was troubled by Egypt, which he did not march against, though it was probably in view as a possible conquest.

We know that Cyrus advanced on Lydia at some point, probably before he took Babylon, although there is no reference to Sardis in the *Cyrus Cylinder*. However, given the very local Mesopotamian interests of the *Cylinder*, that is not necessarily surprising. There might be some support for a date in the 540s through the association of the philosopher/mathematician Thales with Croesus' crossing of the Halys (Thales is thought to have died in the 540s), although Herodotus does himself debunk the part that Thales played in Croesus' campaign (1.75-3-6), and in any case, the ancient testimony for Thales' death are open to doubt.[102] It is interesting that the Roman historian Justin, who summarised the universal history of Pompeius Trogus,[103] places the campaign against Babylon *before* the capture of Sardis (Justin 1.7.3-4). The historicity of Justin/Pompeius Trogus is of doubtful value, but it does show that there was a historical logic which could sequence these campaigns in this way.

Although we cannot confirm the date of the campaign,[104] the army of the Medes played a major part in the fall of Sardis and the conquest of the Greek cities of Asia Minor. As already noted, we know Cyrus had access to roads into northern Mesopotamia in 547 (so after Nabonidus' accession at Babylon in 556, his departure to Teima in 553, Cyrus' defeat of Astyages in 550, but before Nabonidus' return to Babylon from Teima in 543 and his rebuilding of Harran), so could possibly have approached Cappadocia from northern Mesopotamia, from northern Mesopotamia into Armenia, or from Ecbatana into Armenia and then west into Cappadocia. From Assyria to Sardis, he could even have taken what was to become the Persian Royal Road, which probably went from north eastern Mesopotamia to Melitene before taking (probably) other routes to Pteria, where the first confrontation with Croesus took place (1.75-6).

Herodotus tells us that the Lydian king, Croesus, initiated the campaign, and once he crossed the Halys, took the city of Pteria (1.71.1-2, 75-6),[105] although rumours were already circulating among the Greeks about Cyrus' growing power in the east which could threaten western Anatolia (cf. Hdt. 1.163). In fact, Cyrus had also offered the Greek cities terms, which they rejected (Hdt. 1.76.3), except for the Milesians (Hdt. 1.141.4, 169.2). That Croesus knew that crossing the Halys was a move that would threaten Cyrus, and Cyrus' response does seem to suggest that Cyrus (like Cyaxares) thought of Cappadocia as a territory (or at least its roads) under his control.

Cyrus seems to have engaged Croesus in Cappadocia relatively quickly after the Lydian crossed the Halys, which suggests at the least that he had easy access to Cappadocia over roads that could accommodate an army (although we do not know which was his starting point: the palace at Pasargadae in Fars was not completed until after the conquest of the Greek cities; the relative speed with which he reached Cappadocia might suggest Ecbatana by routes through Armenia, but that is just guesswork). After an inconclusive battle, Herodotus says Croesus returned to Sardis to see out the winter, but Cyrus unexpectedly followed him, and after a siege at Sardis lasting fourteen days, Cyrus took Sardis (Hdt. 1.76-84), the violence of which is confirmed by archaeology.[106]

The taking of Sardis and the fate of Croesus quickly became folklore. Ctesias (through Photius) also has a siege, which becomes the backdrop for a trick (!) of Oebaras involving wooden soldiers on poles to frighten the Sardians (F 9 4; cf. F 9a). The favourite story of the fifth century, however, was of Croesus, his wealth, and his rescue from the pyre. An early fifth-century red-figure vase (originating from Athens, but discovered in a burial context in Vulci in Etruria) depicts Croesus on the pyre, which is just being lit (Figure 4.1).

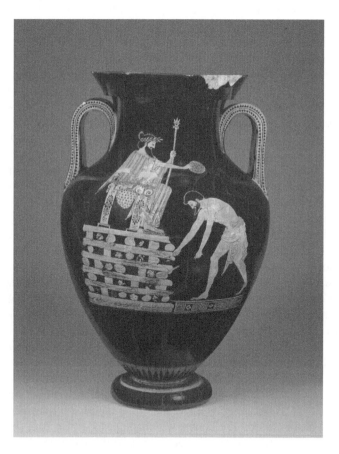

Figure 4.1 Croesus on the pyre. © RMN-Grand Palais (musée du Louvre)/Tony Querrec.

The presentation of Croesus is sympathetic: Croesus wears a laurel wreath and is making a libation, which perhaps speaks to the ambivalence about his receptions in the Greek world. Part of the popular stories about Croesus was about his lavish gift-giving to Greek sanctuaries, and three column bases from the Greek sanctuary of Artemis at Ephesus (Tod i 6), inscribed with dedications from Croesus bear testament to his generosity. On the other hand, Herodotus is clear that Croesus was the first Asian ruler to take away the freedom of the Greeks (1.6).

The fifth-century epinician poet, Bacchylides, included a version of the story of Croesus on the pyre in his ode written to celebrate the Olympic victory of Hieron of Syracuse in 468 BCE (*Ode* 3.23-62), which is significantly different from that later given by Herodotus. In Bacchylides' version, Croesus attempts suicide by self-immolation to escape slavery, but was rescued first by Zeus who sent rain to quench the flames, and then because of his piety, Apollo carried him away with his daughters to settle him among the mythical Hyperboreans. This is often taken to mean that he died in the flames, and much later traditions say that he died at Sardis.[107] In Herodotus, it is Cyrus who builds the pyre, and although he later regrets having lit it, Croesus is rescued by Apollo, who quenches the flames (1.86-7), and saves the king who becomes Cyrus' counsellor. Ctesias (through Photius) does not have a pyre at all, although Croesus does take refuge in the sanctuary of Apollo; he is later released and given a city near Ecbatana, Barnene (F 9.5).

Cyrus and the Medes

Whether or not we take seriously the stories about Astyages' and Croesus' survival,[108] part of the picture that seems to emerge is the international character of Cyrus' army and the inner circle of his court, and especially the prominence of the Medes. Harpagus, the Median commander who seems to have organised the revolt from Astyages of the Median army (Hdt. 1.123-9), was at the siege of Sardis and advised Cyrus about the use of camels (Hdt. 1.80.2).[109] After the fall of Sardis, Cyrus initially gave the important position of looking after the revenues to a Lydian, beside the 'Persian' Tabalus who was left in charge of the city (Hdt. 1.153.3). When the Lydian Pactyes revolted and laid siege to Tabalus, Cyrus sent a Median general, Mazares to help Tabalus; in the face of Mazares and his army, Pacytes fled to the Greek city of Cyme, but was eventually handed over to Mazares by the Chians (Hdt. 1.157-60). Mazares then proceeded to punish the Greek cities who had helped Pactyes: Herodotus says the people of Priene and Magnesia were enslaved (Hdt. 1.161), although van der Spek thinks this means they were deported,[110] and that the plain of the Maeander was plundered. Mazares then died, but he was replaced in Asia Minor by Harpagus, who captured the rest of the Aeolian and Ionian cities (Hdt. 1.162-4, 169), except for Miletus which was not attacked because it had negotiated a treaty with Cyrus (Hdt. 1.141.4, 143.1, 169), and the Phocaeans and Teans who escaped by sea (Hdt. 1.163-4, 168). Caria, Caunia and Lycia suffered a similar fate (Hdt. 1.171.1, 174-6). When the islanders saw the treatment of the mainland Greeks at the hands of Harpagus, Herodotus says they also surrendered (except Samos, where the Aeacid dynasty ruled), even though the islanders had not been subject to the Lydians and had had a 'ritualised friendship' (*xenia*) with Croesus (Hdt. 1.169.2; cf. 1.27.5).

That these actions were undertaken by a *Median* army, together with Median commanders and the violence of their attack, had a lasting impact on the Greeks, who thenceforward characterised the eastern enemy as the 'Mede'.[111] Johannes Haubold has also brilliantly illuminated the importance of the Medes in the *Babylonian* imaginary as the chaotic agents of divine will, especially in relation to their role in the downfall of the Assyrian empire, who themselves succumb to divine retribution.[112] While it is often said that the Medes did not hold a privileged position in the Achaemenid empire, especially as it developed under Darius I, they do seem to have held a special place in Cyrus' army, and continued to do so even in the army of Darius. It is notable at Behistun that Darius says that the army he deploys (even against insurgent Medes) is 'the army of Parsa and Mada' (DB §25.18). It is also often assumed that even from Cyrus' rule, Persians dominated the court.[113] That may well be true from the reign of Darius I. Nevertheless, the rebel Gaumata was a Mede (as well as a Magus), as we know from the Babylonian version of the Behistun inscription (*ma-da-a-a … ma-gu-šu*),[114] and Herodotus sees Medes behind the palace coup in 522 (Hdt. 3.61-79). While it is difficult to know how many of the events that Herodotus provides map onto the real world or real time, we have seen that Herodotus may know something about the reach of the Medes beyond Media, even if he may be wrong to suggest that it is a conventional territorial empire, such as the Assyrian empire in its developed phase. By the same token, we might ask, even though the argument is no longer fashionable, whether it is possible that one of the many things that we are seeing, even if only partially, in 522, whatever the precise details of the coup, is the use of this political upheaval as a means to suppress the importance of the Medes (or the *Umman-manda*) at court in order to fix the interests of the emerging 'Persians'?[115]

In any case, despite what the *Cyrus Cylinder* suggests about the relationship between Cyrus and the Medes at the time of the conquest of Babylon, as we have already seen in the previous chapter, both of the Cyrus' birth stories that we find in our Greek sources were intended to provide a retrospective explanation for Cyrus' succession, at least in terms of the leadership of the army of the Medes. It was also an army of Medes that was remembered, even if metaphorically, as the cosmological threat to Babylon (*Isaiah* 13.17, cf. 21.2; *Jeremiah* 51.11, cf. 51.28; note also *Daniel* 8.20).[116] The army remembered as responsible for the taking of Babylon in the *Nabonidus Chronicle* is the army of Gutium, also called Cyrus' army (*ABC* 7 iii. 15, 17). However, we also know that the Medes were basically city dwellers who also practised transhumance. Although they may not have provided Cyrus with a model for empire, they may have been important (and not just in terms of their wealth) in the movement of the peoples of the southwest Zagros from pastoral nomadism to a more sedentary way of life.

Furthermore, however the Medes imagined their control of at least parts of Asia, Cyrus soon developed a more recognisably territorial model for empire. Herodotus says that at Sardis, Oroetes was appointed as governor (*hyparchos*) (3.120.1, 122.1), and Thierry thinks he was given authority in all of western Anatolia (although later this region was broken into smaller units).[117] After the taking of Babylon, Cyrus also appointed a local governor, Gubaru (Gobryas), who himself set about appointing officials (*ABC* 7 iii.20). Tolini thinks that this man is the same as the commander of the army of the Guti who took Babylon a few weeks before (called Ugbaru in the *Nabonidus Chronicle*: ABC 7 iii.15-16),[118] and whom the *Chronicle* says died a few weeks later (*ABC* 7 iii.22). Either this man or, as Tolini thinks, another Gubaru, remained in office certainly until 525 and probably until the accession of Darius I over all of Babylonia, although later under Darius, new jurisdictions were arranged.[119] In any case, it is clear that Cyrus was by this point thinking in terms of regionally based provinces with governors, which had been one of the hallmarks of the Assyrian empire, and to a lesser extent, the Neo-Babylonian empire.[120] In imperial terms, the taking of Babylon was an important moment. However, there are many stories about its capture, so it is to that city and Cyrus' relationship to Gutium and the *Umman-manda* that we turn next.

Notes

1. See Bosworth (1995), 19.
2. See Briant (2002), 40.
3. Waerzeggers (2021). Note also Larsen (1979, 91), who observes that Mesopotamians did not have a word for 'empire' but instead 'speak of "countries" or "lands"'. Cf. the 'assembly of lands' (Parpola, 1995, 393), although Radner (2011, 371) says this should be understood as a Babylonian (rather than Assyrian) institution. Lecoq (1997, 137) suggests that this is an Iranian title, not a Babylonian one (Babylonian rulers call themselves 'King of Babylon'), but it is known from Assyrian and Urartian contexts: Assyrian examples: Karlsson (2016), 151, 153; Urartian: Tavernier (2013), 64.
4. Roaf (1995), 54–66; Radner (2003).
5. See also Stronach (2003).
6. Levine (1974), 117–9, with Levine (1973), esp. 3–5, associates Mt. Bikni with the Alwand range, just south of Hamadan, although others, including J. Reade (1995), prefer Mt. Damavand near the southern coast of the Caspian Sea. Note also M. Roaf (1995); Lanfranchi (2003), 81–2.
7. Levine (1973); Roaf (1995), 56–7; note also Radner (2003), 40–1.
8. Levine (1973), 3–4; (1974), 99.
9. Levine (1974), 117; note also Gunter (1982), 105.
10. Grayson (1996), 68 (A.0.102.14 at 121).
11. Lanfranchi (2003).
12. Radner (2003), 42: 'Is being a rider what makes a Mede a Mede in the eyes of the Assyrians?' She also speculates on the possibility of religion as a unifying feature of Median culture.

13. Radner (2003); Lanfranchi (2003). On the dynastic nature of the *bēl āli*, see also Lanfranchi (1998), 101–2.
14. http://oracc.org/riao/Q004738/ (accessed 05/08/2022) at iii 27b–36; see Radner (2003), 41–2.
15. See, e.g., Tadmor and Yamada (eds.) (2011), Tiglath-Pileser III no. 41.13–15, no. 47 obv. 38b–39a (including Bactrian camels: ANŠE.*ud-ra-a-ti*), 42; Frame (ed.) (2021), no. 1.191b–94a, no. 2.224b–226a, no. 7.65b–67a, no. 74 iii.54–6; Leichty (ed.) (2011), no. 1 iv.32–9.
16. Greco (2003), 65–78.
17. E.g. Radner (2003), 41–2: '[The Medes] were clearly not nomadic' (41); Lanfranchi *et al.* (2003), 400; note also Potts (2014), 67–81. Note, however, Liverani (2003), 5: 'The basic economic resource was pastoralism, as descriptions of booty and tribute confirm'.
18. Kerkenes Dağ in Anatolia was originally thought to be Median but is now recognised as a city with a Phrygian character (Summers draws back from calling it a 'Phrygian' city), although the excavation team still thinks it should be equated with Herodotus' Pteria. Newsletters on the excavations are available on the Kerkenes Project website: https://sciences.ucf.edu/anthropology/kerkenes/overview/ (accessed 02/02/2018). See also Draycott and Summers (2008); Summers (2008). Kerkenes was a large and obviously important city on the Anatolian plateau which was destroyed in the mid-sixth century, consistent with the story in Herodotus about the conflict between Croesus and Cyrus (Hdt. 1.76), which says that Croesus captured 'the city of the Pterians'.
19. See, for example, Liverani (2003), 2–4.
20. Radner (2003); note also Liverani (2003), 5–6; Adalı (2011), 107–8.
21. For the description of the Medes as 'those who roam the mountain(s) and desert as thieves', see Frame (ed.) (2021), no. 1.189–90, cf. no. 2.222–3 where it has been restored.
22. E.g., Lanfranchi (2003).
23. Liverani (2003), 6.
24. For the *adê* inscriptions found in the temple of Nabû at Kalhu/Nimrud, see Fales (2012). It had been thought that these *adê* inscriptions should be understood as oaths of loyalty sworn by members of the Median elite at the Assyrian court. However, the discovery of another copy on the periphery of the empire at Tell Ta'yinat (in Turkey) means that a new interpretation needs to be found. For the text of the inscriptions at Kalhu, see Parpola and Watanabe (1988), no. 6 (with XIXX–XXX).
25. Liverani (2003), 6.
26. Note also Tuplin (2004), 233.
27. http://oracc.org/ribo/Q005365/: no. 6.19–27, http://oracc.org/ribo/Q005366/: no. 7.17–21 (accessed 14/05/2022). See also Chapter 1.
28. See Waerzeggers (2012). Waerzeggers argues that these *Chronicles* (*ABC* 3-4-5) were composed at Borsippa (rather than Babylon), and date to no later than the mid-sixth century.
29. Asheri in Asheri *et al.* (2007), 155.
30. Cf. Ctesias F 1pα, δ*, ε*, q.
31. On Ashur-uballit's status as crown prince rather than king, see Radner (2018); Levavi (2020), 68–9.
32. On the fall of the Assyrian empire: Oates (1991), 180–8; Kuhrt (1995a), 2.540–6.
33. Weiershäuser and Novotny (eds.) (2020), Nabonidus 3 ii.14–41.
34. Waerzeggers (2012), 294.
35. Beaulieu (2018), 227–8; Dalley (2021), 217–8.
36. Haubold (2013), 80–1.
37. See Grayson (1975b), 72–80; see also Da Riva (2017).

38. See Llewellyn-Jones (2010), 37–40.
39. Asheri thinks this must be the attack Herodotus mentions in 1.103.2 (Asheri in Asheri *et al.* (2007), 152–3) – although there is no reference in the Babylonian chronicle to Herodotus' mention of a Scythian attack on the Median army, which in any case is not consistent with the Medes' later activities either in 614 which resulted in the destruction of Ashur (*ABC* 3.26–7), or their joint campaigning with the Babylonians in 612 and 610 BCE.
40. Amelie Kuhrt (1995b) has argued that Assyria and its cities were neither completely deserted after their defeat, nor completely neglected by the Neo-Babylonian kings, although she does concede that the city of Nineveh was greatly diminished. See also Radner (2015), esp. 6. For the skeletal remains found in the excavations at the Halzi Gate at Nineveh: Pickworth (2005).
41. On the chronological problems in Herodotus for this sequence of events, see Asheri in Asheri *et al.* (2007), 147–8 (*s.v.* 95–106), 153 (*s.v.* 103.3–106.2), 155 (*s.v.* 106.2).
42. See esp. Sancisi-Weerdenburg (1988); Sancis-Weerdenburg (1994); essays in Lanfranchi *et al.* (eds.), (2003); Rollinger (2008), Rollinger (2021).
43. Tuplin (2004).
44. See, e.g., Düring (2020), 112.
45. Parpola (2003, 100–2), for example, argues for a standard procedure that was rolled out across conquered territories from the reign of Tiglath-Pileser III in the eighth century BCE, in which the elite played an important role; see also Postgate (1992). Düring (2020) has argued for greater diversity in 'imperial repertoires' that were used according to regional and local needs, but still sees the role of the elite as crucial in creating the Assyrian imperial project. Deportations seem to have played an important role in assimilating non-Assyrians into Assyrian cultural and political practices. Deportees could be incentivised to resettle, with offers of land, housing and wives: e.g., *2 Kings* 18.32–3 (cf. *Isaiah* 18.16–17, which is a close parallel text); SSA V.210 (http://oracc.org/saao/P334152/ (accessed 20/08/2022)), SAA XIX. 18 (http://oracc.org/saao/P224476 (accessed 20/08/2020); see, e.g., Na'aman and Zadok (1988); Gallagher (1994); Radner (2012). Interestingly, the Babylonian policy on deportation did not emphasise integration, but deportees retained their previous ethnic affiliations and could even be settled in towns with the same names as those from which they had been relocated, as was the case with Judeans deported to Babylon: see Alstola (2020).
46. Herodotus says the final battle came to an end because of an eclipse of the sun predicted by Thales. That Thales would have been able to predict such an eclipse, and even the link between an eclipse and the end of the battle has been doubted: Mosshamer (1981). There was a solar eclipse in 585 BCE, but this date does not work well with other dates given by Herodotus, not least since he also suggests that the fall of Nineveh was late in Cyaxares' career (Hdt. 1.106.2).
47. Zimansky (1985), 48–50.
48. For the failing years of Urartu, see, e.g., S. Kroll (1984); Zimansky (1995a); Çilingiroğlu (2002); A.T. Smith (2003), esp. 253–4; Hellwag (2012).
49. See, e.g., Zimanksy (1995b), esp. 261; A.T. Smith (1999); Tuplin (2004).
50. S. Kroll (2003).
51. Tuplin (2004), 231; cf. Vogelsang (1992), 109–12, 119, 175–7. Note, however, Rollinger (2008), who sees in this episode no evidence for Median control of Armenia, but an attempt by the Armenians to assert their independence.
52. Weiershäuser and Novotny (eds.) (2020), Nabonidus no. 3 ii 1–41, no. 28 I 7–12a. In the pseudo-autobiography of Adad-guppi, mother of Nabonidus, it is said that in the 16th year of the reign of Nabopolassar (that is 610 BCE),

the god Sin became angry with the city and temple and went up to heaven so that the city and its temple fell into ruin: Weiershäuser and Novotny (eds.) (2020), Nabonidus no. 2001 i.1–9.

53. T.M. Green (1992), 20–1, 36–7.
54. Novotny and Jeffers (eds.) (2018), Ashurbanipal nos. 5 ii.2–14, 6 i.65–98, 140, 7 i.39–65, 10 ii.29–iii.14, 23 64–72b; note also Weiershäuser and Novotny (eds.) (2020), Nabonidus no. 28 ii.3–4, no. 29 ii.1–3 (although the text of 29 is heavily restored) where Nabonidus refers to the fact that Ashurbanipal had seen Shalmaneser's foundations.
55. Weiershäuser and Novotny (eds.) (2020), Nabonidus nos. 28 i.38–40, ii.3, 29 ii.1 ii.43b–6.
56. Holloway (1995).
57. Weiershäuser and Novotny (eds.) (2020), Nabonidus no. 3 x.1–51.
58. Holloway (1995), 307–8.
59. Weiershäuser and Novotny (eds.) (2020), Nabonidus no. 2001.
60. See Holloway (1995), 283–4.
61. Mitford (1996), 986, map 64. For roads through Asia Minor, see also French (1998).
62. Weiershäuser and Novotny (2020), Nabonidus no. 28 i.23.
63. See, e.g., Radner (2015), 21–7.
64. For the Assyrian road network in northern Mesopotamia: see Parpola (1987), XIII–XIV, map; Kessler (1997); Radner (2006); cf. Rollinger (2008); see now also Comfort and Marciak (2018), esp. 34–41.
65. Weiershäuser and Novotny (eds.) (2020), Nabonidus no. 28 i.7–29, no. 29 i.1–8, no. 46 i.13a–16; see Beaulieu (1989), 108–15.
66. Beaulieu (2000), 311 n. 7.
67. On the Persian Royal Road, whose course is much disputed: see, e.g., French (1998); Comfort (2009), 106–9; Reade (2015); Comfort and Marciak (2018), 36 with 105–7. For the general east-west axis of roads in northern Mesopotamia and Anatolia in the first half of the first millennium, see Marro (2004), 99–102.
68. He assumes this route because he thinks that Median influence had extended into Urartian territories rather than into Mesopotamia: Tuplin (2004), 236–7. On the Armenian highways: see Sevin (1988); Sevin (1991).
69. Rollinger (2008).
70. Liverani (1988); Parker (2012); note also M.L. Smith (2005).
71. Note, however, Briant (1984), 36–7.
72. Zimansky (1995b), 255.
73. See in general Adalı (2011).
74. See, e.g., Vogelsang (1992), 309, 311.
75. Compare also *Jeremiah* 51.11, 28 (MT): 'kings of the Medes', although note that the Septuagint *Jeremias* 28.11 has the singular 'king of the Medes'.
76. Weiershäuser and Novotny (eds.) (2020), Nabonidus no. 28 i.21–5.
77. On the barbarian peoples of the *Curse of Agade*, see Cooper (1983), 30–3. Note also that in the Standard Babylonian Recension of the *Cuthean Legend*, the *Umman-manda* who are a mountain people, attack Gutium, Elam, and other places: Westenholz (1997), 310–15 (lines 36–62). See also Dalley (1996), 528; Vanderhooft (2006), 361.
78. The transfer of power from the Medes to the Persians in Xenophon's *Cyropaedia* is different from either of the other Greek accounts and is of little use to us here: the Persian Cyrus is bequeathed Media by his childless maternal uncle, Cyaxares, a story which needs to be understood within the context of Xenophon's narrative of obedience: it is important in the *Cyropaedia* that, despite his own success as a leader – and Cyaxares' questionable leadership skills – Cyrus remains obedient to him.

79. Cyrus is here given the epithet ìr-*su ṣa-aḫ-ri* /ARAD-*su ṣa-aḫ-ri*, but the meaning of the phrase is unclear and interpreted variously ('his young servant', 'his servant, second in rank', 'his vassal'). Also, whether it refers to Cyrus' relationship to the god, or to Astyages is unclear: see Beaulieu (2000), 311 n. 7, although Beaulieu does not hesitate in seeing him as a vassal of Astyages in (2018), 241–2; cf. also Schaudig (2001), 417 (2.12 1.27), who translates the epithet 'seinen geringen Diener'; Weiershäuser and Novotny (eds.) (2020), no. 28 i.27: 'a young servant [of Astyages]'; cf. 153 (no. 29.6). Note, however, Haubold (2013), who translates the epithet: 'their [the gods'] insignificant servant' (87), and Waters (2014, 39), says that 'to understand the phrase "his young servant" as a reference to Cyrus being a subordinate of Astyages is not a given. The phrase appears to refer to the god Marduk, who chose Cyrus as the instrument to implement his divine will – a common motif in ancient Near Eastern texts for centuries'.

80. However, see Tadmor (1965), esp. 353–4; cf. Briant (2002), 32. It is also likely that if we accept the date given for Cyrus' attacks on Astyages as given on the *Ehulhul Cylinder* at face value, Astyages' attack on Cyrus in 550/49 as noticed in the *Nabonidus Chronicle* was a response to Cyrus' activities, after Marduk and the gods had raised Cyrus up against (*ú-šat-bu-niš-šum-ma*) the *Umman-manda*, or at least Astyages, as Nabonidus claims (27). So, it is unlikely that, in the first instance, Astyages was the aggressor, but rather was perhaps even responding to a recalcitrant former vassal.

81. Briant (2002), 31–3; cf. Lenfant (2004), lx.

82. See Chapter 3.

83. Flannery (1999).

84. Herodotus says that Astyages ruled for 35 years (1.130.1). Herodotus also says he was married to Aryenis, the daughter of Alyattes of Lydia (Hdt. 1.74.4).

85. Weiershäuser and Novotny (eds.) (2020), Nabonidus no. 28 i.29.

86. Photius has quite a different version of events, although with some interestingly divergent as well as similar themes, which suggests that at this point, Nicolaus of Damascus was not following Ctesias, but perhaps an older tradition; cf. Lenfant (2004), 256.

87. Justin 1.6.16 says he was given the Hyrcanians to rule because he did not want to return to Media. It is doubtful he ruled anyone, but he may have been given a city to provide revenue to support an independent court: see Petit (1990), 27–8; Lenfant (2004), 258–9. Now that the army had gone over to Cyrus, it is unlikely that he represented much of a real political threat.

88. Chapter 2.

89. Chapter 3.

90. On Darius' marriages to two of Cyrus' daughters, Atossa and Artystone (Atossa had also been the wife of her brother Cambyses), and one of his granddaughters: Hdt. 3.88.2–3.

91. Alexander named Sisygambis (mother of Darius III) as his 'mother': Diod. 17.37.5–6; cf. Arrian, *Anab.* 2.12.3–8. He also married two of Darius' daughters: Diod. 17.107.6; Arrian, *Anab.* 7.4.4.

92. Adoption as a means of creating politically significant bonds was not necessarily unusual. In the early fourth century, the Athenian general, Iphicrates, was adopted by Amyntas III, king of the Macedonians. Later, on Amyntas' death, when Eurydice, Amyntas' widow, was put under pressure over the succession (her two surviving sons were small children), she called on Iphicrates as their brother for help, and he drove away Pausanias, the rival for the throne (Aeschin. 2.25–9). The youngest of the two children was to become Philip II, the father of Alexander the Great.

93. Babylonians in Assyria: cf. Kuhrt (1995b); Jursa (2003); see also Rollinger (2008), 57; Adalı (2011), 151–5.
94. See, for example, Rollinger (2008); Dusinberre (2013), 276 n. 58, is not necessarily convinced.
95. For a Mesopotamian east-west road to Harran, whether or not it was an Assyrian 'Royal Road', see Kessler (1997), 131.
96. Rollinger (2008).
97. Beaulieu (1989), 109; cf. Beaulieu (2000), 310. Tadmor (1965, esp. 353–4) thinks the time phrases are metaphorical, although Beaulieu says this understanding of the texts is unnecessary. Asheri, on the other hand, thinks 'the alleged alliance between Cyrus and Nabonidus against Astyages is pure fantasy': Asheri in Asheri *et al.* (2007), 164. Briant (2002, 32), on the other hand, is more equivocal: '... it is not out of the question that Nabonidus, without necessarily going so far as to enter into a formal alliance with Cyrus, did nothing to thwart the undertakings of the Persian king against the Medes of Astyages'.
98. Weiershäuser and Novotny (eds.) (2020), Nabonidus no. 47 i.42–5a.
99. Note also Nabonidus' alleged alliance with Croesus (who also had an alliance with the Egyptians) in the 540s: Hdt. 1.77.2–3.
100. See Briant (2002), 34–5, 39–40.
101. See Lenfant (2004), 257–8.
102. See Kirk *et al.* (eds.) (1983), 76.
103. Pompeius Trogus does seem to have had access to some of the same stories included in Ctesias conveyed through Nicolaus of Damascus (e.g., compare Justin 1.6.13–15 with Ctesias F 8d*§43–4.).
104. The text of the *Nabonidus Chronicle* is damaged at a crucial point in the entry for 547: it is clear that at 7.2.15–7, Cyrus is on campaign but his destination cannot be read. It was long thought that this must have been the year of the Lydian campaign, but an alternative reading of Urartu has gained recent support, although there is still no consensus and the scholarly world is fairly equally divided.
105. Pteria has been associated with Kerkenes Dağ (see n. 18). Kerkenes was a large and obviously important city on the Anatolian plateau which was destroyed in the mid-sixth century, consistent with the story in Herodotus about the conflict between Croesus and Cyrus (Hdt. 1.76), which says that Croesus captured 'the city of the Pterians'. S. Mitchell (1999, 187–8) accepts the city is Pteria, but follows Summers, at the time, in thinking it was Median; later discoveries have made this conclusion unlikely, and Summers has reviewed his earlier conclusions.
106. Greenewalt (1992).
107. E.g., S. West (2003), 418–21; note also Wallace (2016), 178–9.
108. Nabonidus is also said by some sources to have survived the capture of Babylon and was given a residence in Carmenia (Berossus, *BNJ* 680 F 9a; cf. the so-called *Dynastic Prophecy*, Grayson (1975b, 2.17–21), although other texts, and Xenophon in particular, tell a different story – we will return to the fate of Nabonidus in the next chapter.
109. For Bactrian camels in Media, see n. 15.
110. Van der Spek (2014), 258. Priene could not have been completely depopulated. However, since, if Herodotus' information is right, Bias of Priene spoke at a meeting at the Panionium soon after the conquest of Ionia was complete (Hdt. 1.170), and the city contributed ships to the battle of Lade (Hdt. 6.8.1).
111. Graf (1984); Tuplin (1994); Tuplin (1997).
112. Haubold (2013), esp. 78–89.
113. Note the important article by Briant (1988).
114. Von Voigtlander (1978), 14 (line 15).

115. See Asheri in Asheri *et al.* (2007), 458–9, 463 *s.v.* 3.65.6).
116. On the complexities of the composition, and editing, of the Hebrew Bible book of *Isaiah*, see, e.g., Becker (2021), 37–56.
117. See Thierry (1990), 38–42.
118. Tolini (2011), 25–7 and esp. n. 70.
119. Stolper (1989); Jursa (2010b), 80.
120. On Babylonian imperial structures which were, especially in the early years, more ad hoc and included provinces with governors and kingdoms ruled by local kings, see Levavi (2020).

5 Cyrus as Cosmic Warrior

In the Greek tradition, both Cyrus' violence and his diplomacy were remembered, and there was some acceptance of the conqueror. In Asia Minor, Greek political structures, especially the Panionium, were allowed to continue, and, despite the brutality of the conquest, the conquered seemed to settle quickly back into their lives.[1] Xenophanes of Colophon, in one of his poems written at the end of the sixth century, suggests that the Greeks of Asia Minor thought of their conquest by the 'Medes' with melancholy:

> One ought to say such things by the fire in the winter months
> lying on a soft couch, feeling replete,
> drinking sweet wine, quietly chewing on seeds:
> 'Who are you, where are you from? Come, how old are you?
> What age were you when the Mede came?'[2]

However, it was melancholy tinged with acceptance, and Cyrus was even given grudging honour by the Greeks as an idealised leader of cosmic importance. At Athens, for example, Aeschylus in his *Persians* of 472 BCE concedes that, although Cyrus took Ionia by force, god did not hate him because he was 'kindly by nature' (*euphrōn ephu*), and that he was a man blessed (*eudaimōn anēr*) (Aesch. *Pers.* 768-72).

Cyrus was remembered in this way because, at the heart of Cyrus' diplomacy, there was also an understanding of, and willingness to manipulate, the theology of Near Eastern kingship. Cyrus as the companion and partner of the god was an important part of the storytelling surrounding him that justified and legitimated his growing power.

In this theological position as the earthly enforcer of divine will (perhaps even to the point of being divine himself), Cyrus' relationship to Babylon was key, paradoxically both as its destroyer and as its saviour. This theological contradiction was worked out through the storytelling framework of Mesopotamian 'laments', ritual songs which described the destruction and restoration of cities, a literary form which is also pervasive in the Hebrew Bible. As an agent of the gods within this theological context, Cyrus takes on the empowering role of a cosmic warrior, not only enacting the gods' will

DOI: 10.4324/9781003384458-5

(whether that god is Marduk or Yahweh), but also developing his role as a saviour figure, either as the Davidic messiah of the Hebrew Bible's book of *Isaiah*, or positioning himself as the saviour of the city of Babylon (which, ironically, in the Hebrew Bible, he must destroy in order then to become the rescuer of Jerusalem). In fact, it was through the taking of Babylon in 539 BCE that Cyrus acquired a cosmic significance as the human ruler who has a role not only as the agent of divine will in the human sphere, but also the cosmic king who unleashes and controls the divine forces sent by the gods so that he becomes analogous to a god himself.

We will begin this chapter by looking at the role of Babylon in the cosmos, before turning to how it becomes the object of destruction, as well as the recipient of salvation, in the great cosmic game in which Cyrus stands at the centre. In the final sections, we will return to an analysis of the *Cyrus Cylinder* and the way that Cyrus uses it to position himself and his kingship in relation to traditional Mesopotamian kingship, and especially the kingship of Nabonidus and Ashurbanipal: not only is he blessed by gods, but he reaches towards his own divinised status.

Babylon the Great

In the ancient imagination, the city of Babylon loomed large. By the end of the second millennium, it had established itself as the city at the centre not just of the world,[3] but of the cosmos.[4] Its god, Marduk, was recognised in the Babylonian epic of creation, the *Enuma Elish*, as the king of the gods, who defeated Tiamat and founded Babylon as the home of the gods. The focal point of the city was his temple, the Esagil, 'the cosmic abode of the ruler of the universe' and the assembly place of the gods.[5] The ziggurat, also in the temple complex (the 'Tower of Babel' of *Genesis* 11), represented the physical connection between heaven and earth.[6] Its name was Etemenanki, which means 'House, Foundation Platform of Heaven and Underworld'.[7] Nevertheless, the city was razed by the Assyrian Sennacherib in 689 BCE, only then to be rebuilt, first by Sennacherib's son Esarhaddon and grandson Ashurbanipal, and then by the Neo-Babylonian kings, especially Nabopolassar, Nebuchadnezzar (II), and Nabonidus.[8] In fact, as Schaudig has shown, the idea of destruction and renewal was deeply embedded in the Babylonian literary tradition.[9]

For the Greeks, it was the size of the city that caught their attention. Herodotus (who may, or may not, have visited Babylon)[10] was impressed by its size (Hdt. 1.178-83), although the numbers he gives for the length of the walls are wildly exaggerated.[11] Aristophanes in *Birds* has Peisetaerus say that the city of the birds should 'encircle all the air and all this between with a wall of great baked bricks, like Babylon' (551-2).[12] For Xenophon, in his *Cyropaedia*, the taking of Babylon is the dramatic high point of Cyrus' campaigning against the 'Assyrians' (Herodotus also thinks of Babylon as an Assyrian city), and is also struck by the size of the city's wall

(*Cyrop.* 7.5.1-2).[13] Ctesias, who almost certainly did see the city,[14] still gives the walls extraordinary dimensions with a combined length of 360 stades (Ctesias F 1b§7.3),[15] and describes it as playing a prominent role in the shaping of empires, even if (at least in Ctesias' terms) it stood apart from imperial histories.[16] Aristotle thought it was too large to be considered a city; it was so large that it took three days for some of the Babylonians to realise that the city had been taken (*Politics* 3.1276a17-30).[17]

Babylon also held a significant place in the imaginary of the Hebrew Bible. Babylonian campaigning in the Levant at the end of the seventh century resulted in a significant defeat of the Egyptians at Carchemish (on the Euphrates) in 605 BCE (see Chapter 4). Caught between Egypt and Mesopotamia, the king of Judah challenged the Babylonians, which led to Babylonian attacks on Jerusalem in 598-7, and its complete destruction in 586 BCE.[18] The ruin of Jerusalem by the Babylonians became an important theological marker for the Hebrew Bible, and mentions of Babylon, both as a real place, and as a metaphorical one, come second only to those of Jerusalem.[19] In particular, because of Babylon's role at Jerusalem, Babylon becomes itself the object of Yahweh's wrath. In *Isaiah* 13 and 21, for example, the destruction of Babylon becomes a metaphor for the apocalyptic end of the world. In the book of *Jeremiah*, the annihilation of Jerusalem is also intimately linked to the ruin of Babylon. Not only was it inevitable because of the faithlessness of the Israelites (the destruction of Jerusalem by the Babylonians was its punishment), but the Babylonians would also themselves be punished and the destruction of Babylon would be complete (*Jeremiah* 25.12, 28.2-3, 50-1).[20] In fact, in the Hebrew Bible, as a symbol, 'Babylon' is both pervasive and polyvalent. As Sals notes, '... in biblical memory, Babylon could be every and any form of government or society'.[21] However, in the theology of the Hebrew Bible, just as in Babylon's own storytelling, what is certain is that Babylon will be destroyed.

So, as its conqueror, Cyrus plays a special role. Just as in *Jeremiah*, Nebuchadrezzar (Nebuchadnezzar) is named as the 'servant' of Yahweh (*Jeremiah* 25.9), so in *Deutero-Isaiah*, Cyrus is the agent of Yahweh's plan. He will rebuild Jerusalem, especially the temple (*Isaiah* 44.28, 45.13; cf. *Ezra* 1-6; *2 Chronicles* 36.22-3), and, it is implied, destroy Babylon (cf. 46.1-2). Whether or not Cyrus was actually involved in the rebuilding of Jerusalem has been doubted.[22] What is important, however, is the symbolic importance of his involvement in the theology of the Hebrew Bible, where theologically and symbolically Cyrus is a temple-builder at Jerusalem, because, on the one hand, Near Eastern rulers are temple builders,[23] and, on the other, he must be the destroyer of Babylon (and its temples) because of the theological and symbolic need for him to be the restorer of Jerusalem. Nevertheless, at Babylon, he presents himself in the *Cyrus Cylinder* as a temple renewer (just as he needs to be the temple renewer at Jerusalem). So, which is he? Temple builder or temple destroyer? At this point, we need to step aside for a moment to consider Cyrus' role in the taking of Babylon.

The Taking of Babylon

The *Nabonidus Chronicle* says that Babylon (Figure 5.1) was entered by Cyrus' troops on the 16th day of the month Tashritu [VII] (12th October), 539 BCE, the seventeenth year of Nabonidus' reign.[24] The *Chronicle* also includes some information about events leading up to and including the entrance of Ugbaru, Cyrus' general, but, as usual, there is much controversy about details. The Greek sources also talk about the capture of this great city, especially Herodotus and Xenophon. Many commentators have been keen to synthesise and rationalise the Babylonian and Greek accounts, although they do not necessarily sit comfortably with each other. So, we need to spend a few moments trying to sort out (if we can) the stories of what happened in the lead-up to 16th Tashritu, and what happened afterwards.

The Babylonian sources are fairly consistent in their treatment of Cyrus' occupation of Babylon. The first thing to note is that Cyrus' attack on Babylon was probably not a surprise. Although Cyrus and Nabonidus were probably erstwhile allies as we have seen (possibly as recently as 543,[25] and possibly in an attempt by Nabonidus to neutralize Cyrus' growing strength), Nabonidus seems to have been aware of the possibility of an attack, as months earlier, he ordered the statues of the gods to be brought into Babylon both for safe-keeping and to increase the concentration of divine protection for the city (*ABC* 7 iii.9-12, cf. 21-2).[26] Some have also understood the very fragmentary text of the *Nabonidus Chronicle* for year 16 of Nabonidus' reign to mean that Cyrus' troops were active in the south near Uruk,[27] although the text at this point is very uncertain (there is a definite mention of the goddess of Ishtar of Uruk, and a possible mention of Par[sua], although it is almost completely restored). So, there is actually really very little to go on here. Herodotus, for his part, says that Cyrus delayed at the River Gyndes (modern Diyala) to punish it for the drowning of one of his sacred white horses, and spent the summer there creating channels to reduce the strength of the river (1.189, cf. 5.52.6), which some have taken to mean that Cyrus had been massing troops at the Diyala over the summer, an idea which perhaps has some plausibility (although that is not really what Herodotus says) given the relationship of the Diyala to routes through Media and north eastern Assyria, and the fact that Cyrus seems to have come down the Diyala to Opis (which is near the confluence of the Diyala and the Tigris).[28] In fact, the *Nabonidus Chronicle*, at least, tells us that there was a battle at Opis against the Babylonians, that the Babylonians retreated, and that Cyrus 'killed people' (*nišē*.MEŠ *iduk*) (*ABC* 7 iii.13-14), which puts paid, as Kuhrt and others have noted, to any ideas about Cyrus' alleged gentleness.[29]

The *Nabonidus Chronicle* then says that on the 14th day of Tashritu, Sippar (where it seems Nabonidus himself had retreated)[30] was taken without a battle (*ABC* 7 iii.14). The capture of Sippar has been variously interpreted.[31] Kuhrt, for example, suggests that it surrendered out of fear after the devastation at Opis,[32] although Fried thinks that the priests at Sippar

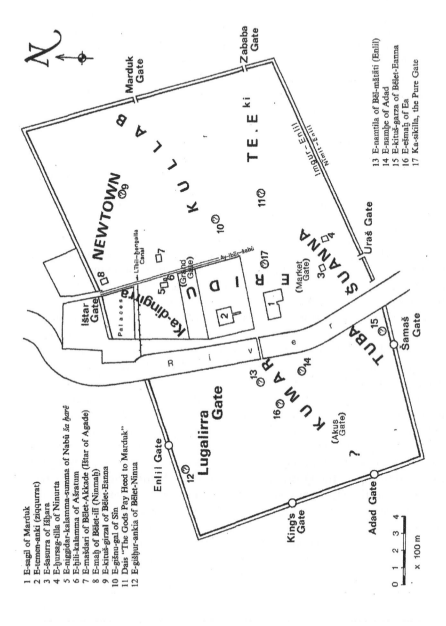

Figure 5.1 Babylon in the sixth century BCE. George (1992) 24; with permission of A.R. George.

must have been sympathetic to Cyrus, and it is possibly of interest that, once the conquest was complete, the priestly officials at Sippar were not replaced as they were at both Babylon and Uruk. Although the evidence for Uruk is less certain, despite Fried's assertion to the contrary, [33] others have seen continuity in the temple administration as evidence of stability and an effort on the part of the conquerors to create stability).[34] These two positions, of course, are not necessarily mutually exclusive.

It is certainly the case that in other temples, the priestly officials remained the same without interruption: at the Eanna temple at Uruk, Nabû-ahu-iddin remained in office from Year 7 of Nabonidus' reign until Year 4 of Cambyses.[35] On the other hand, Jursa makes the point that temple officials were royal appointments (he says: 'All high temple appointments were ... de facto royal appointees')[36] and that retaining temple staff was a way of creating stability through regime change.[37]

The *Chronicle* then says that Ugbaru, the governor of Gutium, entered Babylon without a battle. The identity of Ugbaru has also been much discussed, and particularly how he might relate to the Gubaru, another member of Cyrus' retinue, who was soon to appoint officials in Babylon, and the Gobryas of Xenophon's account of the taking of Babylon.[38] However, this issue will not detain us here, other than to note (as we shall see) that it is probably not possible to synthesise all the different accounts of Babylon's fall. What is important is that Ugbaru was in command of the army, which we saw in the previous chapter was at its heart a Median army (it is later called the army of Gutium, which probably confirms its essentially Median identity),[39] although probably included others from the mountain regions, especially Fars.

That the *Chronicle* says that Babylon was taken without a battle has also raised speculation that the priests of Marduk, in opposition to Nabonidus' promotion of the god Sin, opened the gates to Cyrus' army. In the *Cyrus Cylinder*, Nabonidus is accused of losing reverence for Marduk ('in his mind, reverence for Marduk, king of the gods, came to an end': 7), and in the text known as the *Verse Account of Nabonidus*,[40] a propagandist text likewise written after Babylon's fall, he is accused of trying to replace Marduk with Sin (esp. col. ii). However, as Kuhrt has argued, there is little in Nabonidus' building inscriptions, except perhaps those found at Harran relating to the rebuilding of the temple of Sin there,[41] to suggest that these allegations had any substance.[42] Fried has also made the point that the *Nabonidus Chronicle* says that the army, now called the army of Gutium, laid siege to the precinct of Marduk, Esagil, for two weeks (although the rituals were able to continue), after which Cyrus entered the city, and Gubaru appointed magistrates (*ABC* 7 iii.16-17). All of this taken together probably suggests that, rather than being collaborators, the priests may have initially resisted the occupation,[43] although there is nothing to suggest that they were slaughtered as Fried claims (*ABC* 7 iii.17-18).[44] In fact, the emphasis in a number (if not all) of our texts is on the ultimate peacefulness of the regime change.[45]

Nevertheless, Berossus says that Cyrus destroyed the outer walls of the city (*BNJ* 680 9a), although it is unclear what exactly is meant by 'the outer walls'. If what is meant is Imgur-Enlil (the great inner wall surrounding the city),[46] then Berossus' comments probably cannot be taken at face value. Tolini has argued that the destruction of the walls is confirmed by a private contract to repair the gate of Enlil dating to 538 BCE, by which way, he says Cyrus' troops probably entered the city.[47] Rollinger, however, has used the same building contract to show that, while Cyrus was trying to legitimise his reign by rebuilding the walls in the manner of his Babylonian predecessors (as he is also clearly trying to do in the *Cyrus Cylinder* in his declaration of wall repairs to Imgur-Enlil: 38-40, supported by the *Verse Account of Nabonidus* vi.11), Berossus was trying to show Cyrus as an illegitimate king.[48] The archaeological evidence also does not support the destruction of the walls in this period,[49] and Herodotus says quite explicitly that, while Darius took down the walls, Cyrus had not done so (3.159.1). It would also seem unlikely: George points to the divine nature of these walls,[50] and Cyrus in the *Cyrus Cylinder*, at least, consistently tries to present himself as a supporter and promoter of the gods of Babylon.

So, if Cyrus' army did not enter through a gate, how did it enter Babylon? The Greek texts tell the story of the taking of Babylon differently. As we have already observed, there are points where the Greek account and the Babylonian versions could be seen to be referring to similar events, even if they are talked about in different ways, and there are also points where they diverge significantly. Herodotus, for example, has a battle before the city (at Opis?), which the Babylonians lost, and after which they withdrew into the city (1.190.1). However, contrary to the *Chronicle* (where the fall of Sippar occurs only two days before the entry of Babylon),[51] Herodotus then says that Cyrus laid siege to the city, but, since the Babylonians were prepared, Cyrus was at a loss what to do (1.190.2); we have already noted that the Babylonians seem to have had significant warning of Cyrus' attack.[52]

For Herodotus, it was because of his inability to break the siege that Cyrus came up with the plan of diverting the Euphrates (1.191). Taking most of his army upstream, but leaving a contingent at the point where the river left the city, he diverted the course of the Euphrates so that its water level dropped and Cyrus' army was able to enter the city and escape the notice of the Babylonians because they were taking part in a festival.

But there are good reasons to think that Herodotus has shaped the story of the fall of Babylon to his needs since it is embedded within other storylines about channels and the diversion of water: the stories of Semiramis (1.184) and Nitocris (1.185-7), who Herodotus says were two former queens of Babylon. To Semiramis, Herodotus attributes initial waterworks,[53] but the main work he gives to Nitocris, the mother of Labynetus (= Nabonidus?) son of Labynetus (1.188.1); she is 'more intelligent' than Semiramis because she had left monuments and because, seeing that the empire of the Medes was 'both great and restless (*ouk atremizousa*)',[54] she realised the need to build defences for the city which Herodotus then goes on to describe (1.185.1), building works which are remarkably like those actually undertaken by Nebuchadnezzar. Ironically (and probably intentionally so), Herodotus' Cyrus uses the very principle of diverting the river which Nitocris had used to build her defence works of Babylon, in order to overcome them (1.191.3).[55] But, as Rollinger has shown, even this narrative belongs within a wider one: Cyrus pits his wits against the intelligent Nitocris (and wins), and against the vengeful queen of the Massagetae, Tomyris (as we will see), and meets his death. We will return in the next chapter to Herodotus' fascination with clever, powerful and vengeful women. However, it is the fact that he takes Babylon through his cleverness (an idea which he apparently borrows from Nitocris – Herodotus asks, did someone tell him or did he work it out for himself?: 1.191.1), which eventually leads him towards the *hybris* of thinking he was like a god, and so to his death.

Xenophon, too, has historiographical axes to grind. In the *Cyropaedia*, Xenophon also has Cyrus enter Babylon by diverting the river. While for Herodotus, Cyrus' death is the critical moment in his *logos*, for Xenophon, the taking of Babylon is the dramatic high point of his story, most of which is occupied by the build-up to the taking of Babylon in Cyrus' war against the 'Assyrians', and after which Cyrus sets up Babylon as the principal city of his empire (*Cyrop.* 7.5.55-7). Xenophon does not have the initial battle (his Cyrus actively avoids any military confrontation with the Babylonians), but his Cyrus, although initially talking about a siege, also decides to divert the river to gain access to the city because of the difficulties presented by the walls, even though it is thought that the river presents a better defence than the walls (*Cyrop.* 7.5.7-8). Xenophon's method for diverting the river is also rather different from Herodotus' in that the river was drained into ditches dug beside the walls (*Cyrop.* 7.5.10-16).[56] Two *Assyrian* defectors, Gobyras and Gadatas, who both wanted revenge against the Assyrians,[57] then lead Cyrus' army into the city during a festival in which the Babylonians are enjoying themselves (drunken and revelling),[58] attack the palace guards and kill the unnamed Assyrian king (*Cyrop.* 7.5.20-32), who has been Cyrus' arch-enemy for most of the story. Xenophon is quite explicit that the city was taken by the sword (*dorialōtos*) (*Cyrop.* 7.5.35).

The taking of Babylon, particularly given the size and importance of the city, was such a monumental event that it seems there were a number of explanations which were current in the ancient world, just as Cyrus' birth (and death) also attracted numerous different kinds of stories, which cannot (and should not) simply be synthesised. For example, Herodotus' entrance by means of the river is different from that of Xenophon: they are two distinct stories even if they share some motifs which surely derive from the variety and interplay of oral traditions that we have seen in other Cyrus stories that find their way into the Greek written traditions, where it is shaped again to fit our authors' individual purposes.

For this reason, it is also difficult (if not impossible) to prefer one version to another. The *Nabonidus Chronicle*, while precise regarding dates, is also very vague about some details: it just does not tell us how Cyrus' army entered Babylon. Others have seen Herodotus' story of the capture of Babylon as a completely unbelievable fantasy,[59] both because of the entrance along the river and the story of the festival. The festival can possibly be explained (there was a festival of the autumnal equinox in Babylon in early Tashritu),[60] and Vanderhooft has shown how the riverine entrance (at least as described by Herodotus) might have been possible.[61]

However, he also points out that the Babylonians themselves thought that the river was a weakness in their defences. One of Nebuchadnezzar's building texts refers to the river works:

> I constructed its broad gates, plated immense doors of cedar with bronze and fixed them (in those gates). I checked the outflow(s) of its water and built its embankments with bitumen and baked brick so that no robber (or) sneak thief could enter the outflows of its water, I blocked its outflow(s) with shiny iron. I ...ed (it) with crossbars and ... of iron and reinforced its joint(s). I strengthened the protection of Esagil and Babylon and (thereby) established the lasting fame of my kingship.
>
> (Transl. Weiershäuser & Novotny)[62]

As Vanderhooft has argued, this concern about the vulnerability of the river in the defence of the city may have been precisely the reason why the story of Cyrus' entry into Babylon in this way was created. In fact, there were a number of stories about the diversion of the river: Ctesias (in Diodorus) attributes the founding of Babylon to Semiramis, who completed the building of the city (and the tunnel under the river connecting the palaces) by diverting the Euphrates (F 1b§9.1-3). The possibilities created by the diversion of the river were part of the myth-making of the city. Just as the Hebrew Bible required the destruction of Babylon to requite Jerusalem, and demonstrate that Yahweh was not only in control, but also had the will and the means to avenge the Israelites, there were also other stories of Babylon's capture which were generated out of other kinds of needs and anxieties.

This is also true of the document produced by Cyrus himself, at least in negotiation with the scribal elite. According to the *Cyrus Cylinder*, Cyrus was able to take Babylon because it was abandoned by Marduk. We have already seen in an earlier chapter how Cyrus in the *Cylinder*, through an intertextual reference to the *Enuma Elish*, suggests that he is the one who 'saved' Babylon, just as Marduk was also a saving figure. In fact, the purpose of the whole text is to present Cyrus as the cosmic warrior who saves Babylon, and does so through the theology of the 'laments on the destruction of cities'.

So that we can appreciate fully how Cyrus is positioning himself in the theological matrix of city destroyer and city saviour, we now need to turn aside briefly to consider the city laments, and the role of the *Umman-manda* in the destruction of cities.

Laments on the Destruction of Cities

The 'Laments on the Destruction of Cities' were part of a ritual that confronted the insecurity of the cosmos. In Mesopotamian theology (also reflected in the Hebrew Bible), the essential reason why cities were destroyed was that their god had abandoned them, and so their success and prosperity depended on securing the god's goodwill and continued physical presence in the city.[63] In Mesopotamia, part of this belief system rested on the understanding that the cult statue did not just represent the god, but *was* the god.[64] If the city was destroyed, it meant that the god was angry and had left. For that reason, invading forces also often removed the cult statue (an event sometimes called 'god-napping') and rehoused the god in their own temples, not as captives or hostages but as divine refugees.[65] It is in these terms that Nabonidus in the *Babylon Stele* explains the sack of Babylon in 689 BCE as the removal of the cult statue to Ashur, and its restoration to Babylon in 668 BCE:[66]

> ... [(who) pl]otted evil [to t]ake away the people, his (Sennacherib's) heart thought about sin. [He did] not [have] mercy on the people of the la[nd of Akkad. He approach]ed Babylon with evil [int]ent, laid waste to its sanctuaries, made its ground plans unrecognisable, destroyed (its) rituals, took the prince, Marduk, by the hand, and had (him) enter inside Baltil (Ashur). He treated the land like the wrath of a god. The prince, the god Marduk, did not assuage his divine wrath (and) for twenty-one years he took up residence inside Baltil. The days elapsed and the appointed time arrived. The wrath of the king of the gods, the lord of lords, relented and he remembered Esagil and Babylon, the residence of his lordly majesty.
>
> (Transl. Weiershäuser & Novotny)

The god is the point of focalisation, and it is the god who has agency:[67] it is the god leaving the city which leads to its destruction. When the god returns, this is also known through divination which reveals divine intent. It is significant that when Esarhaddon first attempted to repatriate Marduk, the procession returning him to Babylon was stopped by a bad omen (although Porter also suggests there may have been Assyrian concerns about a Babylonian uprising), and Marduk was taken back to Ashur.[68] Retaining the goodwill of the gods was therefore of paramount importance. We have already observed how, in a Babylonian context, the kings focussed on their work of rebuilding and restoring city walls (which we have noted had divine qualities) and temples, which, because they were built of mud brick, needed constant attention. However, another way of appeasing the gods was through ritual lamentation.

Lamentation

Cultic lamentation was a ritual form of poetry which was both oral and written, concerned with the destruction of a city or temple, and addressed to particular gods.[69] They were often called *balag*s because they were performed by a priest to the accompaniment of a *balag*, which was probably, at least originally, a kind of harp.[70] It was once assumed that the *balag*s derived from the group of laments known as 'City Laments' dating from the Old Babylonian period, which lament the destruction of particular cities (the *balag*s are general), although it is now thought that *balag*s were regularly performed as early as the third millennium BCE, so that 'the City Laments probably represent a literary development of the earlier Cultic Laments, by adapting them to specific historical circumstances'.[71] In any case, the *balag*s also have a close association with the laments of the Hebrew Bible, and scholars have seen connections between the lament tradition of Mesopotamia and that of Israel.[72] The *balag* maintained a continuous tradition in Mesopotamia from the third millennium into the Seleucid period.[73]

The Near Eastern laments shared common themes: destruction, assignment of responsibility for the destruction, abandonment of the city, restoration, return of the god, and presentation of a prayer.[74] As Petter has observed: '... this loose plot revolved around divine abandonment and divine presence. Simply put, the poems speak of death (due to divine abandonment) and the hope for an afterlife (due to the return of the divine presence)'.[75] The *balag*s (although not the City Laments) were incorporated into daily cultic activity, and their main function was to appease the god and prevent communal catastrophe.[76] The destructive forces operate on two levels: in the cosmic realm (the storm) and the human realm (the enemy, described in terrifying terms).[77] For that reason, the final sections of the laments where the god has returned, order is restored and the city is rebuilt is of particular importance in the ritual movement from destruction to renewal.[78]

The tradition of lamentation, and the City Laments, in particular, have been linked to two other important didactic texts from the Mesopotamian world: the *Curse of Agade* (composed and copied as a school text in the Old Babylonian period),[79] a memory of which is retained into the Neo-Assyrian/ Neo-Babylonian period through the so-called *Weidner Chronicle*;[80] and the *Cuthean Legend* (which was first composed in the Old Babylonian period, but continued to be copied – and re-worked – in the Neo-Assyrian and Neo-Babylonian periods).[81] The *Curse of Agade* and the *Cuthean Legend* in particular tell stories about Naramsin (a historical king of the third millennium, who attracted to him a number of completely unhistorical stories), so it is worthwhile summarising the plot lines.

In the *Curse of Agade*, the goddess Inanna suddenly turns against Naramsin, after he becomes king, apparently because Enlil, chief of the gods (later replaced by Marduk) has refused permission for a temple to be built for her and abandons Agade (Akkad). As a result, the gods withdraw their favour and Naramsin sinks into a seven-year depression. Naramsin then performs extispicy (reading of a lamb's liver), hoping that he will be given permission to build the temple. The omens are unfavourable so Naramsin attacks and plunders Enlil's sanctuary of Ekur in Nippur, hoping to change Enlil's mind. Enlil avenges his temple by unleashing the barbarous Guti ('a people who know no inhibitions, with human instincts, but canine intelligence, and monkeys' features – Enlil brought them out of the mountains'). The people of Agade perform a lament, but Enlil retreats into his inner chamber. The gods of Babylonia try to placate Enlil by laying a curse on Agade and Naramsin, whose impiety had been the cause of the destruction; as a result, Agade is completely destroyed. As Cooper notes, the main difference between the thematic structure of the *Curse of Agade* and the City Laments is that a city is destroyed and is never to be rebuilt.[82]

The *Cuthean Legend*, on the other hand, is a pseudo-biographical text in which Naramsin addresses himself to future kings to read his story. He then goes on to recall how the hero Enmerkar came to a bad end, but did not leave a written account of his story so that others could learn from his experiences. Naramsin then tells his own story: how the *Umman-manda* were created as his enemies ('a people with partridge bodies, raven-faced humans', 'suckled by Tiamat', who come from 'the shining mountains'); and Naramsin summons the diviners to perform extispicy, but the results are unfavourable. Nevertheless, Naramsin defies the omens and sends out troops against the invaders and suffers devastating losses. He becomes depressed, and the god Ea intercedes on his behalf. Naramsin then consults the gods again. This time results are favourable; Naramsin attacks the enemy and is successful. Having learned his lesson (to obey the gods), Naramsin resolves not to act without consulting them. Importantly, he is then told not to kill the invaders, as they are Enlil's responsibility ('To Naramsin, descendant of Sargon: Cease! You shall not destroy the accursed people! In the future, Enlil will raise them up for evil. They await the furious heart of Enlil'). Naramsin calls on future kings to read his story, and there is a final blessing. This is a text about kingship which emphasises the impotence of even the king in the face of divine will, and the need for the king to obey the gods' wishes as they are revealed through extispicy, even if that means pacifism in the face of a marauding army, which the gods will themselves punish in their own time and way.

Both of these texts contain the same basic message as the laments, although in reverse:[83] the displeasure of the gods leads to ruin! However, what is of particular interest for our purposes at the moment is the identities of the enemy agents who enact the gods' destructive will. In the *Curse of Agade* (as in the later *Weidner Chronicle*), the enemy of Naramsin are the Guti (in the *Weidner Chronicle*, Naramsin's adversary is the 'army of Gutium', the Guti being those 'who did not know how to honour the gods nor how to perform divine rites and ceremonies correctly'), while in the *Cuthean Legend*, they are the *Umman-manda*.

The *Umman-manda* and the Guti

The first known attestations of the *Umman-manda* are in Old Babylonian extispicy texts, where it was the name given to a remote and attacking army.[84] In the *Cuthean Legend*, as we have seen, they are particularly associated with the army from the mountains which the gods used to punish Naramsin for disregarding the omens.[85] Further, the *Umman-manda*, while the instrument of god's will, are also itself subject to it. The basic message of the *Cuthean Legend* is that the will of the gods, discoverable through omens, always prevails. It is also surely not accidental that the other enemy of Naramsin (in the *Curse of Agade*) is also a barbarian army from the mountains, the army of the Guti.

This link between the *Umman-manda* and the foreign, barbarian army carries over into other texts. As we have seen, in Mesopotamian historical texts, *Umman-manda* could at different times be used to refer to foreign armies, such as the Cimmerians or also the Medes.[86] As we have already noted, in the *Fall of Nineveh Chronicle (ABC 3)*, it is said that Cyaxares (U-makiš-tar) and the *Madaa* (Medes) sacked Ashur (in 614 BCE) before the Babylonians had time to arrive (24-8), but later (38-47), it is Cyaxares with the *Umman-manda* that helped the Babylonians in the taking of Nineveh (in 612 BCE). It was also the *Umman-manda* who were allies of the Babylonians against the Assyrian king Ashur-uballit in 610 (*ABC* 3.65), although we know from other evidence that the Babylonian allies at Harran were none other than the Medes.[87]

Adalı argues that the naming of the *Umman-manda* in texts like the *Chronicles* or other historical texts should be viewed through the prism of the *Cuthean Legend*.[88] Even when the *Umman-manda* clearly refers to the army of the Medes, the connotations of barbarity are contrasted to the civilised and pious actions of the Babylonian king, and this is important for how we should understand these texts. This contrast can be clearly seen in the *Babylon Stele* (which was also discussed earlier in the chapter) in the section which refers to the sacking of Harran in 610:[89]

> He (Marduk) gave him (Nabopolassar) support (and) allowed him to find an ally. He made a king of the *Umman-manda* (LUGAL *um-man-ma-an-da*), who had no opponents, submit to his command and made him come to his aid. Above and below, right and left he overwhelmed Subartu (=Assyria) like the Deluge. He avenged Babylon, he exacted vengeance. The king of the *Umman-manda*, who has no respect for anything (LUGAL *um-man-ma-an-da la a-di-ru*),[90] destroyed the sanctuaries of the gods of the land of Subartu (Assyria), all of them. Moreover, (as for) the cities on the border of the land of Akkad that had become hostile toward the king of the land of Akkad and that had not come to his aid, he destroyed their cultic rites, spared no one, (and) laid waste to their cult centres even more severely than the Deluge. The king of

Babylon (Nabopolassar), envoy for the god Marduk, to whom blas-
phemy is a taboo, did not lay his hand(s) upon any of the rituals of the
gods, wore matted hair (as if in mourning), laid down on a bed on the
ground...

(Transl. Weierhäuser & Novotny)

Here the contrast is made between the pious Babylonian king, Nabopolassar,
who does not attack temples, and the king of the *Umman-manda*, who, while
having no opponents, has no respect for anything,[91] which also calls to mind
the army of the Guti of the *Weidner Chronicle*.

Another Babylonian text that refers to the *Umman-manda*, which we
have also already discussed at a number of different points, is the *Ehulhul
Cylinder*. In this foundation text, Nabonidus describes how the vast *Umman-
manda* are scattered by Cyrus' small army.[92] As Adalı points out, this text
echoes Assyrian inscriptions of Ashurbanipal where 'the *Umman-manda*,
the creation of Tiamat' (here Cimmerians) are 'scattered' by Marduk.[93]
That Nabonidus holds himself aloof (in his text) and allows Cyrus to overcome the *Umman-manda* is again consistent with the *Cuthean Legend* where
Naramsin is told that the *Umman-manda* are not his responsibility, but that
the gods will deal with them, which, in this case, they do through the agency
of Cyrus. However, as we have already seen in other contexts, Cyrus' 'scat-
tering' of the *Umman-manda* is itself a literary trope, not a historical reality:
the army of Astyages came over to Cyrus willingly. This is not a retelling of
what has happened (that is Nabonidus' passivity in the face of the Medes'
control of Harran)[94] so much as a refashioning of events to make Cyrus'
relationship with the *Umman-manda* and Nabonidus' relationship with
Cyrus theologically acceptable.

Viewed through the lens of these texts, steeped as they are in the phrase-
ology and themes of the *Cuthean Legend* and the lament traditions, that it
is Ugbaru of Gutium who enters Babylon first in the *Nabonidus Chronicle* is
significant,[95] and it is a reminder that the *Chronicle* also is not a neutral or
impartial text as has sometimes been claimed.[96] However, it is also a sign of
the relationship between texts and events: texts as literary products reflect
an understanding of the past shaped by that literary past, but this same
literary past can shape the events themselves that are being described.[97]
Furthermore, the *Chronicle* is not the only text to connect Gutium and the
Umman-manda with the capture of Babylon. This is the point, bearing all of
this in mind, where we need to return to the *Cyrus Cylinder*.

The *Cyrus Cylinder*

The structure and internal rhythms of the *Cyrus Cylinder* are unusual by the
standards of other foundation texts.[98] It begins by saying how Nabonidus,
through his impious conduct of the rites, becomes the agent of his people's
destruction ([UN].MEŠ-*šu* ...*u-ḫal-li* -*iq*: 'he destroyed his people' [8]).

As a result, the gods became angry at the mortals' complaints, and they left their shrines (9). As Schaudig has discussed, the wickedness of Nabonidus itself has been drawn from the Babylonian literary tradition, especially the *Weidner Chronicle*.[99] The text then goes on to say that (10-11):

> The god Marduk, the ex[alted one, the Enlil of the god]s, *relented*; [his] (hostile) attit[ude] changed towards all of the inhabited settlements whose dwellings were in ruins and the people of the land of Sumer and Akkad who had become like corpses; he became forgiving.
> (Transl. Finkel with adaptations by Novotny)[100]

The text is very ambiguous here. There seems to be a claim that there was some kind of destruction of temples and that Babylon has been destroyed after all, even if only metaphorically. Cyrus also comes to Babylon as the terrifying destroyer of legend, at the head of an army of the *Umman-manda* and Guti. Schaudig has shown how Cyrus here fits the story patterns of other 'kings of Anshan and Susa' who had destroyed Babylon because of the wickedness of its kings.[101] However, the responsibility for any destruction falls not on Cyrus, but on Nabonidus, because his actions led to the gods' abandonment of the city.

Cyrus, on the other hand, becomes the redemptive figure of lament (Nabonidus destroys, Cyrus redeems). Marduk took the hand of Cyrus, called him by his name (12), made him go to Babylon, and like a 'friend' (*ibru*: 'one of the same status')[102] and companion, he marched at his side into the city. The text goes on:

> 17. Without a fight or battle, he allowed him to enter Shuanna (Babylon). He (Marduk) saved his city, Babylon, from hardship. He delivered Nabonidus, the king who did not revere him, into his (Cyrus') hands.

> 18. The people of Babylon, all of them, the entirety of the land of Sumer and Akkad, (as well as) the nobles and governor(s), bowed down before him (and) kissed his feet. They were happy at him being king (and) their faces shone.

> 19. The lord/ruler (*be-lu*), who through his support revived all the dead/ dying (*mitutan*) (and) universally spared (them) from trouble and hardship, they graciously blessed/prayed to him (and) praised his name.[103]

This is an extraordinary part of the text, although there are variants on the readings of some of the signs,[104] and there is some disagreement about how l. 19 in particular should be translated.[105]

One issue revolves around the identity of *be-lu* (Marduk or Cyrus?) and, related to that, the question of who is lending support (Cyrus or Marduk?) and who is reviving/rescuing all the dead. It is likely that line 19 is deliberately vague and ambiguous precisely so that is unclear who is doing the saving, who is doing the helping, and who is getting the prayers or blessings. In any case, Cyrus seems to be positioning himself on a level with Marduk, whether as his helper or the one who is being helped: he is Marduk's earthly representation (not just his representative, or earthly reflection, but his earthly refraction: 'god on earth').[106] Marduk, the Enlil of the gods ('god of gods'), proclaims Cyrus 'for the kingship of the entirety of everything (*ana ma-li-ku-ti ku-lat nap-ḫar*)' (12). Even the land of Gutium and the *Umman-manda*, the earthly powers that enact Marduk's destruction, are made to submit at his feet (13).

But line 19 is also transitional. At line 20, the tempo of the text changes. Rather than being the recipient and beneficiary of Marduk's actions, Cyrus now assumes agency both within the text and in the role that Marduk has given him of being the restorer of the city. He restates the fact that he and his army entered the city peacefully (22, 24), and that he has been received joyfully into the city (23). The 'unrelenting yoke' which Nabonidus had put on his people (8), Cyrus says he has removed (25-6). All kings submit at his feet (30), and he has made all the lands live peacefully (36). He repaired the temples and returned the statues of the gods (25, 31-4). Cyrus is the opposite of Nabonidus, and, within the logic of the lamentation, becomes a redemptive and divinised figure.

So far from being a text about 'human rights' as is sometimes claimed, the *Cyrus Cylinder* acts as a 'position paper' for Cyrus' kingship in Babylon. The narrative flow of the text relates both to lamentation and the *Cuthean Legend*. It moves from the acts of Nabonidus which cause the gods' wrath and decision to abandon the city. That inevitably leads to its implicit destruction. However, Marduk then finds a king who will not only contain the *Umman-manda*, but also, as his equal on earth, restore both cosmic and earthly order. Cyrus then embodies that role: he, his son, Cambyses, and his whole army are blessed by the god (26-8), and in turn are blessed by the people of Babylon (36).

Cyrus and Kingship in Babylon

Through the *Cylinder*, Cyrus is creating a new vision of kingship in Babylon. He performs all the responsibilities of a Babylonian king in respect of the gods: unlike Nabonidus (6-7), he offers the appropriate sacrifices, and repairs the great outer wall of the city, completing the building work of an earlier unnamed king (38-9).[107] However, he does not present himself completely in the manner of a Babylonian king. We have already noted in an earlier chapter the Assyrianising nature of the titulary he gives himself (20-1), as well as the reference to the building works of Ashurbanipal, which he makes at the end of the *Cylinder*'s text (43). We have also noted that Nabonidus in the *Ehulhul Cylinder* also does both these things: he (unusually) uses Assyrian-style titulary (no. 28, i.1-2), and he says that he rebuilt the Ehulhul which Ashurbanipal also restored, driving home the connection by saying that in his renovations, he found Ashurbanipal's building cylinder (i.33-ii.5a). In fact, the *Ehulhul Cylinder* seems to have an important intertextual relationship with the *Cyrus Cylinder*.

The *Ehulhul Cylinder* was well known within the scribal system. There were at least fifty-three copies made between Sippar and Babylon,[108] which were all produced in the last four years of Nabonidus' seventeen-year reign (they must all date from the period after his return from Teima in 543 BCE). Apart from its near cousin, the single exemplar of another cylinder inscription from Sippar whose text is closely related but not identical,[109] the *Ehulhul Cylinder* is the only text from Nabonidus' reign to mention Cyrus explicitly. As we have already discussed on a number of occasions, Cyrus is named as the one chosen by Marduk to defeat the *Umman-manda* in battle so that Nabonidus can complete the rebuilding of the temple at Harran. We have also noted Nabonidus' apparently passive position (although, as argued earlier, it is likely that this seeming passivity is required by Babylonian theologies rather than being a representation of lived reality).

What is interesting, then, is the way that Cyrus in the *Cyrus Cylinder* does not adopt passivity in the same way. Although he is very careful to disclaim (whatever the actualities) any violence against Babylon or its temples, he is presented in this text as an agent, even if that agency is given to him by Marduk. However, he has already been presented as acting, 'having been stirred up by Marduk' (in the face of Nabonidus' deliberate passivity) in the *Ehulhul Cylinder*. The text of the *Cyrus Cylinder* thus seems to bounce off and even complete the narrative of the *Ehulhul Cylinder*. What were the actual historical realities behind either text are immaterial. Cyrus is using the interplay between the two texts to indicate, at least to the scribal elite, that he is a very different kind of king to his predecessor: his piety resides in his ability to act, while Nabonidus' piety was in his claims of inaction of the kind he had also attributed to Nabopolassar in the *Babylon Stele* in the face of the *Umman-manda*.

The *Umman-manda* provide another point of contact between the two texts: in the *Ehulhul Cylinder* Cyrus defeats the barbarous (and impious) *Umman-manda*. In the *Cyrus Cylinder*, they are made to submit at his feet. Cyrus is a ruler, who unlike even Naramsin, is authorised to control and deal with this barbarian army; indeed, Marduk stirs him up to do just that (while Naramsin was told to leave them, and Nabonidus represents himself as holding himself aloof). Again, the intertextual relationship between the *Ehulhul Cylinder* and the *Cyrus Cylinder* Cyrus is pointing toward his special relationship to Marduk: he is Marduk's earthly incarnation.

Finally, the *Ehulhul Cylinder*, as we have seen, draws a connection between Nabonidus and Ashurbanipal. On Nabonidus' part, this must surely have been related to his need to legitimise his activities in a city so far from Babylon. Whatever Nabonidus may have been trying to do in relation to the cult of Sin at Harran, by drawing the connection with Ashurbanipal, he is laying claim to an Assyrian heritage. Just as Ashurbanipal (and his father Esarhaddon), through the rebuilding of Babylon and the returning of Marduk, seem to have been trying to reintegrate Babylon into the Assyrian Empire,[110] Nabonidus is himself laying claim to Babylon's connection with Assyria in the same kind of way. Harran had been destroyed because of the god's anger and abandonment of the city, which brought about its destruction by the *Umman-manda*.[111] Through a dream, Nabonidus is made aware that Sin wished to return to Harran. As argued here, what happened next (in reality) was that Cyrus (probably Nabonidus' ally) gained control of the *Umman-manda* (the army of Astyages), which solved Nabonidus' problem and allowed him to rebuild the temple. It is important and striking that this was the story told in Babylon and Sippar.

By mentioning Ashurbanipal, Cyrus is probably trying to do something very similar. It is often said that through this reference to Ashurbanipal, Cyrus is trying to remove or negate the Neo-Babylonian kings from Babylonian history. That does not seem to be quite the case, although by not naming Nebuchadnezzar as the builder of Imgur-Enlil, he does seem to be deliberately vague. However, by naming Ashurbanipal, and Ashur and Susa as cities whose gods will be returned,[112] he too is laying claim to Assyrian symbolic icons.[113] However, he is also implying that his style of kingship reflects the active piety of Ashurbanipal, who returned Marduk to Babylon in 688 BCE. Cyrus is doing the same thing in 539: by entering Babylon alongside Marduk he is allowing the god to return to his city, but in doing so, he is taking a share in that divinity himself.

Deeply embedded within Babylonian traditions, and the texts produced by the Babylonian scribal elite, Cyrus through the *Cyrus Cylinder* is making some startling claims about his kind of Babylonian kingship, which seem to hint at divinity. Caroline Waerzeggers has talked about the close and interdependent relationship between the gods, the priesthood and the king at Babylon.[114] The Neo-Babylonian kings were aware of the divinisation of earlier kings, who were worshipped by priests in temples.[115] Nabonidus himself repaired the statue of Sargon of Akkad (who was divinised, possibly in his lifetime), and made offerings.[116]

However, it is not this kind of divinity or worship that Cyrus is intimating. In his self-representation, he is not the unwitting instrument of the deity as he is presented in *Deutero-Isaiah* or the *Ehulhul Cylinder*. Rather, he is actively and purposefully fulfilling the wishes of Marduk as his companion in the divine enterprise of liberating and restoring Babylon. In this way, he seems to be setting himself on a par with Marduk in the earthly realm, just as Alexander the Great was later to do in his relationship with Zeus.[117]

To frame the relationship in another way, from an earthly perspective, Cyrus is presenting himself as more than mortal even if he is not fully divine. As we saw in Chapter 1, Graeber and Sahlins talk about all kings as 'metahumans' and having a status which is beyond their mortal personhood.[118] Peter Machinist seems to be reaching for this kind of idea when he talks about Assyrian kingship, although in the end, he concludes that it was the office of kingship that is divine rather than the person of the king (which is how he solves the conundrum of an apparently divinised king who is not worshipped).[119] It is certainly the case that there are examples from the ancient world where the office of kingship is separated from the person of the king. Clifford Ando has argued that this was the case in imperial Rome.[120]

However, Cyrus is doing more than that. He is claiming his right to rule in Babylon and on a world stage because he is not just the personal choice of god, but Marduk's companion, someone who meets the god on his own terms. In the manner of Greek kingship, Alexander the Great claimed the right to equate himself with Zeus on account of his deeds (and so claimed divinity). He was the ultimate 'hero' king. At Babylon, Cyrus could arguably have done a similar thing. However, at this point, in his own spectacular career, Cyrus chooses instead to present himself as the redemptive figure of lamentation.

Remembering Cyrus and Babylon

The taking of Babylon was an important moment in the growth of Cyrus' empire, but unlike the Cyrus of the *Cyropaedia*, who makes Babylon the centre of his empire, Cyrus has his son Cambyses installed as 'king of Babylon', and himself probably only visits the city on two other occasions.[121] However, the taking of Babylon and his role in its 'destruction' were long remembered. It is also within the context of lamentation that Cyrus appears in *Deutero-Isaiah*. Although Yahweh is saviour and redeemer, Cyrus, as a king in the tradition of Davidic kingship, is the unknowing instrument of Yahweh's salvation, who destroys Babylon, sets free the Israelites from their captivity, and rebuilds Jerusalem (44.24-47.15).[122]

The pairing of Jerusalem and Babylon as twin cities became embedded in the thinking of the early Christian church. In the New Testament book of *Revelation*, the fall of 'Babylon the great' prepares the way for the rise of the 'new Jerusalem' (18, 21). In the fifth century CE, Augustine's *City of God*, Babylon ('whose name means Confusion', 'a first Rome') is contrasted with the heavenly Jerusalem, 'the city of God'. Likewise, Orosius, in his *Historiarum adversum paganos libri VII* (*Seven Books of History against the Pagans*), a work commissioned by Augustine,[123] is interested in Cyrus as the conqueror of Babylon,[124] set in counterpoint to Rome (while Babylon falls, Rome is saved by Christianity:[125] 'Then the *imperium* of the East passed away, and that of the West arose' (2.2.10: *tunc orientis occidit et ortum est occidentis imperium*: 2.3.6)).[126] Orosius' Cyrus (as all his pre-Christian rulers) is an *exemplum*, along with Ninus, Phalaris, Alexander and Romulus and Remus, of a wicked ruler, and it was in this guise (through Orosius) that the memory of Cyrus travelled into the medieval west: Charlemagne's palace at Ingelheim was decorated with paintings of ancient kings, Cyrus included, 'whose wickedness and ambition appear to act as warnings'.[127]

By contrast, a millennium earlier, in Greek sources of the fifth century BCE, for the most part, Cyrus was remembered positively. Herodotus says that Cyrus realised, after taking Croesus captive and was about to burn him on the pyre, that he himself had no greater share of *eudaimoniē*, 'blessedness', than the Lydian king once had, and that human affairs were not stable (Hdt. 1.86.6, cf. 87.3). Indeed, one of Herodotus' programmatic themes for his *Histories* is that *eudaimoniē* never stays in the same place for long (Hdt. 1.5.4), as Cyrus' own career (at least as Herodotus told it) would illustrate. Herodotus also writes that the Persians said that while Darius was a shopkeeper, and Cambyses a master, Cyrus was a 'father', who was gentle (*ēpios*) and arranged all things well for them (3.89.3), although we have already seen that this reputation for gentleness is somewhat contrived.

The Cyrus of the *Cyropaedia* is also mostly a positive figure.[128] Although he is prepared to use fear as a means of controlling men, his great achievement (as we will see further in the next chapter) was to secure their willing obedience (Xen. *Cyrop.* 1.1.1-6). For that reason, Cyrus seemed to be 'a king by nature' (*basileu ... phusei*); like the queen of the bees, whom the bees follow out of 'some terrible passion' (*deinos tis erōs*) to be ruled by her, so men are drawn to Cyrus (Xen. *Cyrop.* 5.1.24-5). We will see more of Cyrus' positive reception in the Greek and Roman traditions in the next chapter.

This positive memory of Cyrus in the Greek world is probably because, in his own time, ideas of divinity swirled around Cyrus. He was not only blessed by gods, but he walked with them. There are even hints of divinisation in his extraordinary palace garden at Pasargadae, an irrigated park of trees and meadow extending from his tomb (cf. Arrian, *Anab.* 6.29.4) to the base of the raised platform of the Tall-i Takht, which included formal gardens and a man-made lake.[129] In a Near Eastern context, garden-building was the politics of kingship and power. At Pasargadae, as Stronach argues, the gardens did not just complement the palace, but the design of the garden was integral to the palace structure in which 'the garden itself became the royal residence'.[130] These gardens probably comprised trees, as well as flower gardens, as are suggested by the reliefs at Persepolis (cf. Xen. *Oec.* 4.4-25). Significantly, there was no wall or defensive boundary, and Stronach argues that Cyrus' wish to set his palace in an undefended garden may have been 'to underline the distance of his capital from any hostile boundary'.[131] However, it also marked out a royal and near-divine space (cf. *Genesis* 3.8), and the king's complete control over it.[132]

However, according to Herodotus, it was thoughts of divinity that led to Cyrus' death. Even though there was in fact nine years between the capture of Babylon and Cyrus' death in December 530, Herodotus, who elides this gap, suggests that it was because Cyrus started to think of himself as divine after the taking of Babylon that he formed the plan of attacking the Massagetae (cf. 1.200).[133] Herodotus says:

> There were many great reasons which stirred and excited him [to attack the Massagetae], first of all his birth, which seemed to be more than mortal, and secondly the good fortune (*eutuchia*) he had experienced in the wars, for whatever race Cyrus purposed to attack were unable to escape him (1.204.2).

For Herodotus, Cyrus' birth and death are linked to each other.[134] When he first approached Cyrus about leading the Persians in a revolt from the Medes, Herodotus has the Median Harpagus say that Cyrus has only survived death as a baby because the gods had looked after him (Hdt. 1.124.1-2, cf. 126.6: Cyrus himself says he was 'born by divine fate' [*theiēi tuchēi gegonōs*]). However, it is Harpagus' comments which sow the seeds which lead Cyrus to his death in this campaign against the Massagetae. Before he crosses the river into Massagetan territory, Cyrus is also warned in a dream about his death, but does not understand the dream's meaning (so the gods *do* look after him, if only he were able to interpret their message: Hdt. 1.209-10).[135] His misinterpretation of the dream, however, is almost willful and driven by what he wants to understand rather than a true or critical appreciation of the warning. In relating his interpretation of the dream to Hystaspes, father of Darius, he says that the gods have given him a sign of Darius' treachery: 'The gods care for me and show me everything that is coming' (Hdt. 1.209.3). However, Herodotus says, what the dream was intended to show was the manner of Cyrus' own death (Hdt. 1.210.1). In fact, by dying at the hands of the Massagetan queen, Cyrus fulfils Herodotean story patterns and exemplifies some of Herodotus' overarching themes: that human happiness never stays in the same place for long, that 'kingship' is an Asian thing, and that one should beware of vengeful women.

In the next chapter, we will look at how Cyrus' life and death became part of the exemplary tradition, particularly of ideal kingship, and how the stories of Cyrus' death became the vehicle in the ancient and medieval worlds for exploring the greatness of a woman, Tomyris, the queen of the Massagetae.

Notes

1. See L. Mitchell (2020a).
2. DK 2 B 22.
3. On the so-called 'Mappa Mundi', which probably dates to the eighth or seventh century BCE, Babylon is depicted near the centre of the world, which is surrounded by encircling ocean: Horowitz (2011), 20–42; see also Pongratz-Leisten (2015), 192–7.
4. George (1997), 125–45.
5. George (1999).
6. Van de Mieroop (2003), 264–5; note also Edzard (1987).
7. George (1993a), no. 1088.
8. George (1993b).
9. Schaudig (2019).
10. See, for example, Dalley (1996); Kuhrt (2002); Henkelman *et al.* (2011).
11. For an analysis of Herodotus' description of Babylon's spatiality: Kurke (1999), 232–5.
12. *Birds* was produced in 414 BCE. Commentators assume Aristophanes was relying on Herodotus' description of the walls, particularly in reference to the use of baked (rather than sun-dried) bricks: Sommerstein (1987), 233; Dunbar (1995), 374.

13. Cyrus the Younger intended to march on Babylon (Xenophon, *Anab.* 1.4.11) in 401 BCE with the Greek army, of which Xenophon was a member. However, Cyrus was killed at Cunaxa, about 40 miles north of Babylon (Xenophon, *Anab.* 2.2.6), and the Greek army then made their retreat north through Babylonia and the Assyrian heartland along the Tigris: see Brennan and Thomas (2021), Appendix P. Consequently, although he came close to Babylon, Xenophon probably did not see the city either.

14. Ctesias was court physician to Parysatis (Ctesias T 7a), sister of Darius II and mother of Artaxerxes II, who owned estates in Babylonia, where she retreated after murdering her daughter-in-law (Plut., *Artox.* 19.10).

15. Lenfant (2004), 238–9 *s.v.* n. 144: 'cette exaggeration des dimensions s'inscrit dans un processus de mythification des murailles de Babylon … Le chiffre de 360 a sans doute d'abord valeur de symbole, puisqu'il correspond à peu près au nombre de jours de l'année'. For a comparison of the measurements given by Greek authors for the walls, see also the summary by MacGinnis (1986), 69.

16. Haubold (2013), 91–4.

17. Compare *Jonah* 3.3: Nineveh was a large city; it took three days to cross it.

18. Beaulieu (2018), 227–9.

19. Sals (2014).

20. See Thelle (2009).

21. Sals (2014), 296.

22. Esp. Edelman (2005), ch. 3; note also van der Spek (2014).

23. See Kuhrt (1983).

24. This date is given by dating formulae from Uruk and the *Nabonidus Chronicle* (*ABC* 7). Note also Berossus *BNJ* 680 F 9a, 9b.

25. On the basis of the dating of the *Harran Stele*: Weiershäuser and Novotny (2020), 188.

26. Beaulieu (1993); van der Spek (2014), 254.

27. For the text, see Glassner (2004), 236–7 (Grayson also thought $^{kur}Pa[rsu(? …]$ preferable at iii.3: *ABC* 282). For analysis, see Fried (2004), 28–9.

28. Cameron (1974) with Beaulieu (1993), esp. 61–2.

29. For example, Kuhrt (1990), 132–5.

30. In any case, the *Chronicle* says that Nabonidus retreated further to Babylon (*ABC* 7 iii.15, 16), although Berossus says that he went to Borsippa (*BNJ* 680 F 9a).

31. Note Beaulieu (1989), 230: 'It is impossible to determine why Sippar surrendered so readily to Cyrus …'.

32. Kuhrt (1990), 133–4; cf. Waerzeggers (2021), 80.

33. Fried (2004), 24–31.

34. Waerzeggers (2015), 190; cf. Bongenaar (1997), 1.

35. Kleber (2008), 19 n. 82.

36. Jursa (2010b), 77.

37. Jursa (2010b): 'The Achaemenid administration manifestly aimed at stability and continuity in this respect' (78; cf. 83).

38. For example, Briant (2002), 41–2;

39. See also Vanderhooft (2006), 364–7.

40. Schaudig (2001), 563–78; English translation: Kuhrt (2007a), 75–80.

41. Especially the *Harran Stele* and the *Adad-Guppi Stele*: Weiershäuser and Novotny (eds.) (2020), Nabonidus nos. 47 and 2001.

42. Kuhrt (1990).

43. Fried (2004), 28–30.

44. Waerzeggers (2015), 198–9.

45. See esp. Jursa (2010b).

46. On the walls at Babylon in the late seventh and sixth centuries, see George (1992), esp. 343–51.
47. Tolini (2005); Tolini (2012), 266.
48. Rollinger (2013), 143–7.
49. Wetzel (1930), 70–5.
50. George (1992), 351.
51. MacGinnis (1986), 79.
52. Cf. Vanderhooft (2006), 355.
53. Ctesias (F 1b (= Diod. 2.2.2–9)) credited the founding of Babylon to Semiramis, and attributed to her also the monumental building works there.
54. Many attempts have been made to identify Nitocris, but, ultimately, she is an imaginary figure: MacGinnis (1986), 78–9; cf. Asheri and Lloyd in Asheri *et al.* (2007), 204 (Asheri), 312 (Lloyd), who both suggest a legendary connection with Adad-guppi, Nabonidus' mother. Note also how Herodotus builds the tension around the fear generated by the 'Medes'; Arganthonius, ruler of Tartessus, gave the Phocaeans money to build a wall around their city after they told him how the power of 'the Mede' was growing: Hdt. 1.163.3.
55. Rollinger (2003); cf. Immerwahr (1966), 91–3.
56. It is unclear how this ditch relates to the moat that surrounded the city.
57. In Xenophon, Gobryas is an Assyrian *eparch*, who goes over to Cyrus because of the role of the Assyrian king in the death of his son, and Gadatas is a young Assyrian prince castrated by the king, and so is persuaded by Gobryas to join Cyrus: e.g., *Cyrop.* 4.6.1–10, 5.1.22–3.21.
58. Once again, Xenophon uses 'the surprise' motif of attacking revellers: see Krentz (2000).
59. Especially Rollinger (1993), 148–66; Rollinger (2014). Vanderhooft (2006), 356, however, points out that Herodotus does seem to have a fairly accurate idea of the waterworks and defences in the city along the river.
60. Cohen (1993), 326–30 (although Parpola's observations, which are cited, about a then unpublished text, have now been shown to be incorrect: van der Toorn (1991), 332 n. 4). Beaulieu, however, thinks the festival in question might be a festival of Sin which Nabonidus had relocated to Babylon: Beaulieu (1989), 226, Beaulieu (1993) 255–6. Note also the famous feast in *Daniel 5*, where Belshazzar's death was predicted (although Belshazzar was in fact the son of Nabonidus). *Daniel 4* on the madness of Nebuchadnezzar is probably a version of the madness of Nabonidus of the *Verse Account* and seems to be confirmed by similar stories about madness relating to Nabonidus and other Babylonian rulers: Beaulieu (2007), 138–9.
61. Vanderhooft (2006), 354–60.
62. http://oracc.org/ribo/Q005487/ (no. 16) i.25–ii.16 (accessed 13/06/2022).
63. Cogan (1974), 9–21.
64. Bottéro (2001), 64–6.
65. Cogan (1974), 22–41.
66. Weiershäuser and Novotny (eds.) (2020), Nabonidus no. 3 i.1–34. On the restoration of Marduk to Babylon, attempted first by Esarhaddon, and completed by his sons Shamash-shumu-ukin and Ashurbanipal, see Porter (1993), 137–48; Schaudig (2019), 57.
67. See Schaudig (2019), 55–72.
68. Porter (1993), 147–8.
69. Cohen (1974).
70. Cohen (1974), esp. 31.
71. Samet (2014), 2–3.
72. The scholarship on this is now extensive: e.g., Ferris (1992); Dobbs-Allsopp (1993); N.C. Lee (2002); Heskett (2011); Petter (2011).

73. Cohen (1974), 6.
74. M.W. Green (1975), 295.
75. Petter (2011), 9.
76. Löhnert (2011); Gabay (2020).
77. Samet (2014), 3, 5.
78. Samet (2014), 4.
79. Cooper (1983), 5, 41–4 with Delnero (2010).
80. For the text and date, see Al-Rawi (1990); Glassner (2004), no. 38 (263–9).
81. Westenholz (1997), 263–368.
82. Cooper (1983), 20–3; cf. Michalowski (1989), 8.
83. See Tinney (1996), 35–6: 'The relationship between [the *Curse of Agade*] and [the *Nippur Lament*] is not one of positive comparisons, but of negative: *CA* shows how not to act when faced with adversity, whereas *NL* offers a paradigm for behaviour in the face of such odds, and an intimation that to follow the paradigm is to bring blessings on oneself and one's subjects. By following the procedure detailed in *CA*, one can be sure of eternal devastation; by following the instructions of *NL*, adversity can be overturned'.
84. Komoróczy (1977), 55–9.
85. Adalı (2011).
86. Adalı (2011), 85–67.
87. Thureau-Dangin (1925).
88. Adalı (2011).
89. Weierhäuser and Novotny (eds.) (2020), Nabonidus no. 3 ii.1–41.
90. For *la adiru*, see *CAD* A1, 218 (*s.v. adiru*).
91. Adalı (2011), 96–100; Haubold (2013), 80–6.
92. Weiershäuser and Novotny (eds.) (2020), Nabonidus no. 28 i.28.
93. Adalı (2011), 98. See http://oracc.org/rinap/Q007632/ no. 224 20–24 (accessed 04/07/2022); cf. Novotny and Jeffers (eds.) (2018), Ashurbanipal no. 21 19–21. The *Umman-manda* (explicitly the Cimmerian king) also appears in the inscriptions of Esarhaddon: e.g., Leichty (ed.) (2011), Esarhaddon nos. 2 ii.1–4, 3 ii.15–16.
94. Cf. Haubold (2013), 87.
95. On the significance of 'Ugbaru of Gutium' as the first to enter Babylon: Dalley (1996), 527.
96. On the literariness of the *Nabonidus Chronicle*, see Waerzeggers (2015); cf. Schaudig (2019), 23–4: 'Babylonian historiography as manifested in the chronicles did not perceive history as a chain of events following upon one another chronologically, but as an expression and manifestation of divine will' (24).
97. Christopher Pelling has drawn my attention to the wonderful article by Jasper Griffin (1976) which discusses how Augustan love poetry shaped contemporary ideas about the experience of love.
98. For a short but excellent analysis of the structure of the *Cylinder*, see: Stolper (2013).
99. Schaudig (2019), 76–85.
100. http://oracc.org/ribo/Q006653/ Cyrus II no. 1 (accessed 01/06/2022).
101. Schaudig (2019).
102. For *ibru*, see *CAD* 7.5.
103. Based on the text of http://oracc.org/ribo/Q006653/ Cyrus II no. 1.17–19 (accessed 01/06/2022), and broadly on the translation of Novotny.
104. See *CAD* 10.143; compare the translation of Brosius (2000), 10 (n. 12).
105. Schaudig (2001), 555: 'Als den Herrn, der durch das (zurecht) in ihn (gesetzte) Vertauen all To(dgeweih)ten am Leben hielt, aus Not und Bedrägnis alle Welt errettete, segneten sie ihn immerzu (auf das) Süß(este), priesen seinen Namen'; Kuhrt (2007a), 71: '"The lord, who through his help has brought the dead to

life, who in (a time of) disaster and oppression has benefited all" – thus they joyfully celebrated him, honoured his name'; Finkel (2013), see also Appendix A, this volume: 'The lord through whose help all were rescued from death and who saved them all from distress and hardship, they blessed him sweetly and praised his name'; van der Spek (2014), 262: 'The lord by whose support all the dead were revived, he spared them all from hardship and distress, they greeted him friendly and praised his name'; Novotny (http://oracc.org/ribo/Q006653/): '(As for) the lord, who through his (Marduk's) support revived the dying (and) universally spared (them) from trouble and hardship, they graciously blessed him (and) praised his name'; Waters (2022), 192: 'All the people joyfully extolled the lord, through whose support, they were restored to life, and by whom they were saved from oppression, and they extolled his name'; cf. Brosius (2000), 10: 'The lord, who through his help has revived the gods (?), who spared them disaster and oppression, they praised again and again in gratitude, honoured his name'.

106. See Parpola (1999).
107. In the *Verse Account of Nabonidus*, mention is also made of completing the building work of Nebuchadnezzar: vi.9–11.
108. Weierhäuser and Novotny (2020), 17–18, 141–4.
109. Weierhäuser and Novotny (eds.) (2020), no. 29.
110. See Porter (1993), 146–8.
111. Weierhäuser and Novotny (eds.) (2020), Nabonidus no. 28 i.7–12a.
112. http://oracc.org/ribo/Q006653/ 30 (accessed 02/06/2022).
113. Ashur was taken by the Medes in 614 BCE according to the *Fall of Nineveh Chronicle* (see Chapter 4). The city remained inhabited after its sack in 614, and the temple active, although the identity of the god is unknown: Kuhrt (1995a), 1.247–8. The gods of Susa taken by the Assyrians after the sacking of the city in 647 BCE were apparently returned by Nabopolassar in the first year of his reign, 626 BCE (*ABC* 2.16–17). For the status of Susa from the mid-seventh to the mid-sixth century, see especially Potts (2016), 282–305.
114. Waerzeggers (2011).
115. For the divinisation of the kings of the Old Akkadian dynasty and the Third Dynasty of Ur (towards the end of the third millennium BCE), see Brisch (2022), 74–8.
116. On the divinisation of Sargon: Westenholz (1984), 75, although note also Brisch (2022), 75–6, who says that it was Naramsin, Sargon's grandson, who was the first living king to be deified. On Nabonidus' repair of the Sargon's statue, and the offerings he made to it, see Chapter 3.
117. See, for example, L. Mitchell (2022), 127–8.
118. Graeber and Sahlins (2017).
119. Machinist (2011).
120. Ando (2000), 24–41.
121. See Chapter 1.
122. On Cyrus as a 'Davidic' king, see I.D. Wilson (2015). On Cyrus, lamentation and *Isaiah*: Heskett (2011), esp. 79–125. On the figure of the 'messiah'/ 'the anointed one' in the ancient Near East, see the collection of essays: Day (ed.) (2013).
123. See the Preface to Orosius' text.
124. Orosius' description of Cyrus' capture of Babylon is very Herodotean (e.g. Cyrus' rages against the river Gyndes/Diyala); as Orosius was unlikely to have been able to read Herodotus' Greek text, his probable source (since Justin is not interested in Cyrus at Babylon) was probably Seneca, *On Anger* 3.21.1–4; see Bruce (2019).

125. Although Orosius structures book one around four empires (Babylonia, Macedonia, Carthage and Rome), the two intermediate empires are only of minor importance since empire is transferred from Babylon to Rome as between an old father and a young son (*quasi inter patrem senem ac filium paruum*) (1.2.4–6, cf. 2.1.4), although as van Nuffelen argues the parallelism is there in order to show that the two cities are in fact opposed: van Nuffelen (2012), 46–53.

126. This equation of Babylon and Rome brings Cyrus into Orosius' account again in Book Two (which restarts with Ninus and the refoundation of Babylon: 2.2.1) as the conqueror of Babylon (Or. 2.6), although immediately afterwards, he himself is overcome by Thamyris (sic), Queen of the Scythians, in a version which emphasises her cunning in revenge and his arrogance (2.7.4).

127. McKitterick (2008), 163–4.

128. It has often been noted, however, there are differences between the Cyrus of the earlier parts of the *Cyropaedia*, and Xenophon's description of his actions and attitudes once Babylon has been taken. Gera (1993, 285–99), for example, notices Xenophon's less positive attitude towards Cyrus, but then concludes (oddly) that Cyrus has become a benevolent despot because that is what is needed for ruling an empire. Nadon (2001, 161–80), on the other hand, thinks that Xenophon (who, for Nadon, is interested in studying the best kind of constitution) uses the discrepancies between his representation of the pre-and post-Babylon Cyrus to show (although not uncritically) that Republic rather than Empire is the best form of rule for achieving the common life of virtue. Azoulay (2004) has argued that in capturing Babylon, we can explain Cyrus' change in behaviour because he was doing something new, and that, as a result, new rules needed to apply, and that Xenophon is making the point that the successful leader of an empire (as opposed to a republic) must change his behaviour and adopt a more 'Median' style.

129. See Boucharlat and Benech (2002); Boucharlat (2009); Boucharlat (2011).

130. Stronach (1989), 480.

131. Stronach (1989), 486; see also Stronach (1990a).

132. See esp. Lincoln (2012), 3–19.

133. On the importance of Babylon in Herodotus' Cyrus narrative, see Avery (1979).

134. Immerwahr (1966), 161–7.

135. On Cyrus' links with the divine, see Harrison (2002), 43–5, 236–7.

6 Cyrus

An Exemplary Death

News of Cyrus' death reached Kish in Babylonia by 19th Arahsamna (VIII), that is, December 4th, 530 BCE, the last date on which Cyrus is mentioned in the dating formulae on documents.[1] Situated in a park at one end of his garden palace, his tomb at Pasargadae (Figure 6.1) became the location for veneration, and perhaps also the Achaemenid royal investiture ceremony (Plut. *Artox.* 3.1-2).[2] Alexander the Great was said to have visited Pasargadae in 330 BCE on his way to Persepolis (he carried away the treasure stored there:[3] Arrian, *Anab.* 3.18.10; Q.C. 5.6.10; Diod. 17.71.1), and again in the winter of 325/4, when he found that Cyrus' tomb had been desecrated (Arrian, *Anab.* 6.29.4-11; Strabo 15.3.7), possibly to prevent Alexander himself holding an investiture ceremony there.[4]

Aristobulus (to whom Alexander had given the task of restoring the tomb: Arrian, *Anab.* 6.29.10) says that Cyrus' body was laid in a gold sarcophagus, with a couch beside it with feet cast in gold, Babylonian coverlets, purple rugs on the floor, a *kandys*, *chiton*s of Babylonian workmanship, Median trousers and jewellery of gold and stone; although when Alexander saw it in 325/4, the tomb had been emptied of everything except the sarcophagus and the couch, and the body of Cyrus had been mutilated (Arrian, *Anab.* 6.29.5-6, 9).

There was also said to be an inscription on the tomb. Aristobulus says that it was in Persian in a Persian script, which he says Alexander had copied in Greek (Strabo, 15.3.7; cf. Arrian, *Anab.* 6.29.8): 'Mortal, I am Cyrus, son of Cambyses who founded the empire for the Persians and was king of Asia; do not begrudge me this monument'. Onesicritus, who also accompanied Alexander on his campaigns, gives a different version of the inscription (which he says was written in Greek, although carved in Persian script, with a second version written in Persian): 'Here I lie, Cyrus, king of kings' (Strabo 15.3.7). The greatest puzzle of all, however, is that on the tomb itself, there is no sign of any inscription at all, and for that reason, it seems unlikely ever to have existed.[5] What all this points to, however, is just the number and level of stories that attracted themselves to Cyrus (as they had previously to Naramsin, as we have seen, and were also to do again to Alexander the Great).

DOI: 10.4324/9781003384458-6

Figure 6.1 Tomb of Cyrus, Pasargadae. Author's photo.

In fact, the circumstances of Cyrus' death are as unclear as every other aspect of his life and career. Just as his life attracted many stories, so did his death. Herodotus says that many stories were told of his death (1.214.5), in addition to the one that Herodotus chooses to tell, which he thinks is 'most plausible' (*pithanōtatos*). This interest in Cyrus as an *exemplum* continued into the Roman world, and then later in the medieval period and early renaissance, although the nature of this interest changed as the Greek texts became less accessible to late Roman and early medieval readers, only to return with renewed vigour in the early fifteenth century when Greek manuscripts were brought from Constantinople to Italy and translated into Latin.

In this chapter, we will consider first the stories of Cyrus' death that were circulating in the Greek world in the fifth and fourth centuries BCE. We will then look at the ways that Cyrus, in life and death, became a means in Greek political thought, as an exemplary king, for working through ideas

about freedom and its relationship to kingship, before turning to Cyrus in
the Roman and medieval exemplary tradition: how his death at the hands
of a woman was used not as much to show his exemplary character, as to
highlight her feminine strength and cunning. It is the Herodotean story
of Cyrus' death which captured the medieval imagination, not because of
Cyrus, but because of this wonderful and terrible woman, who was ultimately greater than he was.

The Cyrus' Death Stories

Herodotus' story of Cyrus' death was certainly the most colourful, where
he is killed in the battle against the Massagetae (1.204-14), a people whom
Herodotus places on the plains to the east of the Caspian Sea (1.201, 204; cf.
Strabo 11.8.6).[6] Herodotus says that Cyrus at first sent Tomyris, the queen
of the Massagetae, an offer of marriage which she turned down. He then, on
the advice of Croesus, made the decision to cross into Massagetan territory,
having devised a trick suggested by Croesus: he left a small part of the army
(those who were unfit), set out a banquet, and then withdrew with the rest.
The Massagetans (commanded by Tomyris' son, Spargapises)[7] attacked
the remnant, who were killed, but sat down to the banquet (according to
Herodotus, the Massagetans drank milk rather than wine: 1.216.4).[8] When
they were asleep, Cyrus' army attacked the Massagetans, taking a number
of captives including Tomyris' son. He requested to be set free, but when
Cyrus granted his request, he committed suicide. Tomyris then attacked
Cyrus' army, and it was defeated. After the battle, Tomyris, the queen of the
Massagetae, had Cyrus' corpse found and beheaded and his head shoved in
a wineskin of blood (Hdt. 1.211-14). We will return to this story in a moment,
not because it probably has any historical validity, but because it was to
become so important in the Cyrus tradition.

Ctesias, on the other hand, has Cyrus die after receiving a thigh wound
(itself a metaphor for political emasculation)[9] in the battle against the
Derbices (Eratosthenes places them next to Hyrcania on the Caspian: Strabo
11.8.8), their king Amoraeus, and a contingent of Indians, although in a
second battle (led by Cyrus' ally Amorges, king of the Sacae), the Derbices
were defeated and Amoraeus and his sons were killed (Ctesias F 9.7). Cyrus'
death followed soon after, but not before a deathbed scene in the army camp
where he appoints his heirs, tells his sons to look after their mother and
utters prayers and curses (F 9.8).[10]

In the *Cyropaedia*, on the other hand, Cyrus' death is almost completely
different. Xenophon's Cyrus returns from Babylon to Persia, and, after he was
forewarned of his death in a dream (a dream which Xenophon's Cyrus inter-
prets correctly), summons his family and appoints his heirs. In this context,
he made a deathbed speech in which he tells his sons to support each other
(and for Tanaoxares to be obedient to Cambyses) and to remember to help
friends and harm enemies. Then he covered himself and died (*Cyrop.* 8.7.1-27).

The deathbed scene is a fitting end for Xenophon's Cyrus and the *Cyropaedia* (although that this is a genuine Xenophontic ending has sometimes been doubted), as Xenophon is able to draw together some of the main themes of his life, especially the lessons learned from his own father: particularly that it is important to help friends and harm enemies (*Cyrop.* 1.6.34), an important theme in the Xenophontic oeuvre more generally.

In the Hellenistic period, Berossus (as we know from a fragment in Eusebius: *BNJ* 680 F 10) has Cyrus die in central Asia (but only gives the notice of his death), on the plain of the Daae, which Strabo says stretches from the Caspian to the land of the Massagetae (11.8.2). Diodorus, on the other hand, says that after the battle against the Scythians, Cyrus was crucified by their queen (Diod. 2.44.2), although she is unnamed.

As we have seen in previous chapters, we have similarities between the stories of Cyrus' death, but also differences and various conflations of mixed metaphors and motifs. In both Ctesias and Xenophon, there is a deathbed scene, where Cyrus arranges the succession and offers advice to his sons. In Herodotus, Cyrus' heir Cambyses is sent home to Persia with Croesus before Cyrus crosses the River Araxes into Massagetan territory (1.208), with all the dangers that the crossing of rivers and other watery boundaries presage. In Ctesias (through Photius), it is Cambyses who arranges that his father's body is returned to Persia (F 13). A number of narratives have Cyrus die somewhere in territories east of the Caspian against the nomads of the steppe, but the object of his interest in each case is different.

However, just as we saw with the stories regarding the capture of Babylon, it is not possible to choose between the variants to find a 'historical narrative'. So, it is also the case with the stories of Cyrus' death. There has been a tendency to regard Herodotus' story of Cyrus' attack on the Massagetae as the most likely (partly because Herodotus himself claims that of the stories he knows, this one is 'most plausible').[11] However, there is a good reason for regarding it as not only an important part of Herodotus' own storytelling about the rise and fall of oriental monarchs,[12] but also itself, in the formation of Herodotus' story, careful crafting of folkloric motifs – one of which is the party trick by which Cyrus has initial success over the Massagetan army (Hdt. 1.211), which we have already seen is a favourite motif in Greek victory-in-battle stories.[13]

In fact, that Cyrus fights a vengeful woman (and perhaps even a Scythian/Scythian-type woman) also looks as if it is a motif from a conventional storyset regarding Cyrus. Heleen Sancisi-Weerdenburg makes the important point that Herodotus' story is not the only one where Cyrus is defeated by a warrior-woman.[14] Ctesias also has Cyrus defeated by Sparethe, wife of Amorges, king of the Sacae, who himself had been captured by Cyrus in an earlier battle. Amorges went on to become Cyrus' ally but the Scythian queen was seeking revenge for the capture of her kinsman (Ctesias F 9.3). The similarities with Herodotus' story are striking enough to make it plausible that Herodotus is drawing on a stock story about the warrior women of the steppe, the most well known of whom were the Amazons.

Herodotus, Cyrus and Tomyris

Herodotus' Tomyris, however, is not an Amazon – he even distinguishes the Massagetae from the Scythians (1.215-16)[15] – and Cyrus' unprovoked attack on her raises questions about the wisdom of his imperial ambition. Tomyris, however, is a clever woman, who is Cyrus' equal. She understands that his marriage offer is a trick (Cyrus realises that his trick (*dolos*)) has not worked: 1.205), and she interrupts his bridge-building (itself perhaps transgressive) to question his desire to extend his empire.[16] She says to him (Hdt. 1.206.1):

> Stop pursuing the things you are pursuing (*pausai speudōn ta speudeis*). You could not know whether these things will end advantageously. Stop, rule your own people and endure seeing me rule those I rule (*hemeas anecheu oreōn archontas tōn per archomen*).

Her words also look forward to the very final chapters of the *Histories* when Cyrus himself advises the Persians not to invade Greece because they would run the risk of being ruled rather than ruling (*ouketi archontas alla archsom-enous*: 9.122.3).[17] However, they also look back to Solon's encounter with Croesus, especially when the Athenian advises Croesus that: 'It is necessary to consider the end of everything and how it will turn out. For many, the god offers happiness (*olbos*) but then utterly overturns them' (Hdt. 1.32.9).[18] Croesus himself gives Cyrus the same advice ('that there is a cycle in human affairs which being turned about does not allow the same people to prosper': 1.207.2). However, he also advises Cyrus to cross the river into Tomyris' country because, at least in part, it could not be endured (*anascheton*) for 'Cyrus son of Cambyses' to give way to a woman, and suggests the banquet because the Massagetae are inexperienced in the good things of Persia (1.207.5-6).[19]

Herodotus' Croesus is not always a perceptive advisor. While he remembers the lesson taught to him about 'the circle of human affairs', he misunderstands Cyrus' own thinking and intentions. He tells the king that if Cyrus had started to think of himself or his army as immortal, then there would be no point in giving advice (Hdt. 1.207.2). However, as we have seen in the previous chapter, Cyrus has already started to consider the possibility of his own divinity. In fact, Cyrus misguidedly thinks that in his attack on the Massagetae the gods are protecting him (Hdt. 1.209.3).

Croesus then goes on to give advice that reflects his own preoccupations with territorial expansion that led him to invade Cappadocia in the first instance: Herodotus says that one of the reasons why Croesus attacked Cyrus was his desire for land (*gēs himerōi*) (1.73.1).[20] Then Sandanis had warned Croesus about the dangers of his expansionism: that if he were to be defeated, he would lose many of the good things (*agatha*) the Lydians enjoyed (Hdt. 1.71.3). However, Croesus is also reflecting his own experience. It was not the crossing of the Halys as such which brought Croesus down and lost him his kingdom, but the confrontation with Cyrus in Sardis (although one led to the other).[21] So, Croesus advises Cyrus to attack Tomyris in her own territory and to trick the Massagetae with these very same good things (Hdt. 1.207.3-7).

Even in suggesting this final trick against the Massagetae, Croesus, although unaware of the implications of his own words, indicates that the conquest of Lydia has corrupted the Persians, and planted the seeds for Cyrus' eventual downfall at the hands of this milk-drinking woman who has not been corrupted. Before the capture of Sardis, the Lydian Sandanis had advised Croesus against attacking the Persians because of the harshness and frugality of their lifestyle: they wore nothing but leather, ate nothing good, drank water, not wine and came from a 'rugged land' (Hdt. 1.71.2-3). He also said that once the Persians had experienced the good things of the Lydians, they would not give them up or leave Lydia (Hdt. 1.71.3). The trick of the banquet itself shows that the Persians (who Croesus says at the taking of Sardis were both aggressive by nature and unused to possessions: Hdt. 1.89.2) have indeed been seduced by good things so that it becomes inevitable that Cyrus is heading for a fate like that experienced by Croesus, and for similar reasons. Cyrus, like Croesus, cannot resist expanding his empire.

Both Croesus and Cyrus also completely underestimate the Massagetan warrior queen. Not only does Croesus not think of women as warriors, but he also is aware that soft living will make men unable to fight. In order to save the Lydians from enslavement, he has already advised Cyrus to educate the Lydian children in playing the kithara and harp, and in becoming shop-keepers: 'you will soon see that they have become women instead of men' (Hdt. 1.155.4), which is the opposite of the Persian education (Hdt. 1.136.2).[22] However, the implication is that, while they will not be sold as slaves (*andrapodisthentas prēthēnai spheas*: 1.156.1), they would also not have agency because of their new education, which, as we will see, was an important element in Herodotus' conception of freedom (so they will become as good as slaves in any case).

Cyrus does then go on to succeed in his trick with the banquet (which leads to the death of Tomyris' son through his suicide at the shame of being duped), but that only stirs Tomyris to take her revenge, and destroy Cyrus' army in battle. She does not run away, as Croesus says she would (Hdt. 1.207.4). Instead, she castigates him for dishonourably using a trick to defeat her son's army rather than facing him in battle,[23] demands that he return her son and leave her country, and warns Cyrus that she will give him his fill of blood (*haimatos koresō*: Hdt. 1.212.3).

Herodotus then tells us twice that Cyrus did not pay any attention to her advice (Hdt. 1.213, 214.1), hammering home his misplaced confidence and arrogance. Tomyris then engaged him in a closely fought battle; finally, the Massagetan army prevailed, most of Cyrus' army was destroyed, and Cyrus himself was killed (Hdt. 1.214.2-3). Tomyris then filled a wineskin with human blood, and put Cyrus' head in it, saying: 'Although I am alive and I defeated you in battle, you have destroyed me having taken my son by trickery (*dolos*); so, even as I threatened, I will give you your fill of blood (*haimatos koresō*)' (Hdt. 1.214.5).[24]

The story of the death of Cyrus in Herodotus is a very powerful one and is 'plausible' within Herodotus' own narrative framework. For Herodotus, Tomyris is not only a queen who shares the cleverness of Nitocris of Babylon, but also the vengefulness and brutality of other queens, both Greek and Persian, whose roles as wives and mothers converge with their royal power to make them terrifying opponents.[25] However, rather than being a 'noble savage' as Deborah Gera claims,[26] the milk-drinking queen is striking for her uncorrupted intelligence and morality, and yet also her determination and ruthlessness. In this way, she is the perfect foil for Cyrus. She is as he was, before he experienced the temptations of empire. It is also significant that this powerful woman is not tempted to cross the river herself and take Cyrus' empire (as he had crossed the Halys). She knows the limits of her rule and does not desire more.

The decapitation, however, is disturbing. Just as Tomyris searches for the body of Cyrus and then shoved his head in the *askos* (Hdt. 1.114.4), so Xerxes (Cyrus' grandson), after his victory at Thermopylae, searches for the body of the Spartan Leonidas, cuts off his head and impales it on a stake (Hdt. 7.238.1). Herodotus says (7.238.2) that Xerxes must have been angered by Leonidas while he was alive, for otherwise, he would not have committed such an outrage against the corpse since Persians honour those who are brave in war. On the other hand, the Spartan Pausanias refuses to decapitate the Persian Mardonius after the Greek victory over the Persians at Plataea, although it is suggested to him as revenge for the decapitation of Leonidas ('these things seem more for barbarians to do than for Greeks': Hdt. 9.79.1). A Persian king is dishonoured in death by a barbarian woman. Another Persian king dishonours a dead Spartan hero. Yet another Spartan refuses to sink to the depths of depravity that mutilating a corpse would suggest. In the honour code of Homeric epic, mutilation and the decapitation of corpses were seen as an acceptable form of revenge.[27] Herodotus has further vengeful queen, but this time a Greek one, Pheretime, the mother of Arcesilas III of Cyrene, mutilate the bodies of her enemies by impaling them on stakes (Hdt. 4.202.1), although Herodotus tells us that she herself died by being infested by worms, since, he says, excessive vengeance is offensive to the gods (Hdt. 4.205).

The point here seems to be that Tomyris and Cyrus are both operating within a world which is outside the Greek one, where a different value system applies. The decapitation may betray Tomyris' barbarity, but Cyrus belongs to her world: Persians also mutilate the dead. The contest between them, however, is out of place and out of time from the perspective of the classical Greek world. His death is the fitting end for his *hybris*, as likewise her final revenge is justified in its very epic character.

Yet for all its interest and the care with which this story is woven into Herodotus' narrative, Herodotus' account of the death of Cyrus is not necessarily either 'true' or historical, and neither should it be preferred to any of the other stories of Cyrus' death, as it often is, without question. David Asheri, in his commentary on Herodotus, Book 1, says:

> That he [Cyrus] invaded Sogdiana (modern Turkestan) may perhaps be indirectly attested by the place name Cyroupolis or Cyreschata on the river Jaxartes ... but we know nothing of the chronology of such a campaign. The general historical value of the [Herodotean] *logos* is very slight.[28]

However, although the story of Cyrus and Tomyris might have little, if any, historical value, it is a story that has captured imaginations, particularly as it demonstrates and explores feminine capabilities in a world of men. Later, in the chapter, we will return to Tomyris as an exemplary figure in her own right, as part of an exemplary tradition about women that extends from Herodotus to the Renaissance and beyond.

Cyrus: An Exemplary Life

We perhaps cannot say anything more about Cyrus' death, except that it was a death told in many stories, just as his birth and life were also played out in many different and contradictory variants. However, in his death, Cyrus completes a life that was of great interest to ancient political thinkers. It was as an exemplary ruler that Cyrus captured the attention of many of the Greek historians and political philosophers, especially in their speculations on kingship. For Herodotus, Cyrus is for the most part an idealised positive representation of oriental kingship (while his son Cambyses is the negative tyrant: e.g., Hdt. 3.31.1-6, 80.2), although Cyrus, like all oriental monarchs, as we have seen, finally over-reaches himself and comes to a bad end. For the Socratics, Plato and Xenophon, he exemplifies the importance of education (although in rather different ways), and for Antisthenes (another Socratic, as also for Xenophon), he is a vehicle for reflecting on ideal kingship.[29] At Athens, in particular, the exploration of monarchy, for which Cyrus provided a positive example, was a means of thinking about whether positive political values could inhere within autocracy, not because they considered monarchy as a realistic political alternative to democracy, but they did see it as a possible threat, and they were very aware of the problems and possibilities of political leadership which meant that one person might stand out from the rest.[30] In this context, Cyrus could represent a moderate form of monarchy, which exhibited the qualities and virtues of constitutional government that the rule of later Persian kings (to the Greek mind) did not. In this section, we will try to tease out the importance of Cyrus in Greek political thought, especially in relation to Greek ideas about leadership and freedom. We will then consider Cyrus in Roman thought as the exemplary leader. This will bring us finally back to Cyrus' exemplary death, and Tomyris, queen of the Massagetae.

For Herodotus, Cyrus brought freedom.[31] At the end of the so-called 'Constitution Debate' in Book 3, Darius argues for monarchy on the basis that it was Cyrus who gave the Persians freedom (from the slavery of Median rule) so that monarchy then became their hereditary constitution (Hdt. 3.82.5, cf. 1.126.5-6, 129.3-4). Before the attack on the Massagetae, Hystaspes (father of Darius) says to Cyrus that no Persian would plot against the king because Cyrus found the Persians as slaves, but made them free, and instead of being ruled by others, they now ruled over all (1.210.2).

However, Cyrus shows that freedom is not just the absence of slavery, but it can also be a positive quality of ruling, and that this kind of freedom could also embody other positive qualities. Cyrus, even as a child, showed himself to be 'very free' when speaking before the king (Hdt. 1.116.1), as the ability to speak freely is itself a show of strength (cf. Hdt. 5.78, 93.2). Even more than this, however, Cyrus has agency, and, because of his freedom, he has the ability to make choices based on his desires, which is why 'he desired' (*epethumēse*) to subdue the Massagetae (Hdt. 1.201).

However, Cyrus' success had an effect on his character. Emily Baragwanath talks about how for Herodotus 'character' is shaped by the constitution in which it has been nurtured, and discusses the ways in which it can change. She observes how Otanes in the Constitution Debate reflects on how, under a monarchy, even the best of men can be corrupted.[32] We can see in what manner monarchy has affected Cyrus. Although in his first encounter with Croesus, Cyrus can understand that Croesus is a man like himself (Hdt. 1.86.6), as we have seen in the previous chapter, his success makes him think that he may even be divine, and so leads him to make the wrong choices, which take him inexorably to his death.

For, Plato too, Cyrus is an ideal leader, who with Lycurgus of Sparta is worthy of emulation for their character (*ēthos*) and statecraft (*politeia*) (*Letters* 4.320d; cf. *Alcibiades I* 105c). In the *Laws*, Cyrus' regime represented a kind of balanced constitutionalism, which brought freedom on much the same terms as the regime of Cyrus of Herodotus. He says:

> [the Persians] became, first of all, free (*eleutheroi*) themselves, and, after that, masters (*despotai*) of many others. When the rulers gave a share of freedom (*eleutheria*) to their subjects and advanced them to a position of equality (*to ison*), the soldiers were more friendly towards their officers and showed their devotion in times of danger; and if there was any wise man amongst them, able to give counsel, since the king was not jealous but allowed free speech (*parrhesia*) and respected those who could help at all by their counsel, – such a man had the opportunity of contributing to the common stock the fruit of his wisdom. Consequently, at that time all their affairs made progress, owing to their freedom (*eleutheria*), friendliness (*philia*) and mutual interchange (*koinōnia*) of reason.
>
> (*Laws* 694a–b, cf. 701e)

Plato's Cyrus achieves through *autocratic* rule values familiar in the context of Greek (and especially Athenian) democracy.

However, Cyrus' freedom is fragile because it does not have the necessary underpinnings. Despite his successes, Plato's Cyrus makes a mistake in the way he educates his children that means his moderate rule becomes after his death a style of ruling that was more extreme and inadvertently paves the way not only for the decline of the Persian monarchy, but also greater authoritarianism and a loss of freedom (*Laws* 694d–695e).

Xenophon also connects Cyrus to freedom. He suggests that by ruling the willing (rather than the unwilling), Cyrus brought freedom. For example, he has Chrysantas (one of his inner circle) say: 'We are different from slaves in that slaves serve their masters unwillingly, but for us, if indeed, we think we are free (*eleutheroi*), it is necessary to do everything willingly which we think it is worthwhile to do' (8.1.4, cf. *Oec.* 21.12).[33] Xenophon says that, despite the size of the empire, all were willing to be ruled by him (*Cyrop.* 1.1.3), and he was able to inspire such enthusiasm for gratifying him that they always thought it right to be governed (*kybernasthai*) by his judgement (*Cyrop.* 1.1.5). Elsewhere, Xenophon says that the ability to win willing obedience is more than mortal but a divine thing (*Oec.* 21.11–12).[34] However, what is important is that Xenophon has used Cyrus as a cipher to change the basis of freedom from rule under law to the obedience of the willing.

What is interesting in all these Greek authors is the use of a *Persian* king to explore *Greek* ideas about freedom. In a Greek context, using a Persian as a vehicle for exploring a Greek political value is particularly poignant given that the Greeks themselves in 479 BCE celebrated their victory over the Persian aggressors as a victory for 'free Hellas'. The victory altar at Plataea (the site of the final major battle between the combined Greek army and the Persians) was inscribed with the epigram:

> This the Hellenes, by the might of Nike, by the work of Ares,
> trusting the courageous spirit of the soul,
> having driven out the Persians, common to free Hellas,
> they built as the altar of Zeus Eleutherius, Zeus of Freedom
> ([Simonides] XV).[35]

The suggestion seems to be that, although ultimately flawed, 'freedom' in Greek thought was the political value which ensured agency, so that the 'Persian King', whose rule could be used to embody slavery and despotism, could also be a positive metaphor for power and strength. To defeat the Persians, and especially the Persian king (which in Herodotus Tomyris was said to do), was then an even more remarkable feat of even greater power and agency.

Cyrus in the Latin Tradition

Because of the kind of interest in Cyrus in the Greek political tradition as an idealised leader and king, Cyrus becomes in the Latin tradition an exemplary figure, though sometimes in rather uncertain ways. Roman society was an exemplary culture in which morality was defined by the actions of exemplary figures, even if the ways that these exemplars were understood were based on a complex understanding of the ethical relationship between individuals and their actions.[36] In the humanist and imperialist movements of the early medieval periods and the Renaissance, Roman exemplarity had an effect on the literary and artistic traditions of the later Roman West.[37]

In this context, Cyrus becomes an exemplary character, both drawing in large part on the Herodotean Cyrus as a figure of power, even if a great man who has been overcome, and also on the more reflective and philosophical Cyrus of Xenophon's *Cyropaedia*. In one sense, it is clear that these two kinds of reflections on Cyrus, one accepted by the Roman audience as in some sense 'historical' and the other as philosophical and ahistorical, are held apart as distinct and different, although it appears that at various points as storylines, they reconnect or at least intersect.

Cyrus as received at Rome was, in the first instance, used as an *exemplum* of good leadership, primarily through Xenophon's *Cyropaedia*. In particular, although Cicero almost certainly knew of Herodotus' story of Cyrus (Cicero famously called Herodotus not only 'the father of history' but also a spinner of 'innumerable fabulous tales': *On Laws* 1.5),[38] nevertheless his interest was in the Cyrus of Xenophon's *Cyropaedia*. In fact, Cicero's allusions to the Cyrus of the *Cyropaedia* seem to assume that Xenophon's work was well known to Cicero's audience. In the *On Old Age* (*De senectute*), Cicero accepts the version of the death of Cyrus in the *Cyropaedia* and explicitly paraphrases the Xenophontic Cyrus' deathbed speech, but reshapes it to bring out and make a point he develops elsewhere that the souls of the most meritorious become divine on death (*De senectute* 79-81).[39] In the *Tusculan Disputations* (2.62), he says that Scipio used Xenophon's work as a handbook for leadership, and in a letter to his brother Quintus (1.8), he says 'that our hero Africanus used perpetually to have those books in his hands, for there is no duty pertaining to a careful and equitable governor which is not to be found in them'.

That is not to say, however, that Cicero approved of kingship as a political model. In fact, it was because kingship could become tyranny that Cicero resolutely rejected it. In the *Republic*, he says that underneath even the best example of kingship, that of the just and wise Cyrus, a tolerable and even a lovable (*amabilis*) king, lies the degeneracy of Phalaris (*Republic* 1.43-44), a contrast that was to have lasting influence. In fact, Cicero was interested in Cyrus, particularly as an idealised leader, and on these grounds, wanted to separate the Cyrus of the *Cyropaedia* from other accounts about him.

A hundred years later, and in a political context, where rule by kings was now a matter of very real contemporary concern, the first-century CE Dio Chrysostom (*Orations* 2.76-77) is also interested in the contrast between Cyrus and Phalaris as part of a more extended discussion of good (Cyrus) and bad (Phalaris) rulers. Plutarch (*Precepts of Statecraft* 821e) also couples

Cyrus and Phalaris, where the implied contrast is between bad and good kingship, and, while he condemns Herodotus' anti-Boeotian sentiment, he nevertheless commends the Cyrus of Herodotus as an ideal ruler (Plut. *On the Malice of Herodotus* 18).

The historians were also interested in the Herodotean Cyrus, although they clearly had access to other accounts outside Herodotus. Pompeius Trogus (we know his work only through Justin, who wrote an epitome of Trogus' *Historiae Philipicae* at some point between the 140s and the 390s CE)[40] obviously knew the Herodotean tradition on Cyrus and uses it as the core of his account of Cyrus, although there are enough divergences to suggest that either Trogus or Justin (or both!) were willing to integrate multiple accounts, or that there were already other intermediary sources now unknown which had already adapted and supplemented Herodotus' account with material from Ctesias and possibly elsewhere. We have already noted that Diodorus in the first century BCE had access to a different variant of Cyrus' death (crucifixion), combined with a tradition about a battle with a 'Scythian' queen (Sparethe? Or Tomyris? Or someone else?).

Trogus/Justin includes a summary in broadly similar terms of Herodotus' story of Cyrus' birth, abandonment, recovery (although, as we shall see later, he makes some important changes to the basic narrative), and the overthrow of his grandfather Astyages. Nevertheless, he also adds some material about Cyrus' accomplice (here Sybares) (1.6.1-3, 7.1), which must come ultimately from the other sequence of traditions which Ctesias knew (Ctesias F 8d*§13), although possibly through an intermediary.[41] Trogus (in the first century BCE) could have had access to Ctesias since copies of the Greek physician's works were still in circulation at Rome in the late Republic so that the Augustan Nicolaus of Damascus had access to them. Trogus/ Justin (and Orosius) also includes another Ctesian story about the Persian mothers who berate the army which was being beaten back by the Medes to shame them into going back to battle by showing them their genitals (Justin 1.6.12-15; cf. Orosius 1.19.9-10), a story which Ctesias/Nicolaus also includes (F 8d*§43-4) although as part of a much more protracted sequence of battles. It is also conceivable that it was Justin himself who was responsible for incorporating the 'Ctesian' material since there were other versions of the story in circulation by the end of the Hellenistic period and at Rome. For example, Polyaenus in his second-century CE *Strategies* (*Strategmata*) completely inverts the Herodotean story and has Tomyris the queen use against Cyrus what in Herodotus is his trick of making the soldiers drunk on wine and so easy to overcome (8.28).

Even more to the point, however, Trogus/Justin places the history of Cyrus within a different (even if related) historical and social framework from Herodotus. For Herodotus, as we have seen, Cyrus is a vehicle for understanding and complicating important Greek political values. Nevertheless, he is also an important element in Herodotus' understanding of empires, and the cycle of historical causation. Trogus/Justin, on the other hand, is interested in a more straightforwardly linear view of history. He like Herodotus was influenced by the so-called 'succession of Empires' or monarchs, of which there were originally perhaps three (as we find obliquely in Herodotus and more explicitly in Ctesias), and later four, and even came to become the justification for an apocalyptic fifth empire (cf. *Daniel*, 2.31-45, 7.1-14). This scheme of three or four world empires (usually Assyria, Media, Persia and Macedonia) probably had its origins in the Near East, but also had an impact on Roman historiography.[42] Justin, probably following Trogus in this temporal structure of a linear succession of empires, overtly makes use of this structure to demonstrate that the main driver in the historical process was a desire for domination (*imperii cupiditate*) (Justin 1.4). It is in this context that he gives us the story of Cyrus' rise to power.

In Justin, Astyages dreams that a vine has sprouted from the womb of his daughter and that this is interpreted as a sign that Astyages' daughter would have a son who would overthrow his grandfather (Justin 1.4.1-4) (in Herodotus, as we have seen, Astyages has two dreams: see Chapter 3). As a result, Astyages marries his daughter to an undistinguished Persian (Justin 1.4.4) (in Herodotus, Cambyses is a noble Persian, but the Persians themselves are considered less distinguished than the Medes: Hdt. 1.107.2). Astyages then plans to kill her baby, and Harpagus is given the baby to expose. Harpagus, afraid of what the king's daughter may do to him, hands the baby over to a herdsman to expose. The herdsman's wife, who also has just had a baby, persuades him to bring the baby to her, and she is so taken with the child that she tells her husband to expose their own child (Justin 1.4.5-14). In Herodotus, on the other hand, the herdsman's baby is stillborn and so is an easy substitute for the live one (Hdt. 1.112.2-3). The switch of the live babies in Justin adds a rather cruel twist to the story and allows Justin to comment on the workings of fate (*fortuna*).

Trogus/Justin then follows the Herodotean account closely, until he introduces Sybares, and in the war against Astyages brings in other material which we know from the 'Ctesian' more extended account found in Nicolaus of Damascus. In all three stories (Herodotus, Ctesias and Justin) Astyages' life is spared by Cyrus, although in Ctesias (now through Photius' summary), Cyrus marries Astyages' daughter after killing her husband (F 9.1), and in Justin, Astyages is made ruler over the Hyrcanians (Justin 1.6.16). Justin is working here outside the traditions of both Herodotus and Ctesias, so may have had access to another tradition which may have already integrated the two Greek traditions. As for Cyrus' death, Justin follows more nearly the Herodotean story of the war against the Massagetae, although in Justin Tamyris (not Tomyris) is the queen of the Scythians (not the Massagetae) and her son is killed by Cyrus (Justin 1.8.8), whereas in Herodotus, he is taken prisoner, but then commits suicide (Hdt. 211-13). In Justin, Tamyris tricks Cyrus (she pretends to retreat, but lures him into a narrow pass and ambushes Cyrus and his army: 8.8.10-11),[43] whereas in Herodotus, the Massagetae are simply stronger than the Persians: they originally fought at a distance with bows and arrows, but then rushed at each other and fought with spears and daggers until eventually the Massagetae prevailed (Hdt. 1.214.2). Frontinus (first century CE) also refers to the story of the ambush (*Stratagems* 2.5.5), which may indicate that this was originally in Trogus. The innovation of the ambush was to have important implications for later versions of the story.

Nevertheless, for Justin, Cyrus is a great man. He concludes his story of Cyrus and Tamyris by saying that throughout the whole of his life, Cyrus was 'wonderfully distinguished' (*admirabiliter insignis*) (Justin 1.8.14). Tamyris, however, is unwomanly in her lack of fear at the approaching enemy (Justin 1.8.2), is willing to use vengeance rather than tears to assuage her grief at the loss of her army and the death of her son (Justin 1.8.9) and completely overcomes Cyrus and his army (Justin 1.8.10-12, 37.3.2). Although Herodotus himself is elsewhere interested in unwomanly women (e.g. Artemisia in Book 8), his focus is more on Cyrus and his arrogance, and his failure to analyse advice and to interpret dreams correctly (Hdt. 1.205-10). For Justin, by contrast, the importance of Cyrus seems to lie in the fact that he was the founder of the Persian empire, the successor empire to the Assyrians and Medes, but himself was completely overcome (the great man overthrown by an equally ruthless 'unwomanly' woman).

Orosius in his work was also following Justin's narrative, and sometimes includes passages copied verbatim. Nevertheless, Orosius' whole purpose differed from that of Trogus/Justin which affected not only how he organised the material, but also what he selected. Orosius claims that his task is to provide the history of the world ('from the beginning of the world to the present day', in order to demonstrate the 'boastful wickedness' (*uaniloqua prauitas*) of men: Preface 9-10, 7.43.19). As we have seen in the previous chapter, Cyrus therefore is an important pagan figure in 'world' history,[44] and Orosius' main interest in Cyrus turns around his role as the conqueror of Babylon, although immediately afterwards, he himself is overcome by Thamyris (sic), Queen of the Scythians, in a version which emphasises her cunning in revenge and his arrogance (2.7.4). Despite the long tradition of Cyrus as an ideal king, who is often contrasted in Greek and Roman authors with the wicked Phalaris of Acragas (cf. 1.20.1, where Orosius synchronises the two),[45] Orosius' Cyrus is exemplary for his wickedness.

Cyrus and the Exemplary Tradition

Cyrus, as an exemplary figure, was an object of interest who combined in his very name all the exemplary traditions about him. In his book about exemplarity in the Renaissance, Timothy Hampton says: 'The reader who comes upon the name of a heroic ancient exemplar in a text has come upon a single sign which contains within it the entire history of the hero's deeds, the whole string of great moments which made the name a marked sign in the first place'.[46] In a slightly different way, Rebecca Langlands (discussing exemplarity at Rome) talks about 'sites of exemplarity', which, she says, are 'part of the field of reference to which a reader or listener has recourse when they encounter an allusion to a particular exemplary figure ...' which '... would describe the entirety of communal knowledge and memory about that figure and his life'.[47] Thus, for Valerius Maximus, 'Cyrus' is both the Cyrus of Herodotus *and* the Cyrus of the *Cyropaedia*: Valerius notes it as a mark of good leadership that Cyrus learned all the names of his soldiers (8.7ext. 16; cf. Xen. *Cyrop.* 5.3.46), but he also knows about the Cyrus of Herodotus (1.7ext. 5), who survived despite the machinations of Astyages (thus demonstrating the workings of fate: *invictae fatorum necessitatis*). By the same token, Trogus/Justin is justified in combining the stories of Herodotus and Ctesias (or an intermediary) because together they form a single exemplary landscape, a 'site of exemplarity'. In fact, Langlands discusses how 'sites of exemplarity' become multilayered so that no single version can take priority over the others: '... there is no Ur-story, only various remediations, so more influential than some, which constitute a site of memory'.[48]

The stories about Cyrus had resonances in the late empire and early medieval period principally through these related strands, but, although Herodotus was known in the fifth century, he was rarely read, especially as a complete text.[49] For example, the fifth-century CE Sidonius Apollinaris, who is prepared to comment on Herodotus' style (*Carmen* 23.135), refers in a slightly garbled form to the story of Cyrus' birth (suckled by a dog) and death (the ambush) as preserved in Justin rather than Herodotus (*Carmen* 9.30-7).

Nevertheless, Herodotus' influence in the Roman world and the Latin West was extensive and influenced the importance of the stories about Cyrus (especially about his death) in the early medieval period. For example, while he condemns Herodotus for his anti-Boeotian sentiments, Plutarch in the second century CE commends the Cyrus of Herodotus as an ideal ruler (Plut. *On the Malice of Herodotus* 18). The Cyrus of Herodotus was also known to Lucian in the second/third century CE, who makes use of the stories of the meeting of Croesus and Solon, Croesus on the pyre, and the death of Cyrus at the hands of Tomyris in his satirical dialogue *Charon* (13). The fourth-/fifth-century CE Boethius also makes reference to Croesus on Cyrus' pyre (*Consolation of Philosophy*, 2.P2), so may also have had access to Herodotus' text,[50] especially since Justin does not provide the story at least in a version which includes the pyre (although of course Trogus, of whose work Justin's is a summary, might have done). On the other hand, while Boccaccio almost certainly used Justin for his biography of Astyages (Boccaccio follows Justin quite closely), his biography of Croesus is probably patched together from a variety of Latin sources (including Boethius),[51] although not Valerius Maximus. For him, Croesus is important as someone who is overcome by fate as foretold in a dream (Val. Max. 1.7ext. 4).

Another important influence in the Roman world was the 'historical' works in Latin, which we discussed earlier, and which survived the fall of the Roman empire to be picked up and disseminated in the ninth and tenth centuries (even if by rather circuitous routes). The Justinian/Orosian remediations, which, although very different kinds of texts, could be bound together in one volume in the medieval western world.[52]

Nevertheless, a memory of Xenophon's Cyrus was retained, although not directly. The educational and political interests and priorities of the elite after the fall of the western Roman empire meant that Greek texts were generally lost, and even the circulation of Latin texts, including Cicero, was severely limited until at least the Carolingian revival of the ninth century, when especially Cicero's philosophical works and the letters, including his *De senectute*, were being circulated again in Carolingian Europe.[53] Furthermore, a large number of Greek texts were known and survived in Constantinople, at least until the fall of the city in 1453: Photius read Herodotus, as well as Ctesias, Xenophon and the Attic orators including Isocrates; Lascaris famously said that he saw a complete copy of Diodorus Siculus in the imperial library in Constantinople in 1453 before the sacking of the city.[54] Nevertheless, through Cicero, there was an awareness of Xenophon's Cyrus at least in general terms in the medieval period and early renaissance; *De senectute*, for example, was translated into French by Laurent de Premierfait in 1405.[55] Although this could not have had much substance until the reintroduction of Xenophon's Greek manuscripts of the *Cyropaedia* in the 1420s,[56] and its translation into Latin, it is astonishing how quickly Xenophon's Cyrus developed his own philosophical importance in not only the political philosophy of Machiavelli, but also more widely in European thinking upon kingship.[57] However, reflections on the exemplarity of Cyrus necessarily bring us back to the exemplary importance of others in the cast of characters around him, and especially the moral focus on the woman who did not cry for her son, but sought vengeance instead.

The Exemplarity of Tomyris

Stories of Cyrus were also known throughout the Hellenistic, Roman and medieval periods through biographies. Although the roots of biographical writing can be traced in Greece as far as the fifth century BCE (and probably then ultimately to the pseudo-autobiographies of the Near East), from at least the first century BCE, if not before, in Roman intellectual circles, it became fashionable to collect short biographies of famous Greek and Roman men as exemplary figures for their fame, skill and moral virtue. Thus, Varro wrote the now-lost *Hebdomades uel de imaginibus libri XV* (cf. Pliny, *Natural Histories* 35.2; Aulus Gellius 3.10), short epigrams to accompany 700 portraits of Greeks and Romans. Nepos wrote an *On Famous Men*, of which *On Eminent Commanders of Foreign Nations*, and two lives of *On the Latin Historians* are extant, as well as a book of *Exempla*, known from Aulus Gellius (6.18.11). The emperor Augustus himself lined his Forum with 100 statues of the 'Greatest Men' (*summi uiri*), each of which was accompanied with an inscription detailing the reasons for their great-ness, which he defined by military prowess.[58]

In subsequent centuries, Valerius Maximus wrote his *Factorum ac dicto-rum memorabilium libri IX* in the first century CE. Suetonius in the first/sec-ond century CE, as well as the extant *On the Life of the Caesars*, wrote the only partially preserved *On Famous Men* which included lives of grammari-ans, orators, poets and historians. Plutarch, at around the same time, wrote in Greek his *Parallel Lives*. He thought that in the writing of the lives of men, he was trying with history, as in a mirror, somehow to adorn his life and make it conform to their virtues (*Aem.* 1.1; cf. *Alex.* 1.2). This taste for lists of famous men continued in a new form into the late Roman and Christian period; in the fourth century, an *On Famous Men* was attributed to Aurelius Victor, and Jerome also wrote an *On Famous Men*, which rather than great men from the Greek and Roman past was a compendium of church fathers and saints, which was later continued by Gennadius of Massilia.

Cyrus features in some of these lists. However, interestingly, it is often other characters in the stories about Cyrus around which these biographical notes are focalised. For example, Valerius Maximus recounts the story of Cyrus' birth, but his interest is just as much in Astyages' inability to prevent Cyrus' rise to power as that Cyrus' fate was preordained by means of a dream (1.7ex 5). When Valerius recounts Cyrus' death, his interest is in the vengeance of the queen, Tomyris (9.10ex. 1). In the influential medieval works of Boccaccio, *On the Fates of Famous Men* (*De casibus virorum illustrium*) and *On Famous Women* (*De mulieribus claris*), Cyrus appears most promi-nently in the stories of others: Astyages, Croesus and Tomyris. Thus, Cyrus himself becomes the object of others' interest, not an object of interest in his own right. In particular, it is the negative exemplary quality of Tomyris which comes into sharpest focus in the art and literature of the fourteenth and fifteenth centuries, and the struggle over the power of women, in what has come to be called 'the power of women topos', where strong men are represented as being overcome by women, a generally misogynist trope to demonstrate the dangers of women.[59]

In fact, just as there were catalogues of famous men, so there were also compilations of the lives of famous women. There had been a long Greek tradition of recording the lives of women, both outrightly mythological and historical, and the various points in between. The sixth-century BCE *Catalogue of Women* was a genealogy of the Hellenes framed around the sto-ries of heroines.[60] Plutarch, in the second century CE, wrote a work on the deeds of famous women, *On the Virtues of Women*, but the genre was wide-spread: Sopater of Syrian Apamea (fourth century CE) in his *Selection of Histories* (Suda *s.v.* Σ 845, cf. 848) noted that there were a number of collec-tions on the deeds of women (Photius 161),[61] which probably were Hellenistic in date, as was the anonymous *Treatise on Women Distinguished in War* (*Tractatus de mulieribus claris in bello*).[62] Ovid's *The Heroines* (*Heroides*) was based upon this catalogue tradition as was Juvenal's sixth *Satire*.

Polyaenus in the second century CE also wrote paradoxographical chapters on women (the 'wonder' of women of military skill) in his *Strategies* (esp. Book 8), and Valerius Maximus includes exemplary women.

Many of these stories had their roots in Herodotus, who showed a deep interest in strong, vengeful, and often also violent, women (e.g., the Assyrian Semiramis, Nitocris, the wife of the Lydian Candaules, Pheretime of Cyrene, Artemisia of Halicarnassus and Amestris the wife Xerxes). Although only Semiramis of Assyria, about whom there were other stories of her building works and military campaigns (Diod. 2.4.2-20.5 [= Ctesias F 1b§5.1-20.3], noting esp. 2.6.2), Candaules' wife and Tomyris, queen of the Massagetae, are retained in Trogus/Justin, other Herodotean women, Argeia, Nitocris the Egyptian, Nitocris the Babylonian, Pheretime and Artemisia are included, for example, in the *Treatises on Women Famous in War*,[63] Polyaenus (earlier) and the fourth-century CE emperor Julian (*Oration* 3.127a-b).

In the anonymous *Treatises on Women Famous in War* (probably Hellenistic in date),[64] Tomyris is undoubtedly the Massagetan queen of Herodotus, whose captured son committed suicide, and who mutilated the corpse of Cyrus in revenge (Gera, *De mulieribus*. 9-10 (no. 12)). One of the striking things about this list of famous women, however, is that, while not all show their qualities through war, they are all queens. Gera says of them: 'All the women show initiative of some kind, and they generally display their intelligence and courage in the public arena, be it political, civic or military. Their chief interest lies in power: the allocation, preservation or establishment of political sovereignty'.[65]

That they had military characteristics is important. In the Greek world, at least, women ideologically did not take part in war (note Hector's words to Andromache in the *Iliad*: '... go to the house and take up your work, the loom and distaff, and tell your servants to set themselves to their work; war is the work for all men, who are Ilium-born, but especially for me' (486–93)), nevertheless, 'glory in war' was also ideologically entrenched, and women were involved in not only encouraging their sons to fight bravely, but could, especially if they were queens, also take to the battlefield as well.[66] Probably, one of the most famous historical warrior queens of the Greek world was Olympias of Macedon (who went to war on behalf of her grandson, the posthumous child of Alexander the Great), but there were others, including Artemisia of Halicarnassus and Pheretime of Cyrene,[67] who also interested Herodotus and others; both Artemisia and Pheretime are included, together with Tomyris, in *Treatises of Famous Women* (Pheretime (no. 10); Artemisia (13)).

Nevertheless, these lists of women were also thought to be paradoxographical, that is outside the range of the normal.[68] In the *Treatise on Famous Women*, the emphasis in the Tomyris vignette is Tomyris' vengefulness at the death of her son but does not include Herodotus' details of Cyrus' trickery or her bag of blood. The first-century teacher of rhetoric, Theon, proposes that if it were desirable to decide whether either the 'race' (*genos*) of men or of women were more brave, then it would be necessary to compare the most brave man to the most brave woman (*Progymnasmata* 114.13-19), which then leads him to compare Tomyris (as the most brave of women) to Cyrus (the most brave of men), and he judges that Tomyris is braver (*andreiotera*) than Cyrus (although he concludes that there are not enough brave women in proportion to men to mean that the *genos* of women is braver than the *genos* of men: 114.30-115.6). Interestingly, Theon had access to both Herodotus' text and Ctesias', as he uses Sparethra wife of Amorges and queen of the Sacae, as another example of a woman who is better than Cyrus (115.1-2), so that Cyrus becomes a king who has been twice beaten by women!

Other stories develop the Massagetan queen's actions in different ways. Polyaenus, in his list of female warriors, focalises his story through Tomyris, and gives her agency, and luring Cyrus' soldiers towards her camp, they discover wine and food and so indulge themselves so that Tomyris is able to kill them in their drunken sleep (8.28). In Herodotus, as we have seen, Tomyris is a wise adviser and a noble queen, who is able to see through Cyrus' deception but does not use trickery herself. Gera says that in the later accounts where Tomyris is herself cast as a deceiver, the queen's character is being refashioned and diminished.[69] However, in a sense, it is not Tomyris' character that matters, but her queenly power.

In the Roman exemplary tradition, Tomyris (like other powerful women) was easier to understand and handle if she did not hold the moral high ground and could be placed on a level with Cyrus, as a ruler in a world where one of the major questions was how did one live under a king: he was cruel and deceptive, but so was she. In this context, powerful women (and their masculinity that was therefore implied) were a problem that fascinated ancient and medieval thinkers. Herodotus, although apparently admiring of her, has Xerxes say of Artemisia, queen of Halicarnassus, during battle Salamis: 'My men have become women, and my women men' (Hdt. 8.88.3). Likewise, even though it is Tomyris' maternal qualities that Herodotus' ascribes to her desire for revenge, that is not how she moves through the Roman period. As we have seen for Trogus/Justin, she too is defeminised: she is a fierce, vengeful and tearless woman.

The tradition of lists of exemplary famous men and famous women continued in the medieval period/early Renaissance.[70] A full study of all these lists would be outside the scope of this study (Tomyris became a staple figure of lists of 'worthy women'), but it is still useful to explore two further examples which show how the Tomyris myth was adapted to problematise her exemplary character, and so the understanding of the role of women (and especially queens) in medieval society. The first of these is the Tomyris biography of the influential Italian humanist of the fourteenth century, Giovanni Boccaccio, and the second is the biography of the Italian-born French writer of the early fifteenth century, Christine de Pizan.

In the fourteenth century, Boccaccio wrote two important texts on famous men and famous women: *On the Fates of Famous Men* (*De casibus virorum illustrium*) and *On Famous Women* (*De mulieribus claris*).[71] As we have already noted, Cyrus does appear in his book on famous men but is not given his own biography, although he is included in the biographies of Astyages and Croesus, even though Boccaccio's interest is in great kings who have come to bad ends. Boccaccio does allude to the story of Cyrus and Tamiris (sic) in *De casibus* (2.21), but defers a full treatment until *On Famous Women* (*OFW*), written in about 1360 CE, as the victim of Tomyris/ Tamyris/Thamiris.[72]

Here both Cyrus and Tamyris are very much the figures of the Roman tradition, and Boccaccio (Chapter 49) relies heavily on Justin (1.8) for the plot of the biography:[73] Tamyris is not frightened of Cyrus, and allows him to cross the river (*OFW* 49.3; Justin 1.8.2); Cyrus then pretends to withdraw in fear and leaves wine and food in the camp and Tamyris sends her son with an army in pursuit (*OFW* 49.4; Justin 1.8.4-5); Tamyris' son and his army enjoy the feast and were killed in their sleep (*OFW* 49.5; Justin 6-9); Tamyris grieves for her son, although she restrains her tears and instead seeks vengeance, pretending to flee but instead ambushing Cyrus and his army and killing them (*OFW* 49.6; Justin 1.8.9-12); Tamyris has Cyrus' head cut off which she puts in a bag of human blood (*OFW* 49.7; Justin 1.8.13).[74]

There are some important differences, however, between Boccaccio's treatment of Tamyris and Cyrus and that of Justin. Boccaccio's story is more abbreviated than Justin's but it is also sharper in tone. For example, Boccaccio describes the Scythians as 'fierce' and 'invincible', although their country is also 'poor' and 'wild' (*OFW* 49.1-2). Tamyris herself is a 'clever woman' (*sagax femina*) (*OFW* 49.3), whose 'anger and lust for vengeance' (*ira et vindicate cupiditas*) made her restrain her tears on the death of her son. Even though Boccaccio says that Cyrus' death satisfied her anger (*OFW* 49.6), it was 'by an engulfing passion' (*efferato animo*) that she had his corpse found and decapitated (*OFW* 49.7). Cyrus, on the other hand, attacked the Scythians because of his need to augment his own glory rather than extend his kingdom (*OFW* 49.2).[75] While for Justin, Cyrus is a great man (*admirabiliter insignis*), Boccaccio ends his biography of Tamyris by saying: 'What can we say further? We have this deed of Thamiris, nothing more, as famous as Cyrus' empire was great' (*OFW* 49.7).

It is the combination of Tamyris' masculine qualities and her ability and willingness to combine civic responsibility with her maternal responsibilities that Boccaccio seems to admire.[76] Boccaccio says that he has dedicated *On Famous Women* to Andrea Acciaiuoli of Florence because her name contains within it the signal of what he considers the greatest virtues, the Greek word for 'men', *andres* (Dedication 5), and he commends its stories of famous women (even the pagan ones) to her as an encouragement to pursue these virtues. This preface has sometimes been taken to mean that Boccaccio is taking the normal misogynist position of the medieval world. However, there is ambiguity in Boccaccio's treatment of Tamyris and Cyrus, which seems to complicate a straightforward misogynist reading of her, in particular. She is clever but cunning and, while not giving in to tears at the death of her son, she is overwhelmed by her emotion at his death, which leads her to have Cyrus decapitated. However, she also shows no fear and her anger is justified. Cyrus, on the other hand, lusts for glory, and in that way, brought about his own downfall, tellingly 'perhaps so that Thamiris might be more famous' (*OFW* 49.2). So, the great man might be great, but she has the greatest glory, not just in defeating him and cutting off his head, but in having the greater fame. Does that make her a figure for women to emulate or men to fear?[77]

For Christine de Pizan, the Italian-born, French writer of the early fifteenth century, however, there is no such ambiguity. In her *Le livre de la cité des dames*, written c. 1405, Tomyris, now Thomyris, has an important place. She is now a queen of the Amazons, and her soldiers are Amazon women. In the early medieval period, the Amazons had an ambivalent reputation. The tradition about the Amazons which found its way into medieval Europe was through the negative treatment of Justin. For him (2.4), the Amazons were warrior women, who, having lost their husbands in war, decided to set up their own constitution (*res publica*) without men, and so killed all their husbands who had not died in the war. To maintain their race, they had children with men of neighbouring nations (although refusing to marry them), but killed any boys that were born and brought up the girls to fight, look after horses and hunt. Justin also tells the story of the early Amazon queens, including the slaughter of the Amazons, and the capture of Hippolyta by Theseus and the death of Penthesilea against the Greeks at Troy. Boccaccio uses Justin's account of the Amazons on more than one occasion, which was influential also on the visual arts of the period.[78]

Christine de Pizan, on the other hand, transforms the Amazon narrative to take the story of Tomyris/Thomyris, which she tells us she has used before, to a new level (*La cité des dames* 26-7). The Amazons are no longer infanticides of boy babies, who they now send to their fathers to bring up (26). Thomyris herself is wise (*sage*), noble (*noble*) and valiant (*vaillante*), and defeats Cyrus through cunning, strength and intelligence. She hears that Cyrus is coming to her land to bring it under his control, Cyrus who has vanquished Babylon the Great. Realising that she would need to defeat him by cunning, she arms the Amazons and sends them to set up ambushes at strategic points in the mountains through which Cyrus and his army would have to pass. Cyrus is taken by surprise. Most of Cyrus' army is killed except Cyrus and his barons, who are captured, and she orders them to be brought to her. It is only at this point we are told that Cyrus had killed one of her beloved sons whom she had previously sent to him: was he then the boy's father? Did he (rather than the Amazon queen) kill his own son? For this reason, she has all his barons decapitated in front of him. She then has him decapitated also and throws his head into a barrel filled with the blood of his barons. That Lydgate's fifteenth-century translation of Boccaccio also has a barrel of blood into which Cyrus' dismembered body is thrown again suggests the complex ways in which images and stories can also interact and

Figure 6.2 Cyrus' dismembered body floating in a tub of blood; illuminated manuscript from Lydgate's fifteenth-century *Fall of Princes*, a translation
into English of Laurent de Premierfait's second French translation of
Boccaccio. © The British Library Board (Harley 1766, f135).

influence each other (see Figure 6.2), just as we have already seen could be
the case for oral and written traditions.

There is no doubt here that Cyrus, a great king, has been overcome by
a greater woman. But there is perhaps in Christine's story of Cyrus and
Tomyris/Thomyris, as in Herodotus', another strand, although they play
themselves out in rather different ways. In earlier chapters, we talked about
Cyrus as the 'stranger-king', who marries the princess (or is the son of the
princess) and so acquires the kingdom. This is the initial 'trick' in Herodotus'
story, which Tomyris sees through, when she refuses Cyrus' original offer of
marriage because 'she realised that it was not her he was courting but the
kingdom of the Massagetae' (Hdt. 1.205.1). In *La cité des dames*, it appears
that not only has he killed her son, but he also has come for her kingdom

as her previous lover and the father of her child which she had sent to him to bring up. The transgressive nature of the 'stranger-king' in this context becomes even more transgressive and threatening. By the same token, her stature as an Amazon queen is even greater. She has not only defeated a conquering king. She has seen off the threat of the 'stranger-king'.

Cyrus' Women

In a book that has been an exploration of ancient kingship, as much as it has been about Cyrus (II), it seems appropriate to finish this discussion of the reception of the life of Cyrus with Tomyris, a queen. We actually know very little about Cyrus' women. He was married to the Achaemenid Casandane, who was probably the mother of the sons who may have fought a contest for the succession (Hdt. 2.1.1, 3.2.2, 3.1). She probably died at Babylon (the *Nabonidus Chronicle* says that one of his wives died soon after the taking of Babylon and that Cyrus ordered public mourning for her from 21st–26th March, 538: *ABC* 7 iii.23-4). Herodotus tells us that he loved her, and when she died, he mourned her (Hdt. 2.1.1). Of course, Amytis could also have been his wife (Ctesias F 9.1).

It is difficult to understand fully Cassandane's part in Cyrus' kingship. Waters argues that it was this marriage which helped promote Cyrus' interests in Fars.[79] This may be the case, at least insofar as the marriage may have been a strategy to settle rivalries between tribal chiefly elite, of the kind suggested by Flannery.[80] By the same token, it could equally be argued that this marriage promoted *Darius'* and the *Achaemenid's* interests, of which they were later able to take advantage. Although the Achaemenids obviously were an elite family (Hystaspes was almost certainly an important member of Cyrus' army and administration: Hdt. 1.209-10; cf. DB §1-2, 35-6), there are indications (for example, from the Cyrus' seal discussed in earlier chapters – PFS 93*) that Cyrus' family was already an important one, and probably a chiefly one, among the tribal nomads of the southwest Zagros (although that does not preclude the possibility that Darius' family was also a nomadic chiefly family and that the two families vied with each other for supremacy).

At least Cyrus' daughters were worth bringing into the courts of his successors to establish their positions. Atossa, his daughter, so well known in Greek literature, was not only the daughter of Cyrus, but also the wife of Cambyses, Smerdis/Bardiya and Darius (Hdt. 3.88.2); Darius 'favourite' wife (according to Herodotus: 7.69.2) was another daughter of Cyrus, Artystone, who we know from the Persepolis Fortification Tablets as Irtashduna, also had access to independent estates.[81] Both these women (Atossa and Artystone) may not have been as powerful as the Greek sources suggest, but the experience of one and the resources of the other would have in any case made them significant players at the court of Darius, especially in the demonstration of his kingship.

But women at the court held a special place. In attempting to theorise the position of women at medieval European royal courts and their relationship to power and sovereignty, Fradenburg has argued for the 'in-betweenness' of queens, especially in terms of gender definitions, and that queens by their nature were neither exclusively masculine nor feminine, in the actual negotiations of functions caused by the exclusiveness of sovereignty.[82] If we return to our opening chapter where we talked about the exceptional, metahuman, status of the king (where he has his own 'in-betweenness'), we can see how the position of the queen (or queens) also becomes even more ambivalent and difficult, and probably harder to pin down, especially if as the wives of stranger-kings, they pass sovereignty on to their husbands. They not only are wives, but also are intimately connected with the production of sons, who will also (hopefully) become kings themselves. It is no wonder that Tomyris as a queen (who, Herodotus says, through the death of her husband acquired sovereignty), remained such an object of fascination. Of course, it is the issue of her biological gender and her maternity, combined with her sovereignty, that both Herodotus, and later Christine de Pizan, are trying to solve. Herodotus' Tomyris is a very regal and clever queen, who takes away Cyrus' sovereignty in fact, and metaphorically, by cutting off his head. As a queen, Tomyris is the perfect match for Cyrus and is indeed more than his equal. So, the evolving stories of Cyrus and his kingship finally come to be about her and her queenship. Although she was almost certainly a mythical figure, by means of the interest in her story through centuries, she takes on the monumentality of a historical queen.

Notes

1. McEwan (1984), 12 (no. 123): 19/08/9.
2. For doubts about the historicity of this ceremony: de Jong (2010), 545–7.
3. This act possibly qualifies any claims beyond simple pragmatism regarding Alexander's alleged reverence for Cyrus.
4. Badian (1996/2012).
5. Stronach (1978), 6; R. Schmitt (1988), 18–25; Stronach (1990b). There have been some ingenious solutions to the problem of the missing inscription, for example, that the inscription was on a stele beside the tomb.
6. On questions surrounding the location of the Massagetae, see R. Schmitt (2018).
7. One wonders whether these are 'meaningful' names? Tomyris (in Greek), 'she who cuts', and her 'baby'. Beckman (2018, 5), while agreeing that they are probably invented names, thinks they are Iranian, as does R. Schmitt (2003, 26–7, cf. 21–2), although he also struggles with deciding on what a putative Iranian root might be.
8. This is presumably the mares' milk drunk by the Scythians: Hdt. 4.2.
9. Felton (2014).
10. The mother in question must be Amytis (cf. Ctesias F 13.9), although she is unlikely to have been the mother of Cambyses and Tanyoxarces/Tanaoxares/Smerdis/Bardiya. Herodotus says their mother was Casandane, daughter of the Achaemenid, Pharnaspes (2.1.1, 3.2.2, 3.1), father also of Otanes, one of

the seven conspirators in the coup which saw Darius take the throne (Hdt. 3.68.1). The *Nabonidus Chronicle* also says that Cyrus' wife died in 538 (*ABC* 7 iii.22–4). That Cyrus may have practised polygamy is unproblematic: see Brosius (1996), 35–7. Even in the classical period, Greek ruling families were often also polygamous: Mitchell (2013a), 100–5.

11. E.g. Briant (2002), 49.
12. See Immerwahr (1966), 148–88.
13. Chapter 3.
14. H. Sancisi-Weerdenburg (1985), 466.
15. Strabo, however, thinks that all the people to the east of the Caspian have the general name of Scythian, including the Massagetae: 11.8.2.
16. See Payen (1991). See also Gera (1997), 190.
17. For the complex interactions of Herodotus' two views of Cyrus: Avery (1979), who argues for a Cyrus of virtues and a Cyrus of vices.
18. For Solon's advice to Croesus about looking to the end, see Pelling (2006), 146–7.
19. Cf. Gera (1997), 194–5.
20. Cf. Gera (1997), 193–4.
21. Pelling (2006), 171–2.
22. For the inversion of Persian education: Kurke (1989), 539.
23. Krentz (2000) shows that trickery, while ideologically considered dishonourable, regularly featured in Greek warfare.
24. Herodotus does not say explicitly that Tomyris decapitated Cyrus, but it is almost certainly implied, especially in comparison with Hdt. 9.78.3–79.1, where *lumainesthai nekrōi* does refer to the mutilation of a corpse by decapitation. Certainly, the imagery of 'shoving his head in an *askos*' probably only works if his head has been removed from his body. This was what was understood by Justin (1.8.13) and Orosius (1.7.6). Is Tomyris a 'cutter' (see n. 7)? On *askoi*, see Lissarrague (1990), 68–76.
25. Compare, e.g., Pheretime of Cyrene, who takes vengeance on the people of Barce for the assassination of her son, Arcesilas (4.162, 165, 200–5); Amestris, the wife of Xerxes, who mutilated the wife of Masistes, Xerxes' brother, after Xerxes had an affair with their daughter (Hdt. 9.108–113).
26. Gera (1997), 187–204.
27. Kucewicz (2016).
28. Asheri, in Asheri *et al.* (2007), 212.
29. On Antisthenes in the Socratic tradition, see recently Atack (2020), 94–6.
30. On the 'monarch in democracy', see L. Mitchell (2008); L. Mitchell (2013), 156–63; L. Mitchell (2019).
31. Freedom in Herodotus was generally regarded as the absence of slavery: L. Mitchell (2014).
32. Baragwanath (2015).
33. Compare Aristotle in the *Politics* who also places weight on the willingness of obedience in relationship to *basileia* ('kingship') and *tyrannis*: 3.1285a25–29, 4.1313a3–11.
34. See also Currie (2005), 176–178, who observes there was in Greek thought a 'sliding scale' between men and gods, and men could become gods through an abundance of *aretē* (cf. Arist. *Nic. Eth.* 7.1145a18–25).
35. See Page (ed.) (1981), 211–13.
36. See in particular Langlands (2015); Langlands (2018); Rowler (2018).
37. See Hampton (1990).
38. E.g., *De Divinatione* 1.121 (Cicero recounts Herodotus' story of Croesus' son foretelling the overthrow of Croesus' empire: Hdt. 1.85); *Tusculan Disputations* 1.47 (Cicero recounts the story of Cleobis and Biton: Hdt. 1.31); Racine

(2016) argues that Cicero probably knew Herodotus Book 1 most thoroughly, although Fleck (1993) has shown that even then he sometimes approaches the text through intermediaries.

39. See generally Powell (1988); see also Cole (2014), 167. Other references to the *Cyropaedia* in Cicero include: *De legibus* 2.56; *Brutus* 112 (cf. 132); *De finibus* 2.92; *Tusculan Disputations* 5.99.
40. On the possible dates for Justin and the relationship to Pompeius Trogus' *Philippic History*, see Develin (1994), 3–10.
41. In Ctesias, Cyrus' henchman is Oebaras: see further Chapter 3.
42. Swain (1940); cf. Haubold (2013), 78–98, who argues for the Near Eastern origins of the 'succession of empires', against Momigliano (1994).
43. Frontinus (first century CE) includes this version (2.5.5), which may indicate that this was originally in Trogus.
44. Orosius only picks up the Cyrus story with the overthrow of his grandfather Astyages (1.19.4–11), although he does include the detail that Cyrus, though Astyages' grandson, was born in Persia and the story of Harpagus (in Orosius, he becomes Harpalus) to whom Astyages served up his son at a feast. Cyrus takes the kingdom of his grandfather in battle, although (following Justin) he places him in charge over the Hyrcanians (1.19.10). For the suggestion of 'universalism' as a rhetorical trope in Orosius, see van Nuffelen (2012), 171–6.
45. Cicero couples together Cyrus and Phalaris of Acragas as examples of good and bad kings (*Republic* 1.43.4). Plutarch (*Precepts of State-craft*, 821e) couples Cyrus and Phalaris, where the implied contrast is between bad and good kingship, as does Dio Chrysostom (*Orations* 2.76–77) as part of a more extended discussion of good (Cyrus) and bad (Phalaris) rulers.
46. Hampton (1990), 25.
47. Langlands (2018), 173–4.
48. Langlands (2018), 178.
49. Racine (2016); Bruce (2019).
50. Cf. Moorhead (2009), 15. The fourth-century CE Ammianus Marcellinus muddles the details: 23.6.7 (he has Cyrus crossing the Bosporus to meet Tomyris).
51. Law (1948), 461–2.
52. Mortensen (1990). The earliest medieval manuscripts of Justin come from Northumbria, from the eighth century CE, probably from the library of Alcuin, who listed both Justin and Orosius among his books in the York Poem, and who later held a prominent place at the court of Charlemagne. Alcuin's York Poem: Godman (ed.), (1983); Lapidge (2001), 105–12; Alcuin's library: M. Garrison (2011). For the eighth-century manuscripts of Justin, see Reynolds (1983), 197–99; Crick (1987).
53. Reynolds (1983), xvi-xviii, xxviii, xxxiii, cf. 116–24.
54. N.G. Wilson (2017), 220 n. 4.
55. See Hedeman (2008), 14–16.
56. Sabbadini, (1905–14), vol. 1, 48.
57. E.g., Newell (2013); Grogan (2014), 32–69.
58. On Augustus' *summi uiri*, see e.g., Geiger (2008); Shaya (2013); Rowler (2018), 116–18.
59. See e.g. S.L. Smith (1995); Ainsworth and Waterman (2013).
60. For the date: M.L. West (1985), 168–71.
61. The Suda makes a distinction between two different men called Sopater of Apamea, but see Wheeler (2010), 18.
62. Gera (1997).
63. For Semiramis and Pheretime, however, the *Tractatus de mulieribus* is drawing on Ctesias and Menecles, the author of a Libyan history, respectively.
64. Gera (1997), 29–30.

65. Gera (1997), 12.
66. See L. Mitchell (2020b).
67. L. Mitchell (2012). On Olympias, see: Carney (2000), esp. 85–8; Carney (2006), esp. 71–85.
68. See Morton (2010), 123–5 on paradoxography, and collections of wondrous women.
69. Gera (1997), 197–8.
70. McMillan (1979).
71. Boccaccio says in the Preface of *OFW* that he was the first to compile such a list of famous women (3), and is seemingly unaware of the ancient tradition.
72. Boccaccio calls her both Tamyris and Thamiris.
73. Boccaccio, however, includes the 'Herodotean' detail that Tamyris was a widow, which is not included in either Justin or Valerius Maximus: Franklin (2006), 90–1.
74. Orosius also follows Justin quite closely but there are differences between Justin and Orosius at points in the story where Justin and Boccaccio are quite similar.
75. See Franklin (2006), 8: although the comment is directed at Boccaccio's women, Franklin argues that for Boccaccio '... power assumed as a matter of duty is legitimate, while that acquired through personal ambition is not'.
76. Franklin (2006), 90–1. Franklin also argues that the work, written in Latin rather than the vernacular, was aimed at a male elite audience: 27–9.
77. Kolsky (2003), 87–90.
78. Franklin (2010).
79. Waters (2022), 42–6.
80. Flannery (1999).
81. Hallock (1969), e.g. PF 1236, 1454, 1835–9, 1857; see also Brosius (1996), 125–7.
82. Fradenburg (1992).

7 Conclusion

Cyrus' life is told in many stories. He is the hero exposed at birth and the beggar boy who makes good. He is the cunning general who conquers the Medes, saves Croesus from the pyre and takes Babylon by means of a trick. He is defeated in battle by Scythian queens and decapitated by an Amazon. He is the destroyer of Babylon and its saviour. He is the refounder of cities and the liberator of the Israelites from their captivity. He is the cosmic warrior who is the instrument of Yahweh and walks beside Marduk. The *Umman-manda* and the Guti bow at his feet. Like Sargon and Naramsin, stories cluster around him, generated out of and given added meaning by a rich storytelling culture, which not only saw kings as heroic figures, but also saw the past, as told through stories, as a means of understanding the present and predicting the future.

For that reason, even though we have accounts of Cyrus' birth, deeds and death, we cannot easily fit these together to create a biography, a coherent story of a life. However, they do tell us important things about Near Eastern culture and especially about kingship, and something about Cyrus himself, his stature and importance, so that, despite the evident violence of his conquest, he was remembered positively. In some sense, the 'greatness' of his deeds justified them and allowed him to embody all the positive qualities of kingship: the king as a gardener, the king as a temple builder, the king as a shepherd and the king as a father.

It is surprising how little of the violence is remembered. He was an empire builder and in twenty years (from his defeat of Astyages to his death), he controlled territories (not necessarily contiguously) and routes from western Anatolia to at least Sogdiana and Bactria in the east. This was political control gained largely, if not entirely, through at least the threat of military force, certainly in western Anatolia and Babylonia, even if the story that he took Babylon itself without a battle is true. Of course, for some, he came as a deliverer (this was especially true of the Israelites), but not for all. Sardis suffered at his attack, and in regard to the Greeks of Asia Minor, he was prepared to enslave (or deport) any who dared to resist.

However, once military control was achieved, Cyrus seems to have moved very quickly to more conciliatory modes. As we have seen in

DOI: 10.4324/9781003384458-7

Chapter 4, governors were installed at Sardis and Babylon (and probably elsewhere), and, almost certainly revenues were collected. However, for that to happen, stability had quickly to be restored. It seems that, for the most part, pre-existing political and economic structures were maintained: the Ionians continued to meet at the Panionium (Hdt. 1.171.1-2) and the mint at Sardis continued to produce electrum Croesids.[1] It is striking that Cyrus appointed at Sardis a Lydian, Pactyes, to be in charge of the revenue (Hdt. 1.153.3), although he almost immediately rebelled. It appears, however, that Cyrus' preference was for appeasement, especially of the local elite. This also seems to have been Cambyses' policy in Egypt, as the inscription on the naophorous statue of Udjahorresnet seems to suggest.[2] Although there was a widespread rebellion at the beginning of Darius' reign as is evident from the inscription at Behistun, the new empire remained settled until 522 BCE.

One possible question that presents itself is the motivation for empire. The Assyrian kings imagined themselves as 'kings of the four quarters', their coronation ritual included a prayer that the king would extend the land, and part of the role of the king was to bring order to the chaos of the world.[3] Cyrus styled himself 'King of Countries' even before he took Babylon, and was later also to style himself 'king of the four quarters' on the *Cyrus Cylinder*. It looks at face value as if his motivation for empire was primarily economic, extending his control west to the Mediterranean and east to Bactria and Sogdiana, which was the source of precious metals and semi-precious stones: an inscription of Darius I from Susa mentions gold from Bactria and lapis lazuli and carnelian from Sogdiana (DSf §3h.35-40).

We know very little about Cyrus' religious beliefs. Some think there are possible indications that he had connections with Mazdean traditions and perhaps the worship of Mithra,[4] although not all agree. The overwhelming impression, however, is that he was very adaptable in religious terms, and was willing to be the instrument of Yahweh and the companion of Marduk. Beyond that, it is hard to say more.

At this point, we need to return to Cyrus' metahumanity. As we discussed in the very first chapter, kingship always implies separation and a separation of a metahuman kind. The king always sits somewhere between divinity and mortality. The question is, however, where did Cyrus place himself on this metahuman spectrum? Did it remain the same throughout his career? One could well imagine that with the taking of Babylon when he thinks of himself as 'King of Countries', he may well also be developing a more strongly divinised sense of himself (as Alexander the Great was to do). In Ashurbanipal's Coronation Hymn, Ashurbanipal says: Ashur is king but Ashurbanipal concedes his mortality.[5] In the *Cyrus Cylinder*, Cyrus pushes the boundaries on his mortality: he walks beside Marduk, not just as his earthly representative, but as his companion.

Finally, however, we need to return to the storytelling about Cyrus. Cyrus told his own story in the *Cyrus Cylinder* about who he was and how he intended to position his metahumanity. In doing that, he was connecting deeply and knowingly with other Near Eastern narratives about kingship, and so was placing himself within an elaborate and full tradition of storytelling, which was both oral and written, and moved creatively between the two modes of story production. Therefore, in reading the stories of Cyrus, it is important to take account of their embeddedness. They cannot be understood simply because they are situated within a tradition which saw the past repeating itself in the present. It was the sense of history repeating itself which gave his kingship such power, authority and legitimacy. Although an outsider, a stranger-king, he was bringing to his kingship all the heroism of the great kings of the Near Eastern past, even to surpass them. By controlling the barbarian Guti and *Umman-manda* – and the mythologies through which they became real – Cyrus became not only the ultimate stranger-king, but also the ultimate Near Eastern king.

For that reason, there is also the larger question about historical methodology raised in the opening chapter which needs to be taken into account when trying to write about a figure like Cyrus whose stories were so strongly steeped in legend that he comes to be a legend himself. But we also need to consider the transmission of these legends: oral stories become written stories and then are adapted as oral versions again. There is no canonical account. In fact, we can also see the shifts and adaptations even within what is thought of as the more static written tradition as different authors in diverse periods require Cyrus and the cast of characters around him to change according to their needs and the concerns of their own time. Storytelling in writing is as flexible and adaptable as oral creations. Interestingly, it is Herodotus' Tomyris who takes on a life of her own, eventually to become a queen of the Amazons who overturns the Amazon myth in order to avenge her son, and demonstrate her full magnificence as the killer of her son's father and murderer.

As a result, what we must not do is try to rationalise these stories to form coherent narratives. They are not coherent, and cannot be, because each of them is a reflection on different aspects of kingship, as part of the creation of the cultural context in which this king can be placed and understood. In a way, this cultural vision of a king is much more potent in its variety and richness than the simple retelling of deeds. Taken together, these stories do create a biography of sorts, but not so much of the man so much as of his kingship. He emerges from them as a king who seems to have developed not only a new style of Near Eastern kingship, drawing fully on a Near Eastern heritage, but also one that is deeply embedded within it. As a historical king, in this way, he passes into legend, but his kingship becomes greater for that, and he becomes truly Cyrus the Great.

Notes

1. J. Kroll (2010).
2. For a translation of the text, Kuhrt (2007), 117–22; see also Lloyd (1982).
3. See Parker (2011), 363–4.
4. Daryaee (2013).
5. See, e.g., Livingstone (1989), no. 11.15. Ashur is given the determinative for a god, but Ashurbanipal for a mortal.

Appendix A
Translation of the Cyrus Cylinder (Irving Finkel)[1]

1 [When ... Mar]duk, king of the whole heaven and earth, the ...... who, in his ..., lays waste his ......

2 [..] broad? in intelligence, ... who inspects (?) the wor]ld quarters (regions)

3 [..] his [first]born (= Belshazzar), a low person, was put in charge of his country,

4 but [..] he set [a (...) counter]feit over them.

5 He ma[de] a counterfeit of Esagil, [and ....] ... for Ur and the rest of the cult-cities.

6 Rites inappropriate to them, [impure] fo[od offerings ....] disrespectful [...] were daily gabbled, and, as an insult,

7 he brought the daily offerings to a halt; he inter[fered with the rites and] instituted [......] within the sanctuaries. In his mind, reverential fear of Marduk, king of the gods, came to an end.

8 He did yet more evil to his city every day; ... his [people ....], he brought ruin on them all without relief.

9 Enlil-of-the-gods became extremely angry at their complaints, and [...] their territory. The gods who lived within them left their shrines

10 angry that he had made them enter into Shuanna (Babylon). Ex[alted Marduk, Enlil-of-the-go]ds, relented. He changed his mind about all the settlements whose sanctuaries were in ruins

11 and the population of the land of Sumer and Akkad who had become like corpses and took pity on them. He inspected and checked all the countries,

12 seeking for the upright king of his choice. He took the hand of Cyrus, king of the city of Anshan, and called him by his name, proclaiming him aloud for the kingship overall for everything.

13 He made the land of Guti and all the Median troops prostrate themselves at his feet, while he shepherded in justice and righteousness the black-headed people

14 whom he had put under his care. Marduk, the great lord, who nurtures his people, saw with great pleasure his fine deeds and true heart

15 and ordered that he should go to Babylon. He had him take the road to Tintir (Babylon) and, like a friend and companion, he walked at his side.

16 His vast troops whose number, like the water in a river, could not be counted, were marching fully armed at his side.

17 He had him enter without fighting or battle right into Shuanna; he saved his city Babylon from hardship. He handed over to him Nabonidus, the king who did not fear him.

18 All the people of Tintir, all of Sumer and Akkad, nobles and governors, bowed down before him and kissed his feet, rejoicing over his kingship and their faces shone.

19 The lord through whose help all were rescued from death and saved them all from distress and hardship, they blessed him sweetly and praised his name.

20 I am Cyrus, king of the universe, the great king, the powerful king, king of Babylon, king of Sumer and Akkad, king of the four quarters of the world,

21 son of Cambyses, the great king, king of the city of Anshan, grandson of Cyrus, the great king, ki[ng of the cit]y of Anshan, descendant of Teispes, the great king, king of the city of Anshan,

22 the perpetual seed of kingship, whose reign Bel (Marduk) and Nabu love, and with whose kingship, to their joy, they concern themselves. When I went as a harbinger of peace i[nt]o Babylon,

23 I founded my sovereign residence within the palace amid celebration and rejoicing. Marduk, the great lord, bestowed on me as my destiny the magnanimity of one who loves Babylon, and I every day sought him out in awe.

24 My vast troops were marching peaceably in Babylon, and the whole of [Sumer] and Akkad had nothing to fear.

25 I sought the safety of the city of Babylon and all its sanctuaries. As for the population of Babylon [..., w]ho as if without div[ine intention] had endured a yoke not decreed for them,

26 I soothed their weariness; I freed them from their bonds (?). Marduk, the great lord, rejoiced at [my good] deeds,

27 and he pronounced a sweet blessing over me, Cyrus, the king who fears him, and over Cambyses, the son [my] issue, [and over] all my troops,

28 that we might live happily in his presence, in well-being. At his exalted command, all kings who sit on thrones,

29 from every quarter, from the Upper Sea to the Lower Sea, those who inhabit [remote distric]ts (and) the kings of the land of Amurru who live in tents, all of them

30 brought their weighty tribute into Shuanna and kissed my feet. From [Shuanna] I sent back to their places to the city of Ashur and Susa,

31 Akkad, the land of Eshnunna, the city of Zamban, the city of Meturnu, Der, as far as the border of the land of the Guti – the sanctuaries across the river Tigris – whose shrines had earlier become dilapidated,

32 the gods who lived therein, and made permanent sanctuaries for them. I collected together all their people and returned them to their settlements

33 and the gods of the land of Sumer and Akkad which Nabonidus – to the fury of the lord of the gods – had brought into Shuanna, at the command of Marduk, the great lord.

34 I returned them unharmed to their cells in the sanctuaries that make them happy. May all the gods that I returned to their sanctuaries

35 every day before Bel and Nabu ask for a long life for me and mention my good deeds and say to Marduk, my lord, thus: 'Cyrus, the king who fears you, and Cambyses his son,

36 may they be the provisioners of our shrines until distant (?) days, and the population of Babylon call blessings on my kingship. I have enabled all the lands to live in peace.'

37 Every day I increased by [... ge]ese, two ducks and ten pigeons the [former offerings] of geese, ducks and pigeons.

38 I strove to strengthen the defences of the wall Imgur-Enlil, the great wall of Babylon

39 and [I completed] the quay of baked brick on the bank of the moat which an earlier king had bu[ilt but not com]pleted its work.

40 [I ...... which did not surround the city] outside, which no earlier king had built, his workforce, the levee [from his land, in/int]o Shuanna.

41 [.. with bitum]en and baked brick I built anew and [completed] its [work].

42 [...] great [doors of cedar wood] with bronze cladding,

43 [and I installed] all their doors, threshold slabs and door fittings with copper parts [.......................]. I saw within it an inscription of Ashurbanipal, a king who preceded me;

44 [...] in its place. May Marduk, the great lord, present to me as a gift a long life and the fullness of age,

45 [a secure throne and an enduring rei]gn [and may I ...... in] your heart forever.

Note

1. With thanks to Dr. Finkel, who gave me permission to reproduce his translation of the *Cyrus Cylinder*, from I. Finkel (2013) (ed.), *The Cyrus Cylinder: The King of Persia's Proclamation from Ancient Babylon*, London and New York, 4–7.

Bibliography

Adalı, S.F. (2011), *The Scourge of God: The* Umman-Manda *and its Significance in the First Millenium BC*, Winona Lake, IN.

Ainsworth, M.W. & J.P. Waterman (2013), *German Paintings in the Metropolitan Museum of Art, 1350–1600*, New York.

Albenda, P. (2018), 'Royal Gardens, Parks, and the Architecture Within: Assyrian Views', *Journal of the American Oriental Society*, 138: 105–20.

Alizadeh, A. (2010), 'The Rise of the Elamite State: Enclosed or Enclosing Nomadism', *Cultural Anthropology*, 51: 353–83.

Alizadeh, K. (2020), 'The Earliest Persians in Iran: Toponyms and Persian Ethnicity', *Dajir* 7: 16–53.

Al-Rawi, F.N.H. (1990), 'Tablets from the Sippar Library. I. The "Weidner Chronicle": A Supposititious Royal Letter Concerning a Vision', *Iraq* 52: 1–13.

Alstola, T. (2020), *Judeans in Babylonia: A Study of Deportees in the Sixth and Fifth Centuries*, Leiden.

Álverez-Món, J. (2010), 'Elite Garments and Headdresses of the Late Neo-Elamite Period (7th–6th century BC)', *Archäologische Mitteilungen aus Iran und Turan*, 1–29.

Ambos, C. (2014), 'Ancient Near Eastern Royal Rituals', *Religion Compass* 8/11: 327–36.

Amiet, P. (1979), 'Archaeological Discontinuity and Ethnic Duality in Elam', *Antiquity* 53: 195–204.

Amrhein, A. (2015), 'Neo-Assyrian Gardens: A Spectrum of Artificiality, Sacrality and Accessibility', *Studies in the History of Gardens & Designed Landscapes*, 35: 91–114.

Ando, C. (2000), *Imperial Ideology and Provincial Loyalty in the Roman Empire*, Berkeley, Los Angeles and London.

Andreas, F.C. (1904) 'Über einige Frage der ältesten persischen Geschichte', in *Verhandlungen des 13. Internationalen Orientalistenkongresses, Hamburg, September 1902*, Leiden, 93–9.

Ansari, A.M. (2012), *The Politics of Nationalism in Modern Iran*, Cambridge.

Armayor, O.K. (1978), 'Herodotus' Persian Vocabulary', *Ancient World* 1: 147–56.

Asadi, A. & B. Kaim (2009), 'The Achaemenid Building Site 64 in Tang-e Bolaghi', *Arta* 2009.003: 1–20.

Asheri, D., A. Lloyd, & A. Corcella (2007), *A Commentary on Herodotus Books I–IV*, Oxford.

Askari Chaverdi, A., P. Callieri & E. Matin (2014), 'Tol-e Ajori: a Monumental Gate of the Early Achaemenian Period in the Persepolis Area. The 2014 Excavation Season of the Iranian-Italian Project "From Palace to Town"', *Archäologische Mitteilungen aus Iran und Turan* 46: 223–54.

———. (2017), 'The Monumental Gate at Tol-e-Ajori, Persepolis (Fars): The New Archaeological Data', *Iranica Antiqua* 52, 205–58.

Atack, C. (2020), *The Discourse of Kingship in Classical Greece*, Abingdon.

Avery, H.C. (1979), 'Herodotus' Picture of Cyrus', *American Journal of Philology* 93: 529–46.

Azoulay, V. (2004), 'Xenophon and the Barbarian World', in C.J. Tuplin (ed.), *Xenophon and his World*, Stuttgart, 147–73.

Azzoni, A. & M.W. Stolper (2015), 'The Aramaic Epitaph ns(y)ḥ on Elamite Persepolis Fortification Documents', *Arta* 2015.004.

Badian, E. (1996), 'Alexander the Great Between Two Thrones and Heaven', in A. Small (ed.), *Subject and Ruler; Journal of Roman Archaeology* Supplement 17, 11–26 = (2012), *Collected Papers on Alexander the Great*, Abingdon and New York, 365–85.

Ballati, S. (2017), *Mountain Peoples in the Ancient Near East: The Case of the Zagros in the First Millennium BCE*, Wiesbaden.

Baragwanath, E. (2015), 'Characterization in Herodotus', in R. Ash, J. Mossman & F.B. Titchener (eds.), *Fame and Infamy: Essays for Christopher Pelling on Characterization in Greek and Roman Biography and Historiography*, Oxford, 17–35.

Beaulieu, P.-A. (1989), *The Reign of Nabonidus, King of Babylon 556–539 BC*, New Haven/London.

———. (1993), 'An Episode in the Fall of Babylon to the Persians', *Journal of Near Eastern Studies* 52: 241–61.

———. (2000), 'The Sippar Cylinder of Nabonidus (2.123A)', in W.M. Hallo and K. Lawson (eds.), *The Context of Scripture*, vol. 2, Leiden, Boston and Köln, 310–3.

———. (2007), 'Nabonidus the Mad King: A Reconsideration of his Steles from Harran and Babylon', in M. Heinz & M.F. Feldman (eds.), *Representations of Political Power. Case Histories from Times of Change and Dissolving Order in the Ancient Near East*, Winona Lake, IN, 137–66.

———. (2013), 'Arameans, Chaldeans, and Arabs in Cuneiform Sources from the Late Babylonian Period', in A. Berlejung & M.P. Streck (eds.), *Arameans, Chaldeans, and Arabs in Babylonia and Palestine in the First Millenium* BC, Wiesbaden, 31–55.

———. (2017), 'Palaces of Babylon and Palaces of Babylonian Kings', *Journal of the Canadian Society for Mesopotamian Studies* 11–12: 5–14.

———. (2018), *A History of Babylon 2200 BC – AD 75*, Chichester, Weinheim and Singapore.

Beckman, D. (2018), 'The Many Deaths of Cyrus the Great', *Iranian Studies* 51: 1–21.

Becker, U. (2021), 'The Book of Isaiah: Its Composition History', in L.-S. Tiemeyer (ed.), *The Oxford Handbook of Isaiah*, Oxford, 37–56.

Benech, C., R. Boucharlat & S. Gondet (2012), 'Organisation et aménagement de l'space à Pasargades: Reconnaissances archéologiques de surface, 2003–2008', *Arta* 2012.003: 1–37.

Bidmead, J. (2014), *The Akītu Festival: Religious Continuity and Royal Legitimation in Mesopotamia*, Piscataway, NJ.

Boardman, J. (2000), *Persia and the West: An Archaeological Investigation of the Genesis of Achaemenid Art*, London.

Bongenaar, A.V.C. (1997), *The Neo-Babylonian Ebbabar Temple at Sippar: Its Administration and its Prosopography*, Leiden.

Borza, E.N. (1990), *In the Shadow of Olynthus: The Emergence of Macedon*, Princeton.

Bosworth, B. (1995), *Commentary on Arrian's History of Alexander, II*, Oxford.

Bottéro, J. (1982), 'L'Oniromancie en Mésopotamie ancienne', *Ktema* 7: 5–18.

———. (2001), *Religion in Ancient Mesopotamia* (transl. T.L. Fagan), Chicago.

Boucharlat, R. (2001), 'The Palace and the Royal Achaemenid City: Two Case Studies – Pasargadae and Susa', in I. Nielsen (ed.), *The Royal Palace Institution in the First Millennium BC: Regional Development and Cultural Interchange between East and West*, Athens, 113–23.

———. (2009), 'The "Paradise" of Cyrus at Pasargadae, the Core of Royal Ostentation', in J. Ganzert and J. Wolshe-Bulmahn (eds.), *Bau-und Gartenkultur zwischen "Orient" und "Okzident": Fragen zu Herkunft, Identität un Legitimation*, Munich, 49–64.

———. (2011), 'Gardens and Parks at Pasargadae: Two "Paradises"?', in R. Rollinger, B. Truschnegg & R. Bichler (eds.), *Herodot und das Persische Weltreich/ Herodotus and the Persian Empire*, Wiesbaden, 557–74.

———. (2014), 'Achaemenid Estate(s) Near Pasargadae?', in M. Kozuh, W.F.M. Henkelman, C.E. Jone, & C. Woods (eds.), *Extraction and Control: Studies in Honor of Matthew W. Stolper*, Chicago, 27–35.

———. (2020), 'Arriving at Persepolis: An Unfortified Royal Residence', in E.R.M. Duisinberre, M.B. Garrison & W.F.M. Henkelman (eds.), *Achaemenid History XVI: The Art of Empire in Achaemenid Persia. Studies in Honour of Margaret Cool Root*, Leuven, 41–71.

Boucharlat, R. & C. Benech (2002), 'Organisation et aménagement de l'espace à Pasargades: Reconnaissances archéologiques de surface, 1999-2002', *Arta* 2002.001, 1–41.

Boyce, M. (1954), 'Some Remarks on the Transmission of the Kayanian Heroic Cycle', in *Serta Cantabrigiensis*, Wiesbaden, 45–52.

———. (1968), 'Middle Persian Literature', in *Handbook of Oriental Studies: The Near and Middle East*, Leiden, 31–66.

Brennan, S. & D. Thomas (2021), *The Landmark Xenophon's* Anabasis, New York.

Briant, P. (1984), *L'Asie centrale et les royaumes proche orientaux du premier millénaire (c. VIIIᵉ-IVᵉ siècles avant notre ère)*, Paris.

———. (1988), 'Ethno-classe dominante et populations soumises dans l'Empire achéménide: le cas de l'Égypte', in A. Kuhrt & H. Sancisi-Weerdenburg (eds.), *Achaemenid History III: Method and Theory*, Leiden, 137–73.

———. (1990), 'Hérodote et la société Perse', in G. Nenci & O. Reverdin (eds.), *Hérodote et les peoples non Grec: neuf exposés suivi des discussions*, Vandoeuvres-Geneva, 69–104.

———. (2002), *From Cyrus to Alexander: A History of the Persian Empire* (transl. P.T. Daniels), Winona Lake, IN.

Brinkman, J. (1984), *Prelude to Empire: Babylonian Society and Politics 747–626 BC*, Philadelphia.

Brisch, N. (2022), 'Gods and Kings in Ancient Mesopotamia', in A.A. Moin & A. Strathern (eds.), *Sacred Kingship in World History: Between Immanence and Transcendence*, New York, 72–93.

Brosius, M. (1996), *Women in Ancient Persia (559–331 BC)*, Oxford.

———. (2000), *The Persian Empire from Cyrus II to Artaxerxes I* (LACTOR 16).

Bruce, S.G. (2019), 'The Dark Age of Herodotus: Shards of a Fugitive History in Early Medieval Europe', *Speculum* 94: 47–67.

Calmeyer, P. (2011), 'Crown', *Encyclopaedia Iranica*, https://www.iranicaonline.org/articles/crown-i#prettyPhoto (accessed 01/09/2022).

Cameron, G.G. (1974), 'Cyrus the "Father" and Babylonia', *Acta Iranica* 1: 45–8.

Canepa, M. (2015), 'Inscriptions, Royal Spaces and Iranian Identity: Epigraphic Practices in Persia and the Ancient Iranian World', in A. Eastmond (ed.), *Viewing Inscriptions in the Late Antique and Medieval World*, Cambridge, 10–35.

Carney, E.D. (2000), *Women ad Monarchy in Macedonia*, Norman.

———. (2006), *Olympias: Mother of Alexander the Great*, New York and London.

Carr, D. (2005), *Writing on the Tablet of the Heart: Origins of Scripture and Literature*, Oxford.

Carter, E. (1994), 'Bridging the Gap between the Elamites and the Persians in Southeastern Khuzistan', in H. Sancisi-Weerdenburg, A. Kuhrt & M.C. Root (eds.), *Achaemenid History VIII: Continuity and Change*, Leiden, 65–94.

Ceccarelli, P. (2014), 'Charon of Lampsakos (262)', in I. Worthington (ed.), *Jacoby Online. Brill's New Jacoby, Part III*, Leiden. http://dx.doi.org.uoelibrary.idm.oclc.org/10.1163/1873-5363_bnj_a262 (accessed 02/02/2022).

Charpin, D. (2010), *Reading and Writing in Babylon* (transl. J.M. Todd), Cambridge, MA and London.

Chiasson, C.C. (2012), 'Myth and truth in Herodotus' Cyrus *logos*', in E. Baragwanath & M. de Bakker (eds.), *Myth, Truth and Narrative in Herodotus*, Oxford, 213–32.

Çilingiroğlu, A. (2002), 'The Reign of Rusa II: Towards the End of the Urartian Kingdom', in R. Aslan (ed.) *Mauerschau: Festschrift für Manfred Korfmann*, 3 vols. Remshalden-Grunbach, 1.483–9.

Codella, K.C. (2007), *Achaemenid Monumental Gateways at Pasargadae, Susa and Persepolis*, PhD diss. University of California, Berkeley.

Cogan, M. (1974), *Imperialism and Religion: Assyria, Judah and Israel in the Eighth and Seventh Centuries BCE* (SBL Monograph Series), Missoula, MT.

Cohen, M.E. (1974), Balag-*compositions: Sumerian Lamentation Liturgies of the Second and First Millennium BC*, Malibu.

———. (1993), *Cultic Calendars of the Ancient Near East*, Bethesda, MD.

Colburn, H.P. (2013), 'Connectivity and Communication in the Achaemenid Empire', *Journal of the Economic and Social History of the Orient* 56: 29–52.

Cole, S. (2014), *Cicero and the Rise of Deification at Rome*, Cambridge.

Comfort, A. (2009), *Roads on the Frontier between Rome and Persia: Euphratesia, Osrhoene and Mesopotamia from AD 363 to 602*, PhD diss. Exeter.

Comfort, A. & M. Marciak (2018), *How Did the Persian King of Kings Get his Wine? The Upper Tigris in Antiquity (c. 700 BCE to 636 BCE)*, Oxford.

Cooper, J.S. (1983), *The Curse of Agade*, London and Baltimore, MD.

———. (1992), 'Babbling On: Recovering Mesopotamia's Orality', in M.F. Vogelzang & H.L.J. Vanstiphout (eds.), *Mesopotamian Epic Literature*, Lewiston, 103–22.

Cooper, J.S. & W. Heimpel (1983), 'The Sumerian Sargon Legend', *Journal of the American Oriental Society* 103, 67–82.

Cribb, R. (1991), *Nomads in Archaeology*, Cambridge.

Crick, J. (1987), 'An Anglo-Saxon Fragment of Justinus's "Epitome"', *Anglo-Saxon England* 16: 181–96.

Crouch, C.L. (2013), 'Ištar and the Motif of the Cosmological Warrior', in H. Barstad & R.P. Gordon (eds.), *Thus Speaks Ishtar of Arbela. Prophecy in Israel, Assyria and Egypt in the Neo-Assyrian Period*, Winona Lake, IN, 129–42.

Currie, B. (2005), *Pindar and the Cult of the Heroes*, Oxford.

Dalley, S. (1994), 'Nineveh, Babylon and the Hanging Gardens: Cuneiform and Classical Sources Reconciled', *British Institute for the Study of Iraq* 56: 45–58.

———. (1996), 'Herodotos and Babylon', *Orientalische Literaturzeitung* 91: 526–32.

———. (2021), *The City of Babylon: A History c. 2000 BC–AD 116*, Cambridge.

Da Riva, R. (2013), *The Inscriptions of Nabopolassar, Amēl-Marduk and Neriglissar*, Boston, MA and Berlin.

———. (2017), 'The Figure of Nabopolassar in Late Achaemenid and Early Hellenistic Historiographic Tradition: BM 34793 and CUA 90', *Journal of Near Eastern Studies* 76: 75–92.

Daryaee, T. (2013), 'Religion of Cyrus the Great', in T. Daryaee (ed.), *Cyrus the Great: An Ancient Iranian King*, Santa Monica, 16–27.

Day, J. (ed.) (2013), *King and Messiah in Israel and the Ancient Near East.* Proceedings of the Oxford Old Testament Seminar, London and New York.

Delnero, P. (2010), 'Sumerian Extract Tablets and Scribal Education', *Journal of Cuneiform Studies* 62: 53–69.

Develin, R. (1994), 'Introduction', in J.C. Yardley & R. Develin, *Justin: Epitome of the Philippic History of Pompeius Trogus*, Atlanta, GA.

Diakonov, I.M. (1985), 'Media', in I. Gershevitch (ed.), *Cambridge History of Iran*, Cambridge, 36–148.

Dobbs-Allsopp, F.W. (1993), *Weep, O Daughter of Zion: A Study of the City-Lament Genre in the Hebrew Bible*, Rome.

Draycott, C.M. & G.D. Summers (2008), *Sculpture and Inscriptions from the Monumental Entrance to the Palatial Complex at Kerkenes Dağ, Turkey* (Kerkenes Special Studies I), Chicago.

Drews, R. (1974), 'Sargon, Cyrus and Mesopotamian Folk History', *Journal of Near Eastern Studies*, 33: 387–93.

Düring, B.D. (2020), *The Imperialisation of Assyria: An Archaeological Approach*, Cambridge.

Dunbar, N. (1995), *Aristophanes: Birds*, Oxford.

Dusinberre, E.R.M. (2013), *Empire, Authority and Autonomy in Achaemenid Anatolia*, Cambridge.

Edelman, D. (2005), *The Origins of the 'Second Temple': Persian Imperial Policy and the Rebuilding of Jerusalem*, London.

Edzard D.O. (1987), 'Deep-rooted Skyscrapers and Bricks: Ancient Mesopotamian Architecture and its Imagery', in M.J. Geller, M. Mindlin, & J. Wandsbrough (eds.), *Figurative Language in the Ancient Near East*, London, 11–20.

Fales, F.M. (2012), 'After Ta'yinat: The New Status for Esarhaddon's adê for Assyrian Political History', *Revue d'Assyriologie et d'archéologie orientale* 106: 133–58.

Felton, D. (2014), 'The Motif of the "Mutilated Hero" in Herodotus', *Phoenix* 68: 47–61.

Ferris, P.W. (1992), *The Genre of Communal Lament in the Bible and Ancient Near East*, Atlanta, GA.

Finkel, I. (2013), 'The Cyrus Cylinder: The Babylonian Perspective', in I. Finkel (ed.), *The Cyrus Cylinder: The King of Persia's Proclamation from Ancient Babylon*, London, 4–34.

Finkelstein, I. (1992), 'Invisible Nomads: A Rejoinder', *Bulletin of the American School of Oriental Research* 287: 87–8.

Finn, J. (2017), *Much Ado About Marduk: Questioning Discourses of Royalty in First Millennium Mesopotamian Literature*, Boston, MA and Berlin.

Flannery, K.V. (1999), 'Chiefdoms in the Early Near East: Why Is It So Hard to Identify Them?', in A. Alizadeh, Y. Majidzadeh & S.M. Shahmirzadi (eds.), *The Iranian World: Essays on Iranian Art and Archaeology Presented to Ezat O. Negahban*, Tehran, 44–63.

Fleck, M. (1993), *Cicero als Historiker*, Stuttgart, 45–53.

Fradenburg, L.O. (1992), 'Introduction: Rethinking Queenship', in L.O Fradenburg (ed.), *Women and Sovereignty*, Edinburgh, 1–13.

Frame, G. (2021), *The Royal Inscriptions of Sargon II, King of Assyria (721–705 BCE)*, Philadelphia, PA.

Franklin, M. (2006), *Boccaccio's Heroines: Power and Virtue in Renaissance Society*, Aldershot and Burlington, VA.

———. (2010), 'Boccaccio's Amazons and their Legacy in Renaissance Art: Confronting the Threat of Powerful Women', *Women's Art Journal* 31: 13–20.

Freedman, S. (1998), *If a City is Set on a Height: The Akkadian Omen Series* Šumma Alu ina Mele Šakin, vol. 1, Philadelphia, PA.

———. (2017), *If a City is Set on a Height: The Akkadian Omen Series* Šumma Alu ina Mele Šakin, vol. 3, Winona Lake, IN.

French, D. (1998), 'Pre- and Early-Roman Roads of Asia Minor: The Persian Royal Road', *Iran* 36: 15–43.

Fried, L.S. (2004), *The Priest and the Great King: Temple-Palace Relations in the Persian Empire*, Winona Lake, IN.

Gabay, U. (2020), 'Defeat Literature in the Cult of the Victorious: Ancient Mesopotamian City Laments', in K. Streit & M. Grohmann (eds.), *Culture of Defeat*, Piscataway, NJ, 121–38.

Gallagher, W.R. (1994), 'Assyrian Deportation Propaganda', *State Archives of Assyria Bulletin* 8: 57–65.

Garrison, M. (2011), 'The Library of Alcuin's York', in R. Gameson (ed.), *The Cambridge History of the Book in Britain*, vol. 1, Cambridge, 633–64.

Garrison, M.B. (1991), 'Seals and the Elite at Persepolis: Some Observations on Early Achaemenid Persian Art', *Ars Orientalis* 21: 1–29.

———. (2011), 'The Seal of "Kuraš the Anzanite, Son of Šešpeš" (Teispes), PFS 93*: Susa – Ansan – Persepolis', in J. Álvarez-Mon & M.B. Garrison (eds.), *Elam and Persia*, Winona Lake, IN, 375–405.

Gates-Foster J. (2014), 'Achaemenids, Royal Power, and Persian Ethnicity', in J. McInerney (ed.), *A Companion to Ethnicity in the Ancient Mediterranean*, Chichester, 175–93.

Geiger, J. (2008), *The First Hall of Fame: A Study of the Statues in the Forum Augustum*, Leiden.

George, A.R. (1992), *Babylonian Topographical Texts*, Leuven.

——. (1993a), *House Most High. The Temples of Ancient Mesopotamia*, Winona Lake, IN.

——. (1993b), 'Babylon Revisited: Archaeology and Philology in Harness', *Antiquity* 67: 734–46.

——. (1996), 'Studies in Cultic Topography and Ideology', *Bibliotheca Orientalis* 53: 363–95.

——. (1997), '"Bond of the Lands": Babylon, the Cosmic Capital', in G. Wilhem (ed.), *Die orientalische Stadt: Kontinuität, Wandel, Bruch*, Berlin, 125–45.

——. (1999), 'E-sangil and E-temen-anki, the Archetypal Cult-centre', in J. Renger (ed.), *Babylon: Focus mesopotamischer Geschichte, Wiege früher Gelehrsamkeit, Mythos in der Moderne*, Berlin, 67–86.

Gera, D.L. (1993), *Xenophon's* Cyropaedia: *Style, Genre and Literary Technique*, Oxford.

——. (1997), *Warrior Women: The Anonymous* Tractatus de Mulieribus, Leiden, New York and Köln.

Gesche, P. (2001), *Schulunterricht in Babylonien im ersten Jahrtausend v. Ch.*, Münster.

Glassner, J.-J. (2004), *Mesopotamian Chronicles*, Atlanta, GA.

Godman, P. (ed.) (1983), *Alcuin: The Bishops, Kings and Saints of York*, Oxford.

Gondet, S., K. Mohammadkhani, M. Djamali, M. Farjamirad, N. Ibnoerrida, H. Gopnik, D. Laisney, F. Notter-Truxa, J.-B. Rigot, Y. Ubelmann (2019), 'Field Report on the 2016 Archaeological Project of the Joint Iran-France Project on Pasargadae and its Surrounding Territory', *Iranian Heritage Studies* 1: 1–28.

Gondet, S., K. Mohammadkhani & H. Gopnik (2022), 'The 2015-2016 Survey Campaigns at Pasargadae: Results and Observations on the Cyrus' Capital Layout and Its Latter Evolutions', in G. Basello, P. Callieri & A.V. Rossi (eds.), *Achaemenid Studies Today*, Naples, 1–21 with figs. 1–10.

Gopnik, H. (2010), 'Why Columned Halls?', in J. Curtis & St. J. Simpson (eds.), *The World of Achaemenid Persia: History, Art and Society in Iran and the Ancient Near East*, London, 195–206.

Graeber, D. & S. Sahlins (2017), *On Kings*, Chicago, IL.

Graf, D.F. (1984), 'Medism: The Origin and Significance of the Term', *Journal of Hellenic Studies* 104: 15–30.

Grayson, A.K. (1975a), *Assyrian and Babylonian Chronicles*, Locust Valley, NY.

——. (1975b), *Babylonian Historical-Literary Texts*, Toronto and Buffalo, NY.

——. (1991), *Assyrian Rulers of the Early First Millennium BC I (114–859 BC)*, Toronto.

——. (1996), *Assyrian Rulers of the Early First Millennium BC II (858–745 BC)*, Toronto.

Grayson, A.K. & J. Novotny (eds.) (2012), *The Royal Inscriptions of Sennacherib, King of Assyria (704–681 BC), Part 1*, Winona Lake, IN.

Greco, A. (2003), 'Zagros Pastoralism and Assyrian Imperial Expansion', in G.B. Lanfranchi, M. Roaf & R. Rollinger (eds.), *Continuity of Empires (?). Assyria, Media, Persia. Proceedings of the International Meeting in Padua, 26th–28th April 2001*, Padua, 65–78.

Green, M.W. (1975), *Eridu in Sumerian Literature*, PhD diss., University of Chicago.

Green, T.M. (1992), *The City of the Moon God: Religious Traditions of Harran*, Leiden, New York and Köln.

Greenewalt, C.H. Jnr (1992), 'When a Mighty Empire Was Destroyed: The Common Man at the Fall of Sardis, ca. 546 BC', *Proceedings of the American Philosophical Society* 136: 247–71.

Griffin, J. (1976), 'Augustan Poetry and the Life of Luxury', *Journal of Roman Studies* 66: 87–105.

Grogan, J. (2014), *The Persian Empire in English Renaissance Writing, 1549–1622*, Basingstoke.

Gunter, A. (1982), 'Representations of Urartian and Western Iranian Fortress Architecture in the Assyrian Reliefs', *Iran* 22: 103–12.

Hall, J. (1997), *Ethnic Identity in Greek Antiquity*, Cambridge.

———. (2002), *Hellenicity: Between Ethnicity and Culture*, Chicago, IL and London.

Hallo, W.M. (1980), 'Royal Titles from the Mesopotamian Periphery', *Anatolian Studies* 30: 189–95.

Hallock, R.T. (1969), *The Persepolis Fortification Tablets*, Chicago, IL.

Hampton, T. (1990), *Writing From History: The Rhetoric of Exemplarity in Renaissance Literature*, Ithaca, NY and London.

Harmatta, J. (1971), 'The Literary Patterns of the Babylonian Edict of Cyrus', *Acta Antiqua Academiae Scientiarum Hungaricae* 19: 217–31.

Harrison, T. (1998), 'Herodotus' Conception of Foreign Languages', *Histos* 2: 1–45.

———. (2002), *Divinity and History: The Religion of Herodotus*, Oxford.

Haubold, J. (2007), 'Xerxes' Homer', in E. Bridges, E. Hall & P.J. Rhodes (eds.), *Cultural Responses to the Persian Wars: Antiquity to the Third Millennium*, Oxford, 47–63.

———. (2013), *Greece and Mesopotamia: Dialogues in Literature*, Cambridge.

Haussker, F. (2017), 'The *Ekthesis* of Cyrus the Great: A Case of Heroicity versus Bastardy in Classical Athens', *Cambridge Classical Journal*, 63: 103–17.

Hedeman, A.D. (2008), *Translating the Past: Laurent de Premierfait and Boccaccio's De Casibus*, Los Angeles, CA.

Hellwag, U. (2012), 'Der Niedergang Urartus', in S. Kroll, C. Gruber, U. Hellwag, M. Roaf & P. Zimansky (eds.), *Biainili-Urartu: Proceedings of the Symposium held in Munich, 12–14 of October 2007, Acta Iranica 51*, Leuven, 227–41.

Henkelman, W.F.M. (2003), 'Persians, Medes and Elamites: Acculturation in the Neo-Elamite period', in G. Lanfranchi, M. Roaf & R. Rollinger (eds.) (2003), *Continuity of Empires (?). Assyria, Media, Persia. Proceedings of the International Meeting in Padua, 26th–28th April 2001*, Padua, 181–231.

———. (2008a), *The Other Gods Who Are: Studies in Elamite Iranian Acculturation Based on the Persepolis Fortification Tablets*, Leiden.

———. (2008b), 'From Gabae to Taoce: The Geography of the Central Administrative Province', in P. Briant, W.F.M. Henkelman & M.W. Stolper (eds.), *L'archive des fortifications de Persépolis: État des questions et perspectives de recherches*, Paris, 303–16.

———. (2011), 'Cyrus the Persian and Darius the Elamite: A Case of Mistaken Identity', in R. Rollinger, B. Truschnegg, and R. Bichler (eds.), *Herodot und das Persische Weltreich/Herodotus and the Persian Empire*, Wiesbaden, 577–634.

Henkelman, W.F.M. & M.W. Stolper (2009), 'Ethnic Identity and Ethnic Labelling at Persepolis: The Case of the Skudrians', in P. Briant & M. Chauveau (eds.), *Organisation des pouvoirs et contacts culturels dans les pays de l'empire achéménide (Persika 14)*, Paris, 271–329.

Henkelman, W.F.M., A. Kuhrt, R. Rollinger & J. Wiesehöfer (2011), 'Herodotus and Babylonia Reconsidered', in R. Rollinger, B. Truschnegg & R. Bichler (eds.), *Herodot und die Persiche Weltreich/Herodotus and the Persian Empire*, Wiesbaden, 499–70.

Heskett, R. (2011), *Reading the Book of* Isaiah: *Destruction and Lament in the Holy City*, New York.

Holloway, S.W. (1995), 'Harran: Cultic Geography in the Neo-Assyrian Empire and its Implications for Sennacherib's "Letter to Hezekiah" in 2 Kings', in S.W. Holloway & L.K. Handy (eds.), *The Pitcher is Broken: Memorial Essays for Gösta W. Ahlström (Journal for the Study of the Old Testament Supplement Series 190)*, Sheffield, 276–314.

Horowitz, W. (2011), *Mesopotamian Cosmic Geography*, 2nd printing with corrections and addenda, Winona Lake, IN.

Huys, H. (1995), *The Tale of the Hero Who Was Exposed at Birth in Euripidean Tragedy: A Study of Motifs*, Leuven.

Immerwahr, H.R. (1966), *Form and Thought in Herodotus*, Cleveland, OH.

Jong, A. de (2010), 'Religion and the Achaemenid Court', in B. Jacobs & R. Rollinger (eds.), *Der Achämendenhof/The Achaemenid Court*, Wiesbaden, 533–58.

Jursa, M. (2003), 'Observations on the Problem of the Median "Empire" on the Basis of the Babylonian Sources', in G. Lanfranchi, M. Roaf & R. Rollinger (eds.), *Continuity of Empire (?). Assyria, Media, Persia. Proceedings of the International Meeting in Padua, 26th–28th April 2001*, Padua, 169–79.

———. (2010a), 'Der neubabylonische Hof', in B. Jacobs & R. Rollinger (eds.), *Der Achämenidhof/The Achaemenid Court*, Wiesbaden, 67–106.

———. (2010b), 'The Transition of Babylonia from the Neo-Babylonian Empire to Achaemenid Rule', in H. Crawford (ed.), *Regime Change in the Ancient Near East and Europe*, Oxford, 73–94.

———. (2011), 'Cuneiform Writing in Neo-Babylonian Temple Communities', in K. Radner & E. Robson (eds.), *The Oxford Handbook of Cuneiform Cultures*, Oxford, 184–204.

Karlsson, M. (2016), *Relations of Power in Early Neo-Assyrian State Ideology*, Boston and Berlin.

Kennedy, D. (1969), 'Realia', *Revue d'Assyriologie et d'archéologie orientale* 63, 79–82.

Kent, R.G. (1950), *Old Persian. Grammar, Texts, Lexicon*, New Haven, CT.

Kertai, D. (2015), *The Architecture of the Late Assyrian Royal Palaces*, Oxford.

Kessler, K. (1997), '"Royal Roads" and Other Questions of the Neo-Assyrian Communication System', in S. Parpola & R.M. Whiting, *Assyria 1995*, Helsinki, 129–36.

Khazanov, A.M. (1994), *Nomads and the Outside* World, 2nd ed. (transl. J. Crookenden), Madison, WI.

Kirk, G.S., J.E. Raven & M. Schofield (eds.) (1983), *The Presocratic Philosophers*, 2nd edition, Cambridge.

Kleber, K. (2008), *Tempel und Palast: Die Beziehungen zwischen dem König und dem Eanna-Tempel im spätbabylonischen Uruk*, Münster.

Köcher, F., A.L. Openheim, & H.G. Güterbock (1957–1958), 'The Old Babylonian Omen Text VAT 7525', *Archiv für Orientforschung* 18: 62–80.

Kolsky, D. (2003), *The Genealogy of Women: Studies in Boccaccio's* De Mulieribus Claris, New York.

Komoróczy, G. (1977), 'Ummān-manda', *Acta Antiqua Academiae Scientiarum Hungaricae* 25: 43–67.

Krentz, P. (2000), 'Deception in Archaic and Classical Greek Warfare', in H. van Wees (ed.), *War and Violence in Ancient Greece*, London and Swansea, 167–200.

Kroll, J.H. (2010), 'The Coins of Sardis', in N.D. Cahill (ed.), *The Lydians and their World*, https://sardisexpedition.org/en/essays/latw-kroll-coins-of-sardis (accessed 20/08/2022).

Kroll, S. (1984), 'Urartus Untergang in anderer Sicht (La chute de l'Urartu: Une autre vue)', *Istanbuler Mitteilungen* 34: 151–70.

———. (2003), 'Medes and Persians in Transcaucasia? Archaeological Horizons in North-western Iran and Transcaucasia', in G. Lanfranchi, M. Roaf & R. Rollinger (eds.), *Continuity of Empire (?). Assyria, Media, Persia. Proceedings of the International Meeting in Padua, 26th–28th April 2001*, Padua, 281–7.

Kucewicz, C. (2016), 'The Mutilation of the Dead and the Homeric Gods', *Classical Quarterly* 66: 425–36.

Kuhrt, A. (1983), 'The *Cyrus Cylinder* and Achaemenid Imperial Policy', *Journal for the Study of the Old Testament* 25: 83–97.

———. (1990), 'Nabonidus and the Babylonian Priesthood', in M. Beard & J. North (eds.), *Pagan Priests*, London, 117–55.

———. (1995a), *The Ancient Near East c. 3000-330*, 2 vols, London.

———. (1995b), 'The Assyrian Heartland in the Achaemenid Period', in P. Briant (ed.), *Dans les pays des Dix-Mille: Peuples et pays du Proche-Orient vus par un Grec, Actes de la Table Ronde internationale Toulouse, 3–4 février 1995 (Pallas: 43)*, Toulouse, 239–54.

———. (2001), 'The Palace(s) of Babylon', in I. Nielsen (ed.), *The Royal Palace Institution in the First Millennium BC: Regional Development and Cultural Exchange between East and West*, Athens, 77–89.

———. (2002), 'Babylon', in E.J. Bakker, I.J.F. de Jong & H. van Wees (eds.), *Brill's Companion to Herodotus*, Leiden, Boston, MA and Köln, 475–96.

———. (2003), 'Making History: Sargon of Agade and Cyrus the Great of Persia', in W. Henkelman & A. Kuhrt (eds.), *Achaemenid History XIII: A Persian Perspective: Essays in Memory of Heleen Sancisi-Weerdenburg*, Leiden, 347–61.

———. (2007a), *The Persian Empire*, Abingdon and New York.

———. (2007b), 'Cyrus the Great of Persia: Images and Realities', in M. Heinz & M.H. Feldman (eds.), *Representation of Political Power: Case Histories from Times of Change and Dissolving Order in the Ancient Near East*, Winona Lake, IN, 169–91.

Kurke, L. (1989), '*Kapēleia* and Deceit: Theognis 59-60', *American Journal of Philology* 110: 535–44.

———. (1999). *Coins, Bodies, Games, and Gold: The Politics of Meaning in Archaic Greece*, Princeton.

Lanfranchi, G.B. (1998), 'Esarhaddon, Assyria and Media', *State Archives of Assyria Bulletin* 12: 99–109.

———. (2003), 'The Assyrian Expansion in the Zagros and the Local Ruling Elites', in G.B. Lanfranchi, M. Roaf & R. Rollinger (eds.), *Continuity of Empire (?). Assyria, Media, Persia. Proceedings of the International Meeting in Padua, 26th–28th April 2001*, Padua, 79–118.

Lanfranchi, G.B., M. Roaf & R. Rollinger (2003), 'Afterword', in G.B. Lanfranchi, M. Roaf & R. Rollinger (eds.), *Continuity of Empire (?). Assyria, Media, Persia. Proceedings of the International Meeting in Padua, 26th-28th April 2001*, Padua, 397–406.

Langlands, R. (2015), 'Roman Exemplarity: Mediating Through General and Particular', in M. Lowrie & S. Lüdemann (eds.), *Exemplarity and Singularity: Thinking Through Particulars in Philosophy, Literature and Law*, Abingdon and New York, 68–80.

———. (2018), *Exemplary Ethics in Ancient Rome*, Cambridge.

Lapidge, M. (2001), 'Surviving Book-lists from Anglo-Saxon England', in M.P. Richards (ed.), *Anglo-Saxon Manuscripts: Basic Readings*, London, 87–167.

Larsen, M.T. (1979), 'The Tradition of Empire in Mesopotamia', in M.T. Larsen (ed.), *Power and Propaganda: A Symposium on Ancient Empires*, Copenhagen, 75–103.

Law, H.H. (1948), 'Croesus: From Herodotus to Boccaccio', *Classical Journal* 4: 456–62.

Lecoq, P. (1997), *Les inscriptions de la Perse achéménide*, Paris.

Lee, H. (2009), *Biography: A Very Short Introduction*, Oxford.

Lee, N.C. (2002), *The Singers of Lamentation: Cities Under Siege, From Ur to Jerusalem to Sarajevo*, Leiden.

Leick, G. (2001), *Mesopotamia: The Invention of the City*, London.

Leichty, E. (ed.) (2011), *The Royal Inscriptions of Esarhaddon, King of Assyria (680–669 BC)*, Winona Lake, IN.

Lenfant, D. (2000), 'Nicolas de Damas et le corpus des fragments de Ctésias: du fragment comme adaptation', *Ancient Society* 30: 293–318.

———. (2004), *Ctésias de Cnide: La Perse, l'Inde, autre fragments*, Paris.

Levavi, Y. (2020), 'The Neo-Babylonian Empire: The Imperial Periphery as seen from the Centre', *Journal of Ancient Near Eastern History* 7: 59–84.

Levine, L.D. (1973), 'Geographical Studies in the Neo-Assyrian Zagros I'; *Iran* 11: 1–27.

———. (1974), 'Geographical Studies in the Neo-Assyrian Zagros – II', *Iran* 12: 99–124.

Lewis, B. (1980), *The Sargon Legend: A Study of the Akkadian Text and the Tale of the Hero that was Exposed at Birth*, Cambridge, MA.

Lewis, D.M. (1997), 'Persians in Herodotus', *Selected Papers in Greek and Near Eastern History* (ed. P.J. Rhodes), Cambridge, 345–61.

Lincoln, B. (2012), *'Happiness for Mankind': Achaemenian Religion and the Imperial Project*, Leuven, Paris and Walpole, MA.

Lindner, R.P. (1982), 'What was a Nomadic Tribe', *Comparative Studies in Society and History* 24: 689–711.

Lissarrague, F. (1990), *The Aesthetics of the Greek Banquet: Images of Wine and Ritual* (transl. Szegedy-Maszak), Princeton, NJ.

Liverani, M. (1988), 'The Growth of the Assyrian Empire in the Habur/Middle Euphrates Area: A New Paradigm', *State Archives of Assyria Bulletin* 2: 81–98.

———. (2003), 'The Rise and Fall of Media', in G. Lanfranchi, M. Roaf & R. Rollinger (eds.), *Continuity of Empire (?). Assyria, Media, Persia. Proceedings of the International Meeting in Padua, 26th-28th April 2001*, Padua, 1–12.

Livingstone, A. (1989), *Court Poetry and Literary Miscellanea (State Archives of Assyria* vol. III), Helsinki.

Llewellyn-Jones, L. (2010), 'Introduction', in L. Llewellyn-Jones & J. Robson, *Ctesias' History of Persia: Tales of the Orient*, Abingdon, 1–87.

Lloyd, A.B. (1982), 'The Inscription of Udjahorresnet. A Collaborator's Testament', *The Journal of Egyptian Archaeology* 68: 166–80.

Löhnert, A. (2011), 'Manipulating the Gods: Lamenting in Context', in K. Radner & E. Robson (eds.), *The Oxford Handbook of Cuneiform Culture*, Oxford, 402–17.

Longman, T. III (1991), *Fictional Akkadian Autobiography: A Generic and Comparative Study*, Winona Lake, IN.

Luckenbill, D.D. (1924), *The Annals of Sennacherib*, Chicago, IL.

Macdonald, M.C.A. (2009), *Literacy and Identity in Pre-Islamic Arabia*, Farnham and Burlington, VA.

MacGinnis, J. (1986), 'Herodotus' Description of Babylon', *Bulletin of the Institute of Classical Studies* 33: 67–86.

Machinist, P. (2011), 'Kingship and Divinity in Imperial Assyria', in J. Renger (ed.), *Assur-Gott, Stadt und Land*, Wiesbaden, 405–30.

Mac Sweeney, N. (2009), 'Beyond Ethnicity: The Overlooked Diversity of Group Identities', *Journal of Mediterranean Archaeology* 22: 101–26.

Margueron, J.-C. (2019), 'Palais 'mésopotamiens': *status questionis*', in. M. Bietak, P. Matthiae & S. Prell (eds.), *Ancient Egyptian and Ancient Near Eastern Palaces, Vol. II*, Wiesbaden, 9–29.

Marro, C. (2004), 'Upper Mesopotamia and the Caucasus: An Essay on the Evolution of Routes and Road Networks from the Old Assyrian Kingdom to the Ottoman Empire', in A. Sagona (ed.), *A View from the Highlands: Archaeological Studies in Honour of Charles Burney*, Herent, 91–120.

Matthews, R. & H.F. Nashli (2022), *The Archaeology of Iran from the Palaeolithic to the Achaemenid Empire*, Abingdon and New York.

Matthews, V.J. (1974), *Panyassis of Halikarnassos*, Leiden.

May, N.M. (2014), 'Gates and their Functions in Mesopotamia and Ancient Israel', in N.M. May & U. Steinert (eds.), *The Fabric of Cities: Aspects of Urbanism, Urban Topography and Society in Mesopotamia, Greece and Rome*, Leiden, 77–121.

McEwan, G.J.P. (1984), *Late Babylonian Texts in the Ashmolean Museum* (Oxford Editions of Cuneiform Texts 10), Oxford.

McHardy, F. (forthcoming), 'Battlefield Decapitation and Mutilation in the Ancient Greek Imagination', in H.-M. Chidwick (ed.), *The Body of the Combatant in the Ancient Mediterranean*.

McInerney, J. (ed.) (2014), *A Companion to Ethnicity in the Ancient Mediterranean*, Chichester.

McKitterick, R. (2008), *Charlemagne: The Formation of a European Identity*, Cambridge.

McMillan, A. (1979), 'Men's Weapons, Women's War: The Nine Female Worthies, 1400–1640,' *Mediaevalia* 5: 113–39.

Michalowski, P. (1989), *The Lamentation Over the Destruction of Ur*, Winona Lake, IN.

———. (2011), 'Early Mesopotamia', in A. Feldherr & G. Hardy (eds.), *The Oxford History of Historical Writing. Volume 1: Beginnings to AD 600*, Oxford, 5–28.

———. (2014), 'Biography of a Sentence: Assurbanipal, Nabonidus and Cyrus', in M. Kozuh, W.F.M. Henkelman, C.E. Jones, & C. Woods (eds.), *Extraction and Control: Studies in Honor of Matthew W. Stolper*, Chicago, 203–10.

Miroschedji, P. de (1985), 'La fin du royaume d'Anšan et de Suse et la naissance de l'Empire perse', *Zeitschrift für Assyriologie und Vorderasiatsche Archäologie* 75: 265–306.

———. (1990), 'La fin de l'Elam: essai d'analyse et linterpretation', *Acta Iranica* 25: 47–95.

———. (2003), 'Susa and the Highlands: Major Trends in the History of Elamite Civilization', in N.F. Miller and K. Abdi (eds.), *Yeki bud, yeki nabud: Essays on the Archaeology of Iran in Honor of William M. Sumner*, Los Angeles, 17–38.

Mitchell, L. (2007), *Panhellenism and the Barbarian in Archaic and Classical Greece*, Swansea.

———. (2008), 'Thucydides and the Monarch in Democracy', *Polis* 25.1, 1–30.

———. (2012), 'The Women of Ruling Families in Archaic and Classical Greece', *Classical Quarterly* 62: 1–21.

———. (2013a), *The Heroic Rulers of Archaic and Classical Greece*, London, New Delhi, New York and Sydney.

———. (2013b), 'Alexander the Great: Divinity and the Rule of Law', in L. Mitchell & C. Melville (eds.), *Every Inch a King. Comparative Studies on Kings and Kingship in the Ancient and Medieval Worlds*, Leiden, 91–107.

———. (2014), 'Herodotus' Cyrus and Political Freedom', in A. Ansari (ed.), *Perceptions of Iran: History, Myths and Nationalism from Medieval Persia to the Islamic Republic*, London, 111–31, 244–7.

———. (2019), 'Political Thinking on Kingship in Democratic Athens', *Polis* 36: 442–65.

———. (2020a), '"What Age Were You When the Mede Came?" Cyrus the Great and Western Anatolia', in A.P. Dahlén (ed.), *Achaemenid Anatolia: Persian Presence and Impact in the Western Satrapies 546–330 BC* (special issue of *Boreas* 37), 199–215.

———. (2020b), 'Peace, War, and Gender', in S. Ager (ed.), *A Cultural History of Peace in Antiquity*, London and New York, 55–70.

———. (2022), 'King, Divinity and Law in Ancient Greece', in A.A. Moin & A. Strathern (eds.), *Sacred Kingship in World History: Between Immanence and Transcendence*, New York, 111–36.

Mitchell, S. (1999), 'Archaeology in Asia Minor 1990-98', *Archaeological Review* 45: 125–92.

Mitford, T.B. (1996), in *The Barrington Atlas of the Greek and Roman World*, Princeton, NJ.

Moin, A.A. & A. Strathern (2022), 'Sacred Kingship in World History: Between Immanence and Transcendence', in A.A. Moin & A. Strathern (eds.), *Sacred Kingship in World History: Between Immanence and Transcendence*, New York, 1–30.

Momigliano, A. (1971), *The Development of Greek Biography*, Cambridge, MA.

———. (1994), 'Daniel and the Greek Theory of Imperial Succession', in S. Berti (ed.), *Essays on Ancient and Modern Judaism* (transl. M. Masella-Gayley), Chicago, IL, 29–35.

Moorhead, J. (2009), 'Boethius's Life and the World of Late Antique Philosophy', in *the Cambridge Companion to Boethius*, Cambridge, 13–33.

Mortensen, L.B. (1990), 'Orosius and Justinus in One Volume. Post Conquest Book Across the Channel', *Cahiers de l'Institut du Moyen Age grec et latin* 60: 389–99.

Morton, J. (2010), 'Polyaenus in Context: The *Strategica* and Greek Identity in the Second Sophistic Age', in K. Brodersen (ed.), *Polyainos. Neue Studien/Polyaenus. New Studies*, Berlin, 108–32.

Mosshamer, A.A. (1981), 'Thales' Eclipse', *Transaction of the American Philological Association* 111: 145–55.

Munson, R.V. (2005), *Black Doves Speak: Herodotus and the Language of the Barbarians*, Washington.

Murray, O. (2001), 'Herodotus and Oral History', in N. Luraghi (ed.), *The Historian's Craft in the Age of Herodotus*, Oxford, 16–44.

Na'aman, N. & R. Zadok (1988), 'Sargon II's Deportations to Israel and Philistia (716-708 BC), *Journal of Cuneiform Studies* 40: 36–46.

Nadon, C. (2001), *Xenophon's Prince. Republic and Empire in the* Cyropaedia, Berkeley, CA, Los Angeles, CA and London.

Newell, W.R. (2013), 'Machiavelli and Xenophon's Cyrus: Searching for the Modern Conceptions of Kingship', in L.G. Mitchell & C. Melville (eds.), *Every Inch a King: Comparative Studies on Kings and Kingship in the Ancient and Medieval Worlds*, Leiden, 129–49.

Nöldeke, T. (1930), *The Iranian National Epic*, Bombay.

Novotny, J. (2014), *Selected Royal Inscriptions of Assurbanipal (L3, L4, LET, Prism 1, Prism T and Related Texts* (State Archives of Assyria Cuneiform Texts, Volume X), Helsinki.

Novotny, J. & J. Jeffers (eds.) (2018), *The Royal Inscriptions of Ashurbanipal (668– 631 BC), Aššur-etel-ilāni (630–627 BC), and Sîn-šarra-iškun (626–612 BC), Kings of Assyria, Part 1*, Philadelphia, PA.

Nuffelen, P. van (2012), *Orosius and the Rhetoric of History*, Oxford.

Nylander, C. (1970), *Ionians in Pasargadae*, Uppsala.

Oates, J. (1991), 'The Fall of Assyria (635–609 BC)', *Cambridge Ancient History* III.2, 2nd ed., Cambridge, 162–93.

Oppenheim, A.L. (1954–56): 'Sumerian: inim.gar, Akkadian: egirrû = Greek: *kledon*', *Archiv für Orientforschung* 17: 49–55.

———. (1956), 'The Interpretation of Dreams in the Ancient Near East', *Transactions of the American Philological Society* 46: 179–373.

———. (1985), 'The Babylonian Evidence of Achaemenian Rule in Mesopotamia', *Cambridge History of Iran*, vol. 2, Cambridge, 529–87.

Page, D.L. (ed.) (1981), *Further Greek Epigrams*, Cambridge.

Panaino, A. (2009), 'A Mesopotamian Omen in the Cycle of Cyrus the Great with an "Appendix on Cuneiform Sources" by Gian Pietro Basello'. *Studia Orientalia Electronica*, 106: 391–8, https://journal.fi/store/article/view/52477 (accessed 12/12/2021).

Parian, S.A. (2017), 'A New Edition of the Elamite Version of the Behistun Inscription (I)', *Cuneiform Digital Library Bulletin* 3, 1–14.

Parker, B.J. (2011), 'The Construction and Performance of Kingship in the Neo-Assyrian Empire', *Journal of Anthropological Research* 67: 357–86.

———. (2012), 'Geographies of Power: Territoriality and Empire during the Mesopotamian Iron Age', *Archaeological Papers of the American Anthropological Association* 22: 126–44.

Parpola, S. (1987), *Correspondence of Sargon II, Part I: Letters from Assyria and the West*, Helsinki.

———. (1995), 'The Assyrian Cabinet', in M. Dietrich & O. Loretz (eds.), *Vom Alten Orient zum Alten Testament: Festschrift für Wolfram Freiherrn von Soden zum 85. Geburtstag*, Kevelaer and Neukirchen-Vluyn, 379–401.

———. (1997), 'The Man Without a Scribe and the Question of Literacy in the Assyrian Empire', in B. Pontgratz-Leisten, H. Kuhne & P. Xella (eds.), *Ana šadî Labnāni lū allik. Beiträge zu altorientalischen und mittelmeerischen Kulturen. Festschrift für Wolfgang Röllig*, Kevaler and Neukirchen, 315–24.

———. (1999), 'Sons of God: The Ideology of Assyrian Kingship', *Archaeology Odyssey Archives* 2/5: 16–27.

———. (2003), 'Assyria's Expansion in the 8th and 7th centuries and its Long-term Repercussions in the West', in W.G. Dever & S. Gitu (eds.), *Symbiosis, Symbolism and the Power of the Past. Canaan, Ancient Israel, and the Neighbours from the Late Bronze Age through Roman Palaestina*, Winona Lake, IN, 99–111.

Parpola, S. & K. Watanabe (1988), *Neo-Assyrian Treaties and Loyalty Oaths*, Helsinki.

Patterson, C. (1985), '"Not Worth the Rearing": The Causes of Infant Exposure in Ancient Greece', *Transactions of the American Philological Association* 115: 103–23.

Payen, P. (1991), 'Franchir, Transgresser, Résister: Autour de Tomyris et Cyrus chez Hérodote', *Mètis* 6: 253–81.

Peat, J. (1989), 'Cyrus "King of Lands", Cambyses "King of Babylon": The Disputed Co-Regency', *Journal of Cuneiform Studies* 41: 199–216.

Pedersén, O. (1998), *Archives and Libraries in the Ancient Near East 1500–300 BC*, Bethesda, MD.

Pelling, C. (1996), 'The Urine and the Vine: Astyages' Dreams at Herodotus 1.107-8', *Classical Quarterly* 46: 68–77.

———. (2006), 'Educating Croesus: 'Talking and Learning in Herodotus' Lydian Logos', *Classical Antiquity* 25: 141–77.

———. (2011), *Plutarch and History: Eighteen Studies*, Swansea.

———. (2023), 'Plutarch and Biography', in F.B. Titchener & A.V. Zadorojnyi (eds.), *The Cambridge Companion to Plutarch*, Cambridge, 11–28.

Petit, T. (1990), *Satrapes et satrapies dans l'empire achéménde de Cyrus le Grand à Xerxès Ier*, Paris.

Petter, D.L. (2011), *The Book of Ezekiel and Mesopotamian City Laments*, Fribourg/ Göttingen.

Pickworth, D. (2005), 'Excavations at Nineveh: The Halzi Gate', *Iraq* 67: 295–316.

Pollinger Foster, K. (2004), 'The Hanging Gardens of Nineveh', *Iraq* 66: 207–20.

Polonsky, J. (2006), 'The Mesopotamian Conceptualization of Birth and the Determination of Destiny at Sunrise', in A.K. Guinan, M. deJ. Ellis, A.J. Ferrara, S.M. Freedman, M.T. Rutz, L. Sassmannshausen, S. Tinney, & M.W. Waters (eds.), *If a Man Builds a Joyful House: Assyriological Studies in Honor of Erle Verdun Leichty*, Leiden and Boston, MA, 297–311.

Pongratz-Leisten, B. (2015), *Religion and Ideology in Assyria*, Boston, MA and Berlin.

Porten, B. & A. Yardeni (1986), *Textbook of Aramaic Documents from Egypt*, vol. 3, Winona Lake, IN.

Porter, B.N. (1993), *Images, Power and Politics: Figurative Aspects of Esarhaddon's Babylonian Policy*, Philadelphia, PA.

Postgate, J.N. (1992), 'The Land of Assur and the Yoke of Assur', *World Archaeology* 23: 247–63.

———. (2007), 'The Invisible Hierarchy: Assyrian Military and Civilian Administration in the 8th and 7th Centuries BC', in J.N. Postgate (ed.), *The Land of Assur and the Yoke of Assur: Studies on Assyria 1971–2005*, Oxford, 331–60.

Potts, D.T. (2010), 'Cyrus the Great and the Kingdom of Anshan', in V. Sarkosh Curtis & S. Stewart (eds.), *Birth of the Persian Empire*, London, 7–28.

———. (2014), *Nomadism in Iran: From Antiquity to the Modern Era*, New York.

———. (2016), *The Archaeology of Elam: Formation and Transformation of an Ancient Iranian State*, 2nd ed. Cambridge.

Potts, D.T., K. Roustaei, C.A. Petrie & L.R. Weeks (eds.) (2009), *The Mamasani Archaeological Project Stage One: A Report on the First Two Season of the ICAR – University of Sydney Expedition to the Mamasani District, Fars Province, Iran* (BAR International Series 2044), Oxford.

Powell, J.G.F. (1988), *Cicero: Cato Maior De* Senectute, Cambridge.

Quigley, D. (2005), 'Introduction: The Character of Kingship', in D. Quigley, *The Character of Kingship*, London, 1–24.

Racine, F. (2016), 'Herodotus' Reputation in Latin Literature from Cicero to the Twelfth Century', in J. Priestley & V. Zali (eds.), *Brill's Companion to the Reception of Herodotus in Antiquity and Beyond*, Leiden, 193–212.

Radner, K. (2000), 'How did the Neo-Assyrian King Perceive his Land and Its Resources?', in R.M. Jas (ed.), *Rainfall and Agriculture in Northern Mesopotamia*, Istanbul, 233–46.

———. (2003), 'An Assyrian View of the Medes', in G. Lanfranchi, M. Roaf & R. Rollinger (eds.), *Continuity of Empires (?). Assyria, Media, Persia. Proceedings of the International Meeting in Padua, 26th–28th April 2001*, Padua, 37–64.

———. (2006), 'How to Reach the Upper Tigris: The Route Through the Ṭūr 'Abdīn', *State Archives of Assyria Bulletin* 15: 273–305.

———. (2011), 'Royal Decision-Making: Kings, Magnates, and Scholars', in K. Radner & E. Robson (eds.), *The Oxford Handbook of Cuneiform Culture*, Oxford, 358–79.

———. (2012), 'Mass Deportation: The Assyrian Resettlement Policy', *Assyrian Empire Builders*, University College London, http://www.ucl.ac.uk/sargon/essentials/governors/massdeportation/ (accessed 20/08/2022).

———. (2013), 'Assyria and the Medes', in D.T. Potts (ed.), *The Oxford Handbook of Ancient Iran*, Oxford, 442–56.

———. (2015), *Ancient Assyria: A Very Short Introduction*, Oxford.

———. (2018), 'Last Emperor or Crown Prince Forever? Aššur-uballiṭ II of Assyria According to Archival Sources', in S. Yamada (ed.), *Neo-Assyrian Sources in Context: Thematic Studies of Texts, History and Culture. (State Archives of Assyria Studies* 28), Helsinki, 135–42.

Raymond, D. (1953), *Macedonian Regal Coinage to 413 BC*, New York.

Reade, J. (1995), 'Iran in the Neo-Assyrian Period', in M. Liverani (ed.), *Neo Assyrian Geography*, Rome, 31–42.

———. (2015), 'Xenophon's Route Through Babylonia and Assyria', *Iraq* 77: 173–202.

Redford, D.B. (1967), 'The Literary Motif of the Exposed Child (cf. Ex. Ii 1-10)', *Numen* 14: 209–28.

Reiner, E. (1973), 'The Location of Anšan', *Revue d' Assyriolgie et d'archéologie orientale* 67: 57–62.

Reynolds, L.D. (1983), *Texts and Transmissions: A Survey of the Latin Classics*, Oxford.

Richards, J. (2002), 'Text and Context in the Late Old Kingdom Egypt: The Archaeology and Historiography of Weni the Elder', *Journal of the American Research Centre in Egypt*, 39: 75–102.

Rigot, J.-B. (2010), 'Dynamique de la rivièr Pulvar et morphogenèse de la plaine de Tang-I Bulaghi (Fars, Iran) à l'Holocene. Premiers résultats', *Géomorphologie: relief, processus, environment* 16: 1–25.

Rigot, J.-B., S. Gondet, M.L. Chambrade, M. Djamali, K. Mohammadkhani & E. Thamó-Bozsó (2021), 'Pulvar River Changes in the in the Pasargadae Plain (Fars, Iran) during the Holocene and the Implications for Water Management in the First Millenium BCE', *Quaternary International*, https://doi.org/10.1016/j.quaint.2021.05.012 (accessed 23/09/2021).

Roaf, M. (1995), 'Media and Mesopotamia: History and Architecture', in J. Curtis (ed.), *Later Mesopotamia and Iran: Tribes and Empires 1600–539 BC*, London, 54–66.

Rollinger, R. (1993), *Herodots babylonischer Logos: Eine kritische Untersuchung der Glaubwürdigkeitsdiskussion*, Innsbruck.

———. (1999a), 'Der Stammbaum des achaimenidischen Königshauses oder die Frage der Legitimität der Herrschaft des Dareios', *Archäologische Mitteilungen aus Iran und Turan* 30: 155–209.

———. (1999b), 'Zur Lokalisation von Parsu(m)a(š) in der Fārs und zu einigen der frühen persischen Geschichte', *Zeitschrift für Assyriologie und Vorderasiatsche Archäologie* 89: 115–39.

———. (2003), 'Herodotus iv. Cyrus According to Herodotus', *Encyclopaedia Iranica*, https://www.iranicaonline.org/articles/herodotus-iv (accessed 28/05/2022).

———. (2008), 'The Median "Empire", The End of Urartu and Cyrus the Great's Campaign in 547 BC (Nabonidus Chronicle II 16)', *Ancient West and East* 7: 51–65.

———. (2013), 'Berossos and the Monuments: City Walls, Sanctuaries, Palaces and the Hanging Garden', in J. Haubold, G.B. Lanfranchi & R. Rollinger & J.M. Steele (eds.), *The World of Berossos: Proceedings of the 4th International Colloquium on "The Ancient Near East between Classical and Ancient Oriental Traditions", Hatfield College, Durham 7th-9th July 2010. Classica et Orientalia, 5*, Wiesbaden, 137–62.

———. (2014), 'Von Kyros bis Xerxes: Babylon in persischer Zeit und die Frage der Bewertung des herodoteischen Geschichtswerkes – eine Nachlese', in M. Krebernik & H. Neumann (eds.), *Babylonien und seine Nachbarn in neu- und spät-babylonischer Zeit (Alte Orient und Altes Testament 369)*, Münster, 147–94.

———. (2018), 'Herodotus and the Transformation of Ancient Near Eastern Motifs: Darius, Oebares and the Neighing Horse', in T. Harrison & E. Irwin (eds.), *Interpreting Herodotus*, Oxford, 125–48.

———. (2021), 'The Median Dilemma', in B. Jacobs & R. Rollinger (eds.), *A Companion to the Achaemenid Persian Empire*, Hoboken, 333–50.

Rowler, M.B. (2018), *Models from the Past in Roman Culture: A World of Exempla*, Cambridge.

Rowton, M. (1974), 'Enclosed Nomadism', *Journal of the Economic and Social History of the Orient* 17:1–30

————. (1976), 'Dimorphic Structure and Topology', *Oriens Antiquus* 15: 17–31.

Sabbadini, R. (1905-14), *Le Scoperte dei Codici Latini e Greci nei Secoli XIV e XV*, 2 vols, Florence.

Sáenz, C. (1991), 'Lords of the Waste: Predation, Pastoral Production, and the Process of Stratification among the Eastern Twaregs', in T. Earle (ed.), *Chiefdoms: Power Economy and Ideology*, Cambridge, 100–18.

Sahlins, M. (1981), 'The Stranger-King or *Dumézil among the Fijians*', *The Journal of Pacific History* 16: 107–32.

————. (2008), 'The Stranger-king or, Elementary Forms of the Politics of Life', *Indonesia and the Malay World* 36: 177–99.

Sals, U. (2014), '"Babylon" Forever, Or How to Divinize What You Want to Damn', in D.V. Edelmman & E. Ben Zvi (eds.), *Memory and the City in Ancient Israel*, Winona Lake, IN, 293–308.

Salzman, P.C. (2002), 'Pastoral Nomads: Some General Observations Based on Research in Iran', *Journal of Anthropological Research* 58: 245–64.

Samet, N. (2014), *The Lament over the Destruction of Ur*, Winona Lake, IN.

Sancisi-Weerdenburg, H. (1985), 'The Death of Cyrus: Xenophon's *Cyropaedia* as a Source for Iranian History', in H.W. Bailey, A.D.H. Bivar, J. Duchesne-Guillemin, & J.R. Hinnells (eds.), *Papers in Honour of Professor Mary Boyce*, Leiden, 459–71.

————. (1988), 'Was There Ever a Median Empire', in A. Kuhrt & H. Sancisi-Weerdenburg (eds.), *Achaemenid History III: Method and Theory*, Leiden, 197–212.

————. (1994), 'The Orality of Herodotus' *Medikos Logos* or: The Median Empire Revisited', in H. Sancisi-Weerdenburg, A. Kuhrt, M.C. Root (eds.), *Achaemenid History VIII: Continuity and Change*, Leiden, 39–55.

Schacht, T. de, M. de Dapper, A. Asadi, Y. Ubelmann & R. Boucharlat (2012), 'Geological Study of the Achaemenid Dam of Sad-I Didegan (Fars, Iran), *Géomorphologie: relief, processus, environment* 18: 1–29.

Schaudig, H. (2001), *Die Inschriften Nabonids von Babylon und Kyros' des Großen samt den in ihrem Umfeld entstandenen Tendenzschriften: Textausgabe und Grammatik*, Münster.

————. (2008), '"Bel Bows, Nabû Stoops!" The Prophecy of Isaiah XLVI 1-2 as a Reflection of Babylonian "Processional Omens"', *Vetus Testamentum* 58: 557–2.

————. (2018) 'The Magnanimous Heart of Cyrus: The Cyrus Cylinder and its Literary Models', in M.R. Shayegan (ed.), *Cyrus the Great: Life and Lore*, Harvard, 67–91.

————. (2019), *Explaining Disaster: Tradition and Transformation of the 'Catastrophe of Ibbi-Sîn' in Babylonian Literature*, Münster.

Schmitt, C. (2005), *Political Theology: Four Chapters on the Concept of Sovereignty* (transl. G. Schwab), Chicago, IL, and London.

Schmitt, R. (1988), 'Achaimenideninschriften in griechischer literarischer Überlieferung', *Acta Iranica* 28: 17–38.

————. (2000), 'Achaemenid Throne Names', in W. Breidbach & Ph. Huyse (eds.), *Selected Onomastic Writings*, New York, 164–75.

————. (2003), 'Die skythischen Personennamen bei Herodot', *Annali dell'Università degli Studi di Napoli 'L'Orientale'* 63, 1–31.

————. (2015), 'Herodotus as Practitioner of Iranian Anthroponomastics', *Glotta* 91: 250–63.

————. (2018), 'Massagetae', *Encyclopaedia Iranica*, https://iranicaonline.org/articles/massagetae (accessed 10/06/2022).

Sevin, V. (1988), 'The Oldest Highway: Between the Regions of Van and Elazığ in Eastern Anatolia', *Antiquity* 62-236: 547–51.

———. (1991), 'The Southwest Expansion of Urartu: New Observations', in A. Çilingiloğlu & D. French (eds.), *Anatolian Iron Ages 2*, Oxford, 97–112.

Shahbazi, S. (2011), 'Clothing ii: In the Median and Achaemenid Periods', *Encyclopaedia Iranica*, https://www.iranicaonline.org/articles/clothing-ii (accessed 01/09/2022).

Shaya, J. (2013), 'The Public Life of Monuments: The *Summi Viri* of the Forum of Augustus', *American Journal of Archaeology* 117: 83–110.

Sims-Williams, N. (1981), 'The Final Paragraph of the Tomb Inscription of Darius I (DNb, 50-60): The Old Persian Text in the Light of an Aramaic Version', *Bulletin of the School of Oriental and African Studies* 44: 1–7.

Smith, A.T. (1999), 'The Making of an Urartian Landscape in Southern Transcausia: A Study of Political Architectonics', *American Journal of Archaeology* 103: 45–71.

———. (2003), *The Political Landscape: Constellations of Authority in Early Complex Polities*, Berkeley, CA.

Smith, M.L. (2005), 'Networks, Territories, and the Cartography of Ancient States', *Annals of the Association of American Geographers* 95: 832–49.

Smith, S.L. (1995), *The Power of Women: A Topos in Medieval Art and Literature*, Philadelphia, PA.

Smith, T.S. (2018), 'Ethnicity: Constructions of Self and Other in Ancient Egypt', *Journal of Egyptian History* 11: 113–46.

Sommerstein, A.H. (1987), *Aristophanes: Birds*, Oxford.

Spek, R.J. van der (2014), 'Cyrus the Great, Exiles and Foreign Gods: A Comparison of Assyrian and Persian Policies in Subject Nations', in M. Kozuh, W.F. Henkelman, C.E. Jones & C. Woods (eds.), *Extraction and Control: Studies in honour of Matthew W. Stolper*, Chicago, IL, 233–64.

Steele, R. (2022), *The Shah's Imperial Celebrations of 1971: Nationalism, Culture and Politics in Late Pahlavi Iran*, London, New York and Dublin.

Stol, M. (2000), *Birth in Babylonia and the Bible: Its Mediterranean Setting*, Groningen.

Stolper, M.W. (1989), 'The Governor of Babylon and Across-the River in 486 BC', *Journal of Near Eastern Studies* 48: 283–305.

———. (2006), 'Parysatis in Babylon', in A.K. Guinan, M. deJ. Ellis, A.J. Ferrara, S.M. Freedman, M.T. Rutz, L. Sassmannshausen, S. Tinney, & M.W. Waters (eds.), *If A Man Owns a Joyful House: Assyriological Studies in Honor of Erle Verdun Leichty*, Leiden, 463–72.

———. (2013), 'The Form, Language and Contents of the Cyrus Cylinder', in T. Daryaee (ed.), *Cyrus the Great: An Ancient Iranian King*, Santa Monica, CA, 40–52.

Strathern, A. (2019), *Unearthly Powers: Religious and Political Change in World History*, Cambridge.

Stronach, D. (1978), *Pasargadae. A Report on the Excavations Conducted by the British Institute of Persian Studies from 1961 to 1963*, Oxford.

———. (1989), 'The Royal Garden at Pasargadae: Evolution and Legacy', in L. de Meyer & E. Haerink (eds.), *Archaeologia Iranica et Orientalis: Miscellanea in honorem Louis Vandem Berghe*, Ghent, 475–502.

———. (1990a), 'The Garden as a Political Statement: Some Case Studies from the Near East in the First Millennium BC', *Bulletin of the Asia Institute* 4: 171–80.

————. (1990b), 'On the Genesis of the Old Persian Cuneiform Script', in F. Vallat (ed.), *Contribution à l'histoire de l'Iran. Mélanges offerts à Jean Perrot*, Paris, 195–203.

————. (2000), 'Of Cyrus, Darius and Alexander: A New Look at the "Epitaphs" of Cyrus the Great', in R. Dittman, B. Hrouda, U. Löw, P. Matthiae, R. Mayor-Opficius & S. Thürwächter (eds.), *Varatio Delectat: Iran und der Westen: Gedenkschrift für Peter Calmeyer*, Münster, 681–701.

————. (2003), 'Independent Media: Archaeological Notes from the Homeland', in G. Lanfranchi, M. Roaf, & R. Rollinger (eds.), *Continuity of Empire (?). Assyria, Media, Persia. Proceedings of the International Meeting in Padua, 26th–28th April 2001*, Padua, 234–48.

————. (2013), 'Cyrus and the Kingship of Anshan: Further Perspectives', *Iran* 51: 51–69.

————. (2018), 'Cyrus, Anshan and Assyria', in M.R. Sheyegan (ed.), *Cyrus the Great: Life and Lore*, Boston, MA and Washington, 46–66.

Stronk, J.P. (2010), *Ctesias' Persian History. Part I: Introduction, Text, and Translation*, Düsseldorf.

Summers, G.D. (2008), 'Periodisation and Terminology in the Central Anatolian Iron Age: Archaeology, History and Audiences', *Ancient Near Eastern Studies* 45, 202–17.

Sumner, W.M. (1972), *Cultural Development in the Kur River Basin, Iran. An Archaeological Analysis of Settlement Patterns*, PhD diss. University of Pennsylvania.

————. (1974), 'Excavations at Tall-I Malyan, 1971–72', *Iran* 12: 155–75.

————. (1988), 'Maljan, Tall-e (Anšan)', *Reallexikon der Assyriologie und Vorderasiatischen Archäologie* 7: 306–20.

Swain, J.W. (1940), 'The Theory of the Four Monarchies: Opposition History under the Roman Empire', *Classical Philology* 35: 1–21.

Szuchman, J. (ed.) (2009), *Nomads, Tribes and the State in the Ancient Near East: Cross-disciplinary Perspectives*, Chicago, IL.

Tadmor, H. (1965), 'The Inscriptions of Nabunaid: Historical arrangement', in H. G. Güterbock & T. Jacobsen (eds.), *Studies in Honour of Benno Landsberger on his 75th Birthday, April 21, 1965*, Chicago, IL, 351–63.

Tadmor, H. & S. Yamada (eds.) (2011), *The Royal Inscriptions of Tiglath-Pileser III (744-727 BC), and Shalmaneser V (726-722 BC), Kings of Assyria*, Winona Lake, IN.

Talon, P. (ed.) (2005), *The Standard Babylonian Creation Myth: Enūma Eliš*, Helsinki.

Tapper, R. (2008), 'Who are the Kuchi? Nomad Self-identities in Afghanistan', *Journal of the Royal Anthropological Institute* 14: 97–116.

Tavernier, J. (2001), 'An Achaemenid Royal Inscription: The Text of Paragraph 13 of the Aramaic Version of the Bisitun Inscription', *Journal of Near Eastern Studies* 60: 161–76.

————. (2011), 'Iranians in Neo-Elamite Texts', in J. Álvarez-Mon & M.B. Garrison (eds.), *Elam and Persia*, Winona Lake, IN, 191–261.

————. (2013), 'Old Persian', in D. Potts (ed.), *The Oxford Handbook of Ancient Iran*, Oxford, 638–57.

Taylor, J. (2013), 'The Cyrus Cylinder: Discovery', in I. Finkel (ed.), *The Cyrus Cylinder: The King of Persia's Proclamation from Ancient Babylon*, London, 35–68.

Thelle, R.I. (2009), 'Babylon in the Book of Jeremiah (MT): Negotiating a Power Shift', in H.M. Barstad & R.G. Kratz (eds.), *Prophecy in the Book of Jeremiah*, Berlin and New York, 187–232.

Thierry, P. (1990), *Satraps et satrapies dans l'empire achéménide de Cyrus le Grand à Xerxès Ier*, Geneva.

Thomas, R. (1992), *Literacy and Orality in Ancient Greece*, Cambridge.

Thureau-Dangin, F. (1925), 'La fin de l'empire Assyrien', *Revue d'Assyriologie et d'archéologie orientale* 22: 27–9.

Tinney, S. (1996), *The Nippur Lament*, Philadelphia, PA.

Toher, M. (1989), 'On the Use of Nicolaus' Historical Fragments', *Classical Antiquity* 8: 159–72.

Tolini, G. (2005), 'Quelques éléments concernant la prise de Babylone par Cyrus (octobre 539 av. J.-C.), *Arta* 2005.03.

——. (2011), *La Babylonie et l'Iran: les relations d'une province avec le coeur de l'Empire achéménide (539-331 avant notre ère)* (volume 1 & 2). Paris I – La Sorbonne.

——. (2012), 'Le discours de domination de Cyrus, de Darius Ier at d' Alexandre le Grand sur la Babylonie (539-323)', in V. Dieudonné, C. Feyel, J. Fournier, L. Graslin, F. Kirbilher & G. Vottéro (éds.), *Communautés locales et pouvoir central dans l'Orient hellénistique et romain*, Nancy, 259–96.

Toorn, K. van der (1991), 'The Babylonian New Year Festival: New Insights from the Old Cuneiform Texts and their Bearing on Old Testament Study', in J. Emerton (ed.), *Congress Volume Leuven 1989* (*Vetus Testamentum* Supplement 43), Leiden, 331–44.

——. (2007), *Scribal Culture and the Making of the Hebrew Bible*, Harvard.

Treadgold, W.T. (1980), *The Nature of the* Bibliotheca *of Photius*, Washington, DC.

Tuplin, C.J. (1994), 'Persians as Medes', in H. Sancisi-Weerdenburg, A. Kuhrt & M.C. Root (eds.), *Achaemenid History VIII: Continuity and Change*, Leiden, 235–56.

——. (1997), 'Medism and Its Causes', *Transeuphratène* 13: 155–85.

——. (1998), 'The Seasonal Migration of Achaemenid Kings: A Report on Old and New Evidence', in M. Brosius & A. Kuhrt (eds.), *Achaemenid History XI: Studies in Persian History. Essays in Honour of D.M. Lewis*, Leiden, 63–114.

——. (2004), 'Medes in Media, Mesopotamia and Anatolia: Empire, Hegemony, Domination or Illusion?,' *Ancient West & East* 3: 223–51.

——. (2005), 'Darius' Accession in (the) Media', in P. Bienkowski, C. Mee & E. Slater (eds.), *Writing and Ancient Near East Society. Papers in Honour of A.R. Millard*, New York and London, 217–44.

——. (2013), 'Xenophon's *Cyropaedia*: Fictive History, Political Analysis and Thinking with Iranian Kings', in L. Mitchell & C. Melville (eds.), *Every Inch a King. Comparative Studies on Kings and Kingship in the Ancient and Medieval Worlds*, Leiden, 67–90.

Tzonis, A. (2018), 'Buildings We Call Palaces', in M. Bietak & S. Prell (eds.), *Ancient Egyptian and Ancient Near Eastern Palaces, Vol. I*, Vienna, 1.9–21.

Vallat, F. (2011), 'Darius, l'héritier légitime, et premiers Achéménides', in J. Álvarez-Mon & M.B. Garrison (eds.), *Elam and Persia*, Winona Lake, IN, 263–84.

Vanderhooft, D. (2006), 'Cyrus II, Liberator or Conqueror? Ancient Historiography Concerning Cyrus in Babylon', in O. Lipschits & M. Oeming (eds.), *Judah and the Judaeans in the Persian Period*, Winona Lake, IN, 351–72.

Van de Mieroop, M. (2003), 'Reading Babylon', *American Journal of Archaeology* 107: 257–75.

———. (2016), *A History of the Ancient Near East, ca. 3000-323 BC*, 3rd ed., Malden and Oxford.

Veldhuis, N. (2011), 'Levels of Literacy', in K. Radner & E. Robson (eds.), *Oxford Handbook of Cuneiform Culture*, Oxford, 68–89.

Vogelsang, W.J. (1992), *The Rise and Organisation of the Achaemenid Empire: The Eastern Iranian Evidence*, Leiden, New York and Köln.

Voigtlander, E.N. von (1978), *The Bisitun inscription of Darius the Great: Babylonian version*, London.

Waerzeggers, C. (2011), 'The Pious King: Royal Patronage of Temples', in K. Radner & E. Robson (eds.), *The Oxford Handbook of Cuneiform Culture*, Oxford, 725–51.

———. (2012), 'The Babylonian Chronicles: Classification and Provenance', *Journal of Near Eastern Studies* 71: 285–98.

———. (2015), 'Shaping Political Memory in the Nabonidus Chronicle', in J.M. Silverman & C. Waerzeggers (eds.) *Political Memory in and after the Persian Empire*, Atlanta, GA, 95–124.

———. (2017), 'The *Prayer of Nabonidus* in the Light of Hellenistic Babylonian Literature', in M. Popović, M. Schoonover & M. Vandenberghe (eds.), *Jewish Cultural Encounters in the Ancient Mediterranean and Near Eastern World*, Leiden, 64–75.

———. (2021), 'The Day Before Cyrus Entered Babylon', in U. Gabbay & S. Gordon (eds.), *Individual and Institutions in the Ancient Near East: A Tribute to Ran Zadok*, Boston, MA and Berlin, 79–88.

Walker, C.B.F. (1981), *Cuneiform Brick Inscriptions in the British Museum*, London.

Wallace, R. (2016), 'Redating Croesus: Herodotean Chronologies, and the Dates of the Earliest Coinages', *Journal of Hellenic Studies* 136: 168–81.

Waters, M.W. (1996), 'Darius and the Achaemenid Line', *Ancient History Bulletin* 10: 11–8.

———. (1999), 'The Earliest Persians in Southwestern Iran: The Textual Evidence', *Iranian Studies* 32: 99–107.

———. (2011), 'Parsumaš, Anšan, and Cyrus', in J. Álvarez-Mon & M.B. Garrison (eds.), *Elam and Persia*, Winona Lake, IN, 285–96.

———. (2014), *Ancient Persia: A Concise History of the Achaemenid Empire, 550–330 BCE*, Cambridge.

———. (2017), *Ctesias' Persica and its Near Eastern Context*, Madison and London.

———. (2022), *King of the World: The Life of Cyrus the Great*, New York.

Weiershäuser, F. & J. Novotny (eds.) (2020), *The Royal Inscriptions of Amēl-Marduk (561–560 BC), Neriglissar (559-556 BC), and Nabonidus (555–539 BC), Kings of Babylon*, Pennsylvania.

West, M.L. (1985), *The Hesiodic Catalogue of Women*, Oxford.

West, S. (2003), 'Croesus Second Reprieve and Other Tales of the Persian Court', *Classical Quarterly* 53: 416–37.

Westenholz, J.G. (1983), 'Heroes of Akkad', *Journal of the American Oriental Society* 103: 327–36.

———. (1984), 'Review of: B. Lewis, *The Sargon Legend*', *Journal of Near Eastern Studies* 43: 73–9.

———. (1997), *Legends of the Kings of Akkade*, Winona Lake, IN.

Wetzel, F. (1930), *Die Stadtmauern von Babylon*, Leipzig.

Wheeler, E. (2010), 'Polyaenus: *Scriptor Militaris*', in K. Brodersen (ed.), *Polyainos. Neue Studien/Polyaenus. New Studies*, Berlin, 5–54.

Widmer, P. (2012), 'Etymologische und Historishes zum Namen der Perser', in V. Sadovski & D. Stifter (eds.), *Iranistische und indogermanistiche Beiträge in Memoriam Jochem Schindler (1944–1994)*, Vienna, 445–59.

Wilson, I.D. (2015), 'Yahweh's Annointed: Cyrus, Deuteronomy's Law of the King, and Yehudite Identity', in J.M. Silverman & C. Waerzeggers (eds.), *Political Memory In and After the Persian Empire*, Atlanta, GA, 325–59.

Wilson, N.G. (1994), *Photius: The Bibliotheca. A Selection Translated with Notes*, London.

———. (2017), *From Byzantium to Italy: Greek Studies in the Italian Renaissance*, 2nd ed., London and New York.

Windfuhr, G. (2006), 'Iran vii. Non-Iranian Languages (1) Overview', *Encyclopædia Iranica*, XIII/4, 377–86, available online at http://www.iranicaonline.org/articles/iran-vii1-non-iranian-languages-overview- (accessed on 30 December 2021).

Winter, I.J. (1993), '"Seat of Kingship"/"A Wonder to Behold": The Palace as Construct in the Ancient Near East', *Ars Orientalis* 23: 27–55.

Yarshater, E. (1988), 'The Development of Iranian Literatures', in E. Yarshater (ed.), *Persian Literature*, New York, 3–37.

Zadok, R. (1976), 'On the Connections between Iran and Babylonia in the Sixth-century BC', *Journal of Persian Studies* 14: 61–78.

———. (2001), 'On the Location of NA Parsua', *Nouvelles Assyriologiques Brèves et Utilitaires* no. 28.

Zawadski, S. (1996), 'Cyrus-Cambyses Coregency', *Revue d'Assyriologie et d'archéologie orientale* 90: 171–83.

———. (2010), 'The Portrait of Nabonidus and Cyrus in Their (?) Chronicle. When and Why the Present Version was Composed', in P. Charvát & P. Maříková Vlčková (eds.), *Who Was King? Who Was Not King? The Rulers and the Ruled in the Ancient Near East*, Prague, 142–54.

Zimansky, P.E. (1985), *Ecology and Empire: The Structure of the Urartian State*, Chicago.

———. (1995a), 'An Urartian Ozymandias', *Biblical Archaeologist* 58: 94–100.

———. (1995b), 'Xenophon and the Urartian Legacy', *Pallas* 43: 255–68.

Zournatzi, A. (2011), 'Early Cross-cultural Political Encounters along the Paths of the Silk Road: Cyrus the Great as a "King of the City of Anshan"', in D. Akbarzadeh (ed.), *Proceedings of the First International Conference "Iran and the Silk Road"*, Tehran, 1–15.

Index